Women, Vulnerabilities and Service Systems

This book studies welfare systems in Europe and beyond from the standpoint of women in vulnerable positions in society. These systems are under major transformations with new models of service delivery and management, austerity measures, requirements for cost-effectiveness, marketisation, and the prio̶ ̶ ̶ ̶ ̶ ̶ of services.

Divided into thᵢ ̶parts̶:

- Welfare service systems (not) respo̶n̶d̶i̶n̶g̶ ̶t̶o̶ ̶v̶u̶l̶n̶e̶r̶a̶b̶l̶e̶ ̶s̶i̶t̶u̶a̶tions of women
- Women's encounters with the welfare service system
- Contradictions of informal support

This book considers the experiences and encounters with the service system of women in poverty, homeless women, women with substance use problems, women sentenced of crime, girls and young women in care, and refugees and asylum-seeking women.

Drawing upon research and critical discussions from Finland, Canada, Israel, Slovenia, Spain and the UK, this book provides new empirical findings and critical insights, and a valuable resource for the academics and students in social work, social policy, sociology and gender studies, but also for policy makers and professionals in social and health care.

Marjo Kuronen is a Professor of Social Work at the University of Jyväskylä, Finland.

Elina Virokannas is a University Lecturer at the University of Helsinki, Finland.

Ulla Salovaara is a Post-doctoral researcher at the University of Jyväskylä, Finland.

Routledge Advances in Social Work

For more information about this series, please visit: https://www.routledge.com/Routledge-Advances-in-Social-Work/book-series/RASW

Women, Vulnerabilities and Welfare Service Systems

Edited by
**Marjo Kuronen, Elina Virokannas
and Ulla Salovaara**

Routledge
Taylor & Francis Group

LONDON AND NEW YORK

First published 2021
by Routledge
2 Park Square, Milton Park, Abingdon, Oxon OX14 4RN

and by Routledge
52 Vanderbilt Avenue, New York, NY 10017

Routledge is an imprint of the Taylor & Francis Group, an informa business

British Library Cataloguing-in-Publication Data
A catalogue record for this book is available from the British Library

Library of Congress Cataloging-in-Publication Data
Names: Kuronen, Marjo, editor. | Virokannas, Elina, editor. | Salovaara, Ulla, editor.
Title: Women, vulnerabilities and welfare service systems / edited by Marjo Kuronen, Elina Virokannas, Ulla Salovaara.
Description: New York : Routledge, 2020. |
Series: Routledge advances in social work | Includes bibliographical references and index.
Identifiers: LCCN 2020020050 (print) | LCCN 2020020051 (ebook) | ISBN 9780367228026 (hardback) | ISBN 9780429276910 (ebook)
Subjects: LCSH: Public welfare—European Union countries. | Women—European Union countries—Social conditions. | Poor women—Services for—European Union countries. | European Union countries—Social policy—21st century.
Classification: LCC HV238 .W66 2020 (print) | LCC HV238 (ebook) | DDC 362.83094—dc23
LC record available at https://lccn.loc.gov/2020020050
LC ebook record available at https://lccn.loc.gov/2020020051

ISBN: 978-0-367-22802-6 (hbk)
ISBN: 978-0-429-27691-0 (ebk)

Typeset in Times New Roman
by codeMantra

Contents

Contributors

Kate Brown is a Senior Lecturer in Social Policy and Criminology at the University of York, UK. She has been researching and writing about how vulnerability is lived, theorised and governed for around a decade, particularly focusing on the lives and perspectives of those who are deemed 'vulnerable'. She previously worked as a practitioner and manager in the voluntary sector and continues to be active in services for vulnerable women and children.

Estibaliz de Miguel-Calvo is an Assistant Professor in the Department of Sociology II at the University of the Basque Country, Spain. She previously worked for almost 10 years as a social worker and social educator for prisoners in a non-governmental organisation. She is a member of GEISPE, International Thematic Network on Gender and the Penal System. Her research interests include women in prison, gender and the penal system, the sociology of emotions and love.

Katie Ellis is a Research Fellow and Lecturer at the University of Sheffield, UK. She uses research to advocate for young people living in out-of-family environments and has received funding from the Leverhulme Trust, ESRC and British Academy. Ellis is interested in concepts of vulnerability, responsibilisation and resilience, and her research considers the relevance of these themes to children in care.

M. Victoria Gómez is a Senior Lecturer in the Department of Social Analysis at the University Carlos III of Madrid, Spain. She is one of the coordinators of the European Sociological Association Research Network on Urban Sociology. Her current research interests include local belonging, vulnerability, urban inequality, urban sustainability and neighbourhood dynamics.

Teija Karttunen holds a PhD in Social Work from the University of Jyväskylä, Finland. Her dissertation focuses on women's substance abuse treatment from a women-specific perspective. She currently holds a position as a social work manager in psychosocial services for the City of Vantaa. She has extensive experience as a social worker and manager in substance abuse treatment services and in family and child protection services. Her research interests include intervention research, substance abuse and issues of gender and parenting in substance abuse treatment services.

Suvi Krok holds a PhD in Social Work from the University of Tampere, Finland. She has worked as a senior researcher and lecturer in social work at the universities of Tampere and Jyväskylä. She also has extensive experience as a social worker and project manager. Her research interests include poverty, coping strategies of low-income lone mothers, social work and social benefit systems.

Marjo Kuronen is a Professor of Social Work in the Department of Social Sciences and Philosophy at the University of Jyväskylä, Finland, and PI of the research project *Transforming welfare service system from the standpoint of women in vulnerable life situations* (Academy of Finland 2016–2020, project no 294407). Her research interests include the relationships between women, family and the welfare state, local welfare policies and feminist theorising and methodology in social work research, especially institutional ethnography.

Einat Lavee is an Assistant Professor in the Department of Human Services at the University of Haifa, Israel, and Co-Director of the Research and Training Unit at the Interdisciplinary Center for the Study of Poverty and Social Exclusion. Her research interests include the welfare state and social policy, as well as class and the labour market, with a specific interest in low-income workers and mothers. Beyond her academic work, she also advises governmental agencies on poverty and social policy, particularly among low-income mothers.

Vesna Leskošek is a Professor in the Faculty of Social Work at the University of Ljubljana, Slovenia. Her main research interests are social inequalities, poverty, the welfare state and gender. Her recent research is on care work and food poverty.

Vesna Mejak obtained her PhD in Sociology at the University of Ljubljana, Slovenia. Her dissertation addressed the motherhood of women drug users. She works as a social worker at the University Psychiatric Clinic in Ljubljana, in the Centre for Treatment of Drugs. Her specific areas of interest are women and substance use, pregnancy and parenthood.

Ulla Salovaara is a Post-doctoral Researcher in the Department of Social Sciences and Philosophy at the University of Jyväskylä, Finland. She has master's degrees in social policy, ethnology and social work from the University of Jyväskylä. Her PhD dissertation in Social Work focuses on the experiences of women sentenced of crime and their possibilities for re-entering society, using van Gennep's rites of passage as her theoretical framework. Her research interests include women re-entering society after prison, gender and power, and women's homelessness. She has extensive experience as a social worker in probation work, child protection and social work with adults.

Kate Smith is a Research Fellow (asylum and migration) in the Centre for Applied Childhood, Youth and Family Research at the University of Huddersfield, UK. Working also as a Practitioner Manager at a women's centre, (please remove the capitals) she has more than 20 years of experience developing collaborative projects with women migrants. Her research interests centre (please cut broadly) on (please cut 'the areas of') migration, asylum and refugee studies, and she has published and presented widely on these topics. Smith uses visual and participatory methodologies and engages with theories and practices of narrative/storytelling, resistance and vulnerability.

Mandi Veenstra is a PhD Candidate and Teaching Fellow in the Department of Sociology at Queen's University in Ontario, Canada. Her research interests involve intensive mothering, risk prevention, child welfare and comparative social policy. Her current project recognises mothers' experiences with child welfare services as valuable in shaping family policy reform.

Elina Virokannas is a University Lecturer in the Faculty of Social Sciences at the University of Helsinki and a docent (adjunct professor) at the University of Jyväskylä, Finland. Her research interests are related to substance use and motherhood, and the peer supporter–professional relationships in street work. Recently, she has been researching the treatment views of female substance users.

Acknowledgements

This book originates from the research project *Transforming welfare service system from the standpoint of women in vulnerable life situations* funded by the Academy of Finland (project no 294407). We are most grateful to the Academy of Finland for making our research project possible and supporting the writing and editing of this book.

In addition to our Finnish research team, we invited, as authors, colleagues whom we knew have studied and published on related topics. Some of them we knew personally and had worked with before, while others we only knew through their previous publications. We would warmly like to thank you all for your positive response to our invitation, comments on early versions of the chapters, extremely good cooperation throughout the whole writing and editing process and, most of all, for your important substantial contribution.

We also want to acknowledge the work of our research assistant, Anu Karhinen-Soppi, whose contribution to the final stages of editing this book has been most important and valuable. Many mistakes have been avoided, thanks to your careful reading, editing and organising.

On behalf of all the authors, we wish to express our gratitude to all those women and practitioners who have shared their experiences with us.

Marjo Kuronen
Elina Virokannas
Ulla Salovaara

1 Introduction

Women, vulnerabilities and welfare service systems

Marjo Kuronen and Elina Virokannas

Why this book?

Over the years and even decades, much has been written about the relationship between women and the welfare state and the categorisations of different welfare states and their 'generosity' towards women (e.g. Wilson 1977; Hernes 1987; Sainsbury 1999; Esping-Andersen 2009). In recent years, the focus has been on caring, care work and care services. Important feminist conceptualisations of care began in the late-1970s (e.g. Finch and Groves 1983; see also Dahl and Eriksen 2005). Since then, care services have become a political agenda globally, with increasing academic interest first in childcare and more recently in care for older people because of aging societies (e.g. Lewis 1999; Michel and Mahon 2002; Pfau-Effinger and Rostgaard 2011; Kutsar and Kuronen 2015). In addition to care policies, other major recent issues have included family policies, pensions and employment policies, which are all often considered from the perspective of the economy and the promotion of labour market participation (see e.g. Natali and Bonoli 2012). In spite of the strong feminist tradition in social policy research, the gender perspective is still often lacking in these academic and policy debates.

The main interest in academic research as well as social policy debates has been the welfare services and social security for the 'majority' whereas those on the margins of society have gained less attention. There has also been more research on women as care providers than on women as care receivers or as individuals in need of care and other welfare services for themselves, or on women as service users of different welfare service institutions and women's encounters with these institutions' professionals. Even less is known about the services for and service needs of women on the margins of society and in vulnerable life situations. These women include poor women, women with substance abuse issues, homeless women, women with experiences of violence and abuse, women as forced migrants and asylum seekers, women who have been convicted of a crime, who have experiences of interventions by child protection either as children or as mothers of these children and so on. Often their vulnerable situations intertwine and women have experiences of several of these hardships over their life course, some of which might continue over generations.

This book is about those women and their daily lives, but it is especially about their needs for social protection, support and services and their experiences as service users. Most of the chapters in this book begin from the experiences of these women. However, the aim is not to simply report the experiences and struggles of their daily lives and give them a 'voice'. Instead, their experiences are the 'point of entry' (Smith 1987, 157) to how the welfare service systems operate for them. The aim is to show how the service systems in different countries, their institutions and professional practices organise women's daily lives and define them as women and as service users. With the empirical research done by the authors, we wish to show what the welfare service system looks like from the standpoint of these women, and how it should be developed to better meet the complex needs these women have in order to improve their lives.

From vulnerable women to vulnerabilities and vulnerable life situations

Vulnerability is a widely used concept but it is also a complex, criticised and problematic one. It is defined in various ways in different disciplines, contexts and research fields (e.g. Fineman and Grear 2013; Butler, Gambetti, and Sabsay 2016; Cole 2016; Henrickson and Fouché 2017; Virokannas, Liuski, and Kuronen 2020). In this book, the primary aim is not to delve into theorising or dig deep into the conceptual discussions of vulnerability, which many authors have done elsewhere. In this book, the critical element consists of the reflections by social policy and social work academics, who have been warning about the risk of using the concept of vulnerability in association with specific individuals or groups in a stigmatising way (Fawcett 2009; Brown 2011; Virokannas, Liuski and Kuronen 2020).

We emphasise that vulnerability is not something static but contextual, intertwined and changing in time and place. Referring especially to Martha Fineman's (2010) theorising of the concept, we see vulnerability as a universal human condition meaning that, in some stages of our life and in some situations, we might all end up being vulnerable. This is not to deny the consequences of social inequalities and that some of us are more at risk of vulnerabilities than are others (Cole 2016). According to Fineman, "our individual experience of vulnerability varies according to the quality and quantity of resources we possess or can command" (Fineman 2010, 269).

When discussing the daily lives, problems and service needs of the women studied in this book, we understand them as women in vulnerable life situations instead of as vulnerable individuals or groups. Vulnerability is not their individual characteristic or part of their identity. Thus, the authors use either vulnerable situations or positions, 'vulnerable' in quotation marks or vulnerabilities in plural or specified, for example, as 'economic vulnerability' or 'situational vulnerability'. Vulnerability is conceptualised and used in slightly different ways in different chapters. Some of the authors analyse its connections with other concepts, such as marginality, risk or social exclusion. However, all the authors share a critical approach and the commitment of not seeing vulnerability as an individual or group characteristic but rather as something that is (re)produced, governed and constructed in social structures, relations and practices.

It is also important to recognise that the concept of vulnerability is used differently in different countries and languages. In some countries, especially in the UK, it is used not only as an academic concept but also in many policy areas, law and professional practices in defining service users and their access to services (Herring 2016; Brown, Ecclestone and Emmel 2017). In other countries, for example, in Finland, where many of the authors come from, vulnerability is a concept that has only been adopted recently, and it is difficult to even translate into Finnish accurately. Academics have learned to use it while reading books and articles in English, but the nearby concepts such as 'marginality', 'social exclusion' or 'people with special needs' or most recently 'people in need of special support' have been more common in academic and policy texts. Thus, in this book, we find it important to define the social and cultural context where and how the concept is used, especially when used in legislation or in the service system for classifying entitlement to services, care and benefits.

The perspective of this book is strongly on how women themselves understand, experience and define their vulnerable life situations without putting any labels on them. The vulnerability of these women is not taken for granted but the authors are asking what is causing vulnerable situations or positions, how some women or groups of women become defined as vulnerable, what are the consequences of such definitions and how women themselves are responding to them. We want to analyse and understand the processes and conditions that lead women to vulnerable situations. We also see women as active agents in their own lives and as service users instead of as powerless victims of the 'system' or social conditions. Several authors show how women resist being labelled as vulnerable or they analyse the coping strategies women have developed to protect themselves and survive in vulnerable situations.

Welfare service systems from the standpoint of women

Instead of 'vulnerable women', we turn our attention towards societies, social conditions and institutions. We give special attention to the welfare service systems that are expected to prevent and reduce vulnerability and social problems, but that might also generate and (re)produce them with their own actions or through a lack of services and gaps in them.

In this book, welfare service systems or specific parts of them are studied from the standpoint of the women that need them, use them or, in some cases, are forced to use them. These women include poor women, especially poor lone mothers, women with substance abuse issues, women convicted of a crime, young women considered vulnerable, sexually exploited girls and young women, and girls and women who have experiences of interventions of child protection either as children or as mothers of these children. These women encounter severe obstacles in coping, and face stigma, social inequalities and oppression in their everyday life. They are often seen as 'the margin of the margins', not only because they face social problems but because they are women with these problems. Sometimes, as in the case of women with substance abuse issues or a criminal background, they are a marginal group in numbers, but their marginality or vulnerable situations also have specific features. Because of their marginality, they are easily forgotten in the service system and often ignored even in social science research.

The welfare service system is broadly understood in this book as all health and social services, including social security and benefits that women have needed, used or applied for in different life situations. The system includes universal services for all residents such as public health services or maternity care, as well as more specific services, such as those for substance abusers, refugees or homeless people and social work and child welfare/protection for children and families. In some cases, the use of the services is not their own choice but a state intervention into their lives. In general, there is a thin line between women seeking and applying for services and being forced to do so. In many cases, they would rather not use the services and apply benefits, which they might find controlling, stigmatising and even humiliating. As many of the chapters show, women sometimes try to avoid encounters with the service system and its professionals and instead search for other coping strategies. Thus, the standpoint in analysing the welfare service systems is in the women's daily lives and their use and need for services, not in the analysis of the service system or its specific institutions as such. Some of the chapters focus on specific parts of the service system while others analyse it more broadly.

The focus is on public services and social security, and the responsibility of the national or local governments to provide them, but in many countries, non-governmental organisations also have an important role in providing services. The chapters of this book cover the welfare systems in Finland, Canada, Israel, Slovenia, Spain and the UK and their service provision and benefits differ considerably. However, the starting point of this book is not the comparison of different welfare states and their service systems but women's experiences of their service needs and use. Our aim is to show that even if the vulnerable situations and welfare service systems differ, women still have shared experiences as service users.

There are also similarities in how social policies and welfare systems in different countries have been transformed in recent decades. Welfare service systems all over Europe and beyond have experienced new models of service delivery and management, austerity measures, requirements for cost-effectiveness, marketisation and priorisation of services (e.g. Natali and Bonoli 2012; Martinelli, Anttonen and Mätzke 2017; Taylor-Gooby, Leruth and Chung 2017). Too often, these transformations have meant hard times for people who already struggle in their daily lives and who are most in need of services and financial support from the state. The divide between the deserving and undeserving poor has returned to the welfare policies of many countries, personal responsibility for one's welfare has increased and cuts in services and benefits have most affected those in vulnerable situations (e.g. Kamali, Jönsson and Alseth 2018). The authors of this book are not able to show whether, and to what extent, the problems women face as service users are consequences of or directly influenced by these transformations. However, the 'times of austerity' (Martinelli, Anttonen and Mätzke 2017) are the context in which women's experiences are located.

Yet the authors of this book are able to show, based on empirical findings from different countries, that the societies, their policymaking and welfare systems are involved in (re)producing or worsening vulnerable situations and the risks for vulnerabilities of these women by not providing adequate services and support that would recognise women's specific needs. The welfare state, its institutions and professionals should take responsibility to improve the life situation of these women, empower them and provide them with means to improve their lives (Fineman 2010). Instead, when seeking services and benefits, women often experience rejection, the complexity of the system and stigmatisation.

There are strong cultural and moral expectations regarding adequate womanhood and motherhood, which influence the ways these women are seen in society but also as service users (e.g. Smith 2006; Lavee 2017). Women are judged for not fulfilling the cultural and social expectations of 'proper' women. Often their sexuality and sexual behaviour is under suspicion and surveillance. Most often, these women become visible for the welfare service system as mothers or as potential mothers, who are seen as putting the health and welfare of their children at risk. The poverty of families headed by lone mothers has also raised concern among both academics and policymakers primarily because of the risk of social exclusion for the children of these families (e.g. Hakovirta et al. 2020). This means that women often receive, are offered or even forced to use services for the sake of their children, not because of their own needs. It may also be that the needs of the children and mothers are seen to be the same. As mothers, women are able to receive services more easily than other women are, but their motherhood is also strictly monitored. In contrast, women without young children or women whose children are not living with them often receive less attention in the service system.

For women in vulnerable situations, it is typical that they have multiple service needs. They would require intensive care, support and empowerment from the professionals and social protection, women-specific services and interventions from the service system. Instead, there is often a lack of services or weak integration of different services. The women are easily turned away when searching for services; they do not have their individual needs for help, protection and support sufficiently met; or their specific life situations are not recognised. Women experience exclusion and are labelled and stigmatised as 'unfit' women and often as 'bad' mothers. In the welfare service system, women's individual and particular experiences are also easily transformed into categories, generalised definitions and labels. They become classified and labelled as vulnerable, being at risk, excluded and so on. The aim of this book is to make these service gaps visible and show how women in vulnerable situations are seen and defined as service users.

The authors in this book are committed to the standpoint of women (Smith 1987, 2005). We want to hear what women have to say about their daily lives, their experiences of lived vulnerabilities and their encounters with the service system: How do they themselves understand these vulnerable situations? What do they expect from the welfare system and its professionals? What kind of strategies do they use to cope as active actors of their own life? This is especially important when doing research with and for people who are in marginalised, vulnerable and powerless position in society, as the women discussed in this book are.

Contents of the book

Drawing upon research and critical discussions from Finland, Canada, Israel, Slovenia, Spain and the UK, this book provides empirical findings and critical insights into how women in vulnerable life situations are encountered and seen in their welfare service systems and how the system works from their standpoint. The book is divided into three sections that share the book's main theme but each with a different focus.

Part I consists of four chapters looking at how welfare service systems in different countries respond (or not) to vulnerable life situations of women and understand as well as interpret these vulnerabilities. Chapter 2 is by Kate Brown, Katie Ellis and Kate Smith. They take a critical look at how vulnerability is framed in UK welfare policy and explore vulnerability from the perspective of sexually exploited young people, girls in secure accommodation and women seeking asylum and refugees. The authors find gender to be a major structuring dimension of vulnerability and show how it intersects with other dimensions such as class, race, ethnicity, age and sexuality. They also show how women and girls respond to these vulnerability classifications and expectations with varying strategies and resistances. Brown, Ellis and Smith emphasise the need to move beyond an essentialised understanding of vulnerability in policy and practice and to create spaces for women and girls that address their own needs and self-understanding.

In Chapter 3, Elina Virokannas, Ulla Salovaara, Suvi Krok and Marjo Kuronen analyse the Finnish welfare service system from the standpoint of women in varying vulnerable life situations: women with severe substance abuse problems, women sentenced for committing a crime and poor lone mothers living with basic social benefits. The authors emphasise the similarities in the hardships these women face with the service system, which are related to the complexity of the system, receiving only limited support for their basic needs, feelings of stigmatisation and problems in face-to-face interaction with professionals. As a result of their negative experiences, women had lost trust in the service system, which even led them to avoid it.

The context of Chapter 4 is Spain, with a local focus on its capital city of Madrid. M. Victoria Gómez and Marjo Kuronen analyse vulnerable situations that women face in urban life from three perspectives: as presented in local government policy documents, as seen by the welfare professionals and as experienced and expressed by women themselves. Their findings show that the local policy statements remain at the broad, descriptive and categorising level whereas professionals and women themselves bring these vulnerable situations into the actualities of women's daily lives. The authors emphasise the role of local policymaking in recognising and drawing attention to gender-specific problems and answering the vulnerable situations that women face by providing adequate support, protection and services.

The first part concludes with Chapter 5 by Mandi Veenstra, in which she discusses the relationship between maternity, vulnerability and definitions of risk in child welfare policies and service provision in Ontario, Canada. According to Veenstra, the cultural expectations of motherhood and standards of adequate care for children continue to rise, and caregiving remains chiefly the responsibility of women. Even if 'vulnerability' and 'risk' seem to be used as synonymous in policy and professional discourses, mothers in child welfare services are more likely to be defined as risky rather than as vulnerable. Veenstra calls for a more responsive state that includes "partnering with mothers and not just policing them".

Part II includes four chapters that analyse women's encounters with and within the welfare service system more closely, each focusing on a specific part of it. It begins with Chapter 6 by Vesna Mejak and Vesna Leskošek, who have studied drug-using mothers' experiences of health care and social welfare services, especially maternity care in Slovenia, based on interviews with both drug-using mothers and practitioners. The chapter focuses on institutional practices that create a stigma in women's lives and even exacerbate their vulnerable situation. The pregnancies of women who use drugs and their desire to become mothers were judged, and mothers' subsequent fear of losing the child made them avoid the service system and hide from it. The authors call for a more holistic approach and non-stigmatising services for drug-using mothers and their children.

Women sentenced for a crime find it hard to re-enter society, and such re-entry requires both their own motivation and intensive professional support to succeed. In Chapter 7, Ulla Salovaara analyses this process of re-entry based on Finnish women's narratives. The focus is on women's experiences after being released from prison, their service needs and their encounters with different authorities and professionals. Salovaara highlights the service system's structural problems to meet even the basic needs of women as well as attitudes towards former prisoners. She suggests a stronger role for social work and emphasises the need for integrated, women-specific services for women with a criminal background, which are currently very limited.

In the recent reform of the income benefit system in Finland, the administration of the basic financial support was transferred from municipal social work to the National Social Insurance Institution (Kela). In Chapter 8, Suvi Krok analyses the consequences of this reform for the economic vulnerability of low-income lone mothers. She shows how the mothers found the new system frustrating, bureaucratic and ignorant of their individual life situations, and how they sought alternative coping strategies. From the standpoint of lone mothers, the system failed to support their coping strategies to protect their independence, income flexibility, security and self-respect.

Part II closes with Chapter 9 in which Teija Karttunen focuses on women's substance abuse and treatment issues in the context of Finnish society and its welfare service system. She observes that instead of the dominant medical framework, women's substance abuse should be understood to be connected with vulnerability and examined by tracing its social, structural and cultural determinants. Karttunen further argues that the invisibility of gender prevails in Finnish society, including in substance abuse treatment, the professional practices of social and health care professionals and social policy strategies. As do several other authors in this book, she calls for effectively coordinated and integrated social and health care services that would recognise women's individual treatment needs and gender-specific issues.

Especially in situations where the welfare service system does not provide adequate support and protection for women in vulnerable situations, the women develop other strategies for coping and survival, for which informal support is vital. The chapters in Part III focus on women's survival strategies that are based on informal support. However, as the authors of these chapters show, these strategies, which rely on support from male partners, family members and the peer support of other women, are not without their own contradictions and tensions.

The section begins with Chapter 10 by Einat Lavee, who focuses on the exchange of sex for material resources. Lavee illustrates recent policy reforms in Israel where state economic support has been reduced, and poor women – lone mothers in particular – have had to find other survival strategies, such as material support received from men. She shows how women's dependency on male resources increases and results in sexual exchange, exploitation and isolation from interpersonal networks. Lavee defines women's actions as an oppressive survival strategy and connects it to increasing gender and class inequality.

In Chapter 11, Estibaliz de Miguel-Calvo discusses formal and informal support for women prisoners in the Basque Autonomous Community in Spain. According to the author, women use formal and informal support to practice their agency in their aspiration for a 'normal life' after serving a prison sentence. However, formal services for them are limited, which increases the importance of informal support. They have especially high expectations for a romantic relationship with a male partner. The author recognises that these relationships can also be harmful and violent, but for the women, they offer symbolic resources that are especially valuable in the prison context.

Part III concludes with Chapter 12 by Elina Virokannas where she focuses on how peer support is provided among women with a long history of drug use and multiple service needs. Peer support is a form of unofficial survival strategy that supports women's autonomy and sense of community. According to her findings, professionals and authorities of the welfare service system did not play any significant role in how women discussed their coping in difficult life situations. Instead, sharing peer advice, information and empathy were significant for them. Virokannas emphasises that providing spaces for informal support among women as well as utilising experience-based knowledge in organising and providing services is essential, but it should not mean replacing professional services and support with voluntary and unpaid peers.

Book closes with brief concluding remarks by Marjo Kuronen and Ulla Salovaara where they call for improvements in the welfare service systems including more extensive women-specific services.

References

Brown, Kate. 2011. "'Vulnerability': Handle with Care." *Ethics and Social Welfare* 5 (3): 313–321. doi:10.1080/17496535.2011.597165

Brown, Kate, Katryn Ecclestone, and Nick Emmel. 2017. "The Many Faces of Vulnerability." *Social Policy and Society* 16 (3): 497–510. doi:10.1017/S1474746416000610

Butler, Judith, Zeynep Gambetti, and Leticia Sabsay. 2016. *Vulnerability in Resistance*. Durham, NC and London: Duke University Press.

Cole, Alyson. 2016. "All of Us Are Vulnerable, But Some Are More Vulnerable than Others: The Political Ambiguity of Vulnerability Studies, an Ambivalent Critique". *Critical Horizons* 17 (2): 260–277. doi:10.1080/14409917.2016.1153896

Dahl, Hanne Marlene, and Tine Rask Eriksen, eds. 2005. *Dilemmas of Care in the Nordic Welfare State: Continuity and Change*. Aldershot: Ashgate.

Esping-Andersen, Gøsta. 2009. *Incomplete Revolution: Adapting to Women's New Roles*. Cambridge: Polity.

Fawcett, Barbara. 2009. "Vulnerability: Questioning the Certainties in Social Work and Health." *International Social Work* 52 (4): 473–484. doi:10.1177/0020 872809104251

Finch, Janet, and Dulcie Groves, eds. 1983. *A Labour of Love: Women, Work and Caring*. Henley on Thames: Routledge and Kegan Paul.

Fineman, Martha Albertson. 2010. "The Vulnerable Subject and the Responsive State." *Emory Law Journal* 60 (2): 251–275. Emory Public Law Research Paper No. 10–130. Available at SSRN: https://ssrn.com/abstract = 1694740.

Fineman, Martha Albertson, and Anna Grear, eds. 2013. *Vulnerability: Reflections on a New Ethical Foundation for Law and Politics*. Surrey: Ashgate.

Hakovirta Mia, Christine Skinner, Heikki Hiilamo, and Merita Jokela. 2020. "Child Poverty, Child Maintenance and Interactions with Social Assistance Benefits among Lone Parent Families: A Comparative Analysis." *Journal of Social Policy* 49 (1): 19–39. doi:10.1017/S0047279419000151

Henrickson, Mark, and Christa Fouché. 2017. *Vulnerability and Marginality in Human Services*. London and New York: Routledge.

Hernes, Helga. 1987. *Welfare State and Woman Power: Essays in State Feminism*. London: Norwegian University Press.

Herring, Jonathan. 2016. *Vulnerable Adults and the Law*. Oxford: Oxford University Press.

Kamali, Masoud, Jessica H. Jönsson, and Ann Kristin Alseth, eds. 2018. *Neoliberalism, Nordic Welfare States and Social Work: Current and Future Challenges*. London and New York: Routledge.

Kutsar, Dagmar, and Marjo Kuronen, eds. 2015. *Local Welfare Policy Making in European Cities*. Switzerland: Springer.

Lavee, Einat. 2017. "Low-Income Women's Encounters with Social Services: Negotiation over Power, Knowledge and Respectability." *British Journal of Social Work* 47 (5): 1554–1571. doi:10.1093/bjsw/bcw131

Lewis, Jane. 1999. *Gender, Social Care and Welfare State Restructuring in Europe*. Repr. Aldershot: Ashgate.

Martinelli, Flavia, Anneli Anttonen, and Margitta Mätzke, eds. 2017. *Social Services Disrupted. Changes, Challenges and Policy Implications for Europe in Times of Austerity*. Cheltenham: Edward Elgar Publishing.

Michel, Sonya, and Rianne Mahon. 2002. *Child Care Policy at the Crossroads: Gender and Welfare State Restructuring*. New York: Routledge.

Natali, David, and Giuliano Bonoli. 2012. *The Politics of the New Welfare State*. Oxford: Oxford University Press.

Pfau-Effinger, Birgit, and Tine Rostgaard, eds. 2011. *Care between Work and Welfare in European Societies*. Basingstoke: Palgrave Macmillan.

Sainsbury, Diane. 1999. *Gender and Welfare State Regimes*. Oxford and New York: Oxford University Press.

Smith, Dorothy E. 1987. *The Everyday World as Problematic. A Feminist Sociology*. Oxford: Open University Press/Milton Keynes.

Smith, Dorothy E. 2005. *Institutional Ethnography. A Sociology for People*. Lanham, MD and Oxford: AltaMira Press.

Smith, Nora A. 2006. "Empowering the "Unfit" Mother. Increasing Empathy, Redefining the Label." *Affilia: Journal of Women and Social Work* 21 (4): 448–457. doi:10.1177/0886109906292110

Taylor-Gooby, Peter, Benjamin Leruth, and Heejung Chung, eds. 2017. *After Austerity: Welfare State Transformation in Europe After the Great Recession*. Oxford: Oxford University Press.

Virokannas, Elina, Suvi Liuski, and Marjo Kuronen. 2020. "The Contested Concept of Vulnerability – A Literature Review." *European Journal of Social Work* 23 (2): 327–339. doi:10.1080/13691457.2018.1508001

Wilson, Elizabeth. 1977. *Women and the Welfare State*. London: Tavistock Publications.

Part I

Welfare service systems (not) responding to vulnerable situations of women

2 Vulnerability as lived experience

Marginalised women and girls in the UK

Kate Brown, Katie Ellis and Kate Smith

Introduction

In a turbulent period for the welfare state in Europe and beyond, there has been a creeping normalisation and intensification of insecurity for the most vulnerable in society. In a welfare context such as the UK, characterised by weak social rights and little distribution of income, concerns about the conduct and behaviour of 'problem' groups are increasingly at the heart of social interventions, with rights to social welfare more tightly linked to personal responsibility in a 'constrained' welfare state (Dwyer 2016, 44). These developments have had a powerful effect on the most disadvantaged citizens. At the same time, the concept of vulnerability has spread into a multitude of policy arenas (Brown 2015). New models of service delivery, regimes of regulation and security, austerity measures, marketisation and prioritising of services now form a backdrop against which marginalised people, especially women and girls, are surveilled, supported and controlled. Despite policy gesturing to a more caring or inclusive approach to vulnerable groups, underpinning this rhetoric is a range of practical measures that move us towards a more excluding society for these citizens (Harrison and Sanders 2014). In this context, vulnerability has become a frame through which disadvantage is understood, responded to and generated; a contemporary reworking of distinctions drawn between the deserving and undeserving in society (Brown 2015; Smith and Waite 2018). As vulnerability management approaches also often connect with the advancement of protection for minority groups (see Bartkowiak-Théron and Asquith 2012), they have particular relevance for women and girls.

This chapter draws together insights from empirical research in the UK which explored vulnerability in relation to marginalised groups of women and girls. We draw on composite findings from co-authors' empirical research to critically explore how vulnerability is framed in UK policy and experienced by women and girls themselves. The studies included qualitative research studies with 'vulnerable' young people (Brown 2014, 2015, 2017) and sexually exploited young people (Brown 2019), girls in secure accommodation (Ellis 2016, 2018) some of whom were sexually exploited (Ellis 2020) and women seeking asylum and refugees (Smith 2015, 2016, 2017). These studies were distinct from one another but shared similar approaches in their use of qualitative methods to focus on the lived experiences of those seen as the most vulnerable. All of the studies were subject to a strict system of ethical review, focused on protecting participants as a central concern. In the chapter, girls and young women are people who self-identify as such.

We discuss vulnerability in terms of two principal manifestations (see Brown 2017, 668). First, to refer to a *policy or practice category* used officially or informally to describe or define situations that might involve people being subject to actual or potential insecurity or harm. Second, as a means of describing people's *lived experiences* of insecurity or harm, which are carved out by biological and bodily frailties, social inequalities and institutional forces, which persist over time, and which are shaped by the choices, views and experiences of individual social actors.

This chapter begins by providing a brief overview of vulnerability as a concept in contemporary UK welfare and disciplinary systems, using examples from research to highlight exemplars of vulnerability management in action. Second, we draw on our research findings to explore the dimensions of vulnerability as it is lived, highlighting structural factors. Following this, we move on to consider the different strategies used by women and girls to respond to difficult circumstances. Our findings raise questions of how contemporary interventions with 'the vulnerable' may actually increase vulnerability for some women and girls who are excluded and harmed in society. Our composite research findings highlight the ways in which these women and girls respond to structural conditions which create vulnerability with varying strategies and resistances, which enable them to get by as best they can in the circumstances they are faced with. We make the case that social policy needs to take account of this in order to respond to the lived realities of women and girls' vulnerability more effectively.

Vulnerability management in the UK policy and practice

Discussions of vulnerability have been burgeoning within pockets of policy, practice and academic writing, both in the UK and internationally (see Brown 2017; Brown, Ecclestone, and Emmel 2017). There are longstanding debates about how far the welfare system is bound together with the social control of marginalised groups (see Fox Piven and Cloward 1972; Flint 2006, 2019), with gender often featuring in discussions of how and why welfare serves the control of morality and behaviour (Hunt 1999). 'Protective' interventions are often propped up by the continuing spread of the psy-disciplines and social science understandings of human behaviour, ideas operating along with notions of the independent, economically active, male citizen, which together propel more intense surveillance and sanction of those who are seen as a problem (Wacquant 2009). Welfare scholars and criminologists have called these developments 'coercive welfare'

(Phoenix 2008, 282), 'authoritarian therapeutism' (Wacquant 2013, 249) and 'new behaviourism' (Harrison with Hemingway 2014). In an era where social problems are increasingly constructed as individual failings (Harrison and Sanders 2014), concepts of vulnerability have taken root in ways that downplay structural emphasis, which has important implications in terms of how the notion increasingly operates to (re)frame ideas about 'problem' groups of women and girls in particular. For example, in the UK, children can be imprisoned from the age of 10 for breaking the law, yet little account is given of the circumstances in which they are entrenched before offending takes place.

Vulnerability is an important classifier in a number of policy and practice arenas, both in the UK and in international development, human rights law and global anti-poverty initiatives (see Brown 2015, 2017). Although vulnerability governance mechanisms do not explicitly focus on gender, women and girls feature as a high priority in many initiatives that rely heavily on the concept. Judith Butler (2016, 2) explores feminist debates about the concept of vulnerability, arguing that there is something both 'risky and true' in claiming that women and other socially disadvantaged groups are especially vulnerable. Lived experiences of vulnerability can otherwise be overlooked and marginalised, but telling accounts of vulnerability may also further a turn to paternalistic political and social institutions that intensify disempowerment and stifle collective political solutions, entrenching feminine oppression and masculine domination rather than resisting or subverting it (see also Phipps 2019).

Social policy illustrates tensions between care and control in the management of vulnerability. The concept of vulnerability plays a central role in the governance of child protection or safeguarding policy and practice in the UK (Daniel 2010; Brown 2015; Ellis 2018), including those related to child sexual exploitation (CSE). Critical accounts note how CSE policy is grounded in preoccupations with transgression of traditional ideals of femininity (Melrose 2013). The language of exploitation establishes young people (usually girls) as always and inevitably passive, positioning them as either forced/coerced or irrational (Melrose 2013), meaning that normative ideas about vulnerability can result in an exclusion of those whose behaviours and coping mechanisms for dealing with adversity may not conform a victim typology (see Phoenix 2002; Brown 2019; Ellis 2020). The context for this vulnerability management though is a comparatively punitive response to young people who transgress. In contrast to much of Europe (where children are criminally accountable from around age 14), children in the UK are granted criminal responsibility from the age of 10 (Hazel 2008). Secure accommodation (Ellis 2018) is a key tool in responding to the 'most vulnerable' young people, providing intensive therapeutic placements for children aged 10–16 who break the law (offending placements), and also for others who have not committed crime but are deemed to be vulnerable and therefore unsafe in a community setting (welfare placements). Tensions between the managerial responses to children caught between the state of responsibility and vulnerability become particularly prominent when considering provision offered by secure accommodation, with gendered implications. Although secure units often provide mixed-gender accommodation, welfare placements are commonly awarded to girls (Ellis 2020), with efforts focussed on reforming behaviour rather than tackling social-structural causes of exploitation.

In UK refugee policy, women refugees are considered one of the most vulnerable groups of refugees (UNHCR 2019). Officials, such as the United Nations Refugee Agency, United Nations Population Fund and the Women's Refugee Commission (2016), have outlined a detailed list of women and girls considered to be particularly at risk of gender-related persecution, both in countries of origin and also in flight. Categorising women as 'the most vulnerable' has become the moral justification for a model of care and control, with increasingly punitive regimes of immigration regulation and security, alongside stronger social control mechanisms for refugees. This is exemplified through the UK government's high-profile Syrian Vulnerable Persons Resettlement Programme, which solidified a two-tier system in the UK. Making explicit divisions between people spontaneously seeking asylum (the less deserving) and those who are prioritised by the government, UK policy identifies the exceptionally vulnerable (deserving beneficiaries) for resettlement in the UK; most specifically: women, children, disabled and elderly affected by the conflict in Syria (see Smith and Waite 2018). The concept of the vulnerable women refugee has important implications for those who fit and do not fit the template of vulnerability.

Such vulnerability management exemplars highlight the trend that Butler (2016) flags in her work; that contemporary understandings of vulnerability are frequently framed in ways that are disempowering for women and girls. Alongside growing recognition about the needs of minority groups, including women and girls, there have been progressive movements to recognise difference and diversity, prioritising and tailoring interventions for women and girls who are seen as in need. At the same time though, we see paternalistic power and social control mechanisms bolstered further, with special controls and obligations in operation for the most vulnerable, often in practice women and girls. We now move to explore how these dynamics play out in the lived experiences of girls and women defined as vulnerable.

Gendered dimensions of vulnerability

The backdrop for debates about vulnerability is one of wider social change and disciplinary developments in welfare, through which individuals are controlled and disciplined, which can have a disproportionate effect on marginalised groups, including women and girls. Decades of feminist research have shown how abuse, violence and exploitation are informed by patriarchal structural forces (Herman 1981; Saphira 1981), with gender of central importance to how vulnerability is lived. In recent decades in the UK, social policy has increasingly intensified the burden of vulnerability falling on women and girls. The conditions of economic liberalism bear down on some populations more than others (Harrison and Sanders 2014; Flint 2019), with gendered implications. As one example, the privatisation of asylum support has had a devastating social and material effect on women seeking asylum and their children (Grayson 2017; Smith and Lockwood forthcoming). Similarly, the crucial role of many social work services is now outsourced to private companies in the UK, leading to a deterioration of services for the public that threaten the safety and well-being of those believed to be the most vulnerable (Jones 2018). Following the 2009 global financial crisis, austerity measures in the UK are widely shown to have a disproportionate effect on those who are intersectionally disadvantaged, including women and girls, and women and girls of colour in particular (Cooper and Whyte 2017; Women's Budget Group and Runnymead Trust 2017).

Whilst gender is an important structuring dimension of vulnerability, this intersects with other axes of social disadvantage, such as race and ethnicity, social class, age, sexuality and disability. For example, Brown (2019) and Ellis (2020) show that when researching CSE, there were hints of social class being important in how young women's experiences were understood by the professional working with them. Ellis (2020) found that girls were judged by the clothes that they wore, with care workers making judgements about their perceived (lack of) innocence:

> She thinks that I'm a bit of a slapper ... I can tell by the way she talks to me and she'll always make comments about the way I dress ... They said that if they'd been sexually exploited that they wouldn't be wearing clothes that would attract men.
>
> (Lola, aged 13)

Girls in Brown's study (2015) indicated that they were aware of how attention to their vulnerability could subject them to a scrutiny that was gendered in nature. Alicia, who had been in care and used heroin with an older boyfriend commented:

> I don't think I've ever heard of someone saying "he's a vulnerable lad" ever, but I've heard loads and loads of people say 'oh, she's a vulnerable girl' and all this.
>
> (Alicia, aged 16)

Similarly, research shows how the asylum-seeking application process requires applicants to tell "a coherent, consistent and plausible account of past and present experiences" (Rogers, Fox, and Herlihy 2015, 2), with women who provide evidence of their violations and bodily damage more likely to be seen as 'legitimate' in deserving protection (Kea and Robert-Holmes 2013).

Those women and girls who do not conform to vulnerability expectations may experience further exclusion and/or discipline as a result. For example, one young woman described being 'manipulative' as a teen: "you've got to go out and do that. It's how you fight" (Phoenix, aged 23, in Brown 2015), but she described how this led her to be judged as 'unstable'. She described an interaction with a male therapist:

> I threatened him and I told him, "You ask me the same question again, I'll pick the chair up, launch it at you and then I'll throw it outside. I really don't mind". I was escorted off the premises. Yes, I was mentally unstable apparently, not the fact that I had PTSD.
>
> (Phoenix, aged 23)

This quote illustrates a 'double suffering' (Frost and Hoggett 2008, 449) for some women and girls, where exploitation and abuse result in coping strategies which are out of step with expectations attached to how they should behave as vulnerable people, which they are in turn judged and disciplined.

Resisting the label? Responses to being labelled as vulnerable

Presented with a narrow framework within which to make sense of their lives, marginalised women and girls are consistently directed to see themselves as vulnerable. For example, it may be unsurprising that in Smith's (2015, 2016, 2017) research, women refugees spoke of their vulnerabilities. Shimmar, who had been trafficked into the UK for an early/forced marriage, described herself as a child in order to talk about the vulnerability she experienced and reinforce claims of gender-related persecution:

> I was very small girl, very small girl... Baby girl honestly.... I don't speak English... my picture from my marriage, I cried 'cos I little I am really small girl, really small girl... I don't know nothin' about marriage, nothin' about the sex.
>
> (Shimmar)

In Brown's CSE research (2019), some young women were receptive to the concept of vulnerability as a means of clearly delineating their victimisation. Phoenix talked about grooming by older men on the day of her father's funeral:

> They can see how vulnerable you are. You don't need it tattooing on your head. You can pick it out pretty much straightaway.
>
> (Phoenix, aged 23)

For her, the concept clearly offered a means of making sense of the exploitation and abuse she had suffered.

Refutations of vulnerability and the associated categorisations pose risks to some women and girls. For example, girls in secure care were keen to point out that age is an inaccurate marker of vulnerability, and each professed that they could look after themselves:

> I know I ain't vulnerable… I know about me and nobody can tell me what I am, they don't know me … if anyone called me vulnerable I'd say "you don't know me to call me vulnerable."
>
> (Lauren, aged 15)

Resistance to vulnerability classifications was also a major theme in Brown's research (2019), raising questions about how age or other social factors might shape a person's inclination to perform in line with dominant vulnerability classifications. Charlie, a young woman who had grown up in care said she would tell her workers to 'shut up' if the said she was vulnerable:

> I'm not vulnerable. They just chat a load of shit… I think I'm doing well for myself, and if [Social Worker] just said that I was vulnerable, then it'd make me feel like I'm doing loads of things I shouldn't be.
>
> (Charlie, aged 16)

Professionals working with girls in secure care reported that the girls' experiences of CSE had proved their vulnerability. However, the girls themselves argued that they had managed their own circumstances in ways that secured their safety (Ellis 2020). Young people's ideas of safety were often different to those views held by professionals, and even after months of therapy, girls defended their choices, believing that they had made particular decisions in light of their circumstances at the time:

> I mean there was crap going on but it wasn't crap that I couldn't stop going on.
>
> (Lola, aged 13)

In the secure unit, Lola and others felt that professional and policy depictions of age were an ineffective indicator of maturity (Ellis 2018). For those on welfare orders, absconding was cited as being the main contributing factor for secure placements and frequently those detained under welfare orders had been recorded as 'missing' more than 100 times in the 12 months prior to entry. Professionals acted to restrict the liberty of these girls due to concern about the risks that they were exposed to whilst absconding, and particularly around concerns about how they would secure basic amenities like food and shelter. Girls expressed frustration at being secured for absconding and resented that their age was used to justify the severity of intervention received:

> This is her favourite saying "you're only thirteen" and I'm like "yeah and your point is?" I hate it when people say that "you are only thirteen" and then they don't follow it up with anything, it's like it's just a statement and I'm like "thank you, but I did know my own age"... they mean, you shouldn't be dressing like that, you shouldn't be doing that, you shouldn't be having boyfriends, you shouldn't be smoking, you shouldn't be drinking, you shouldn't be going out to clubs, but that's just an easy way of saying it.
>
> (Lola, aged 13)

There are clearly traditional ideas about femininity as well as age at work here, which form a key part of Lola's resistance to her worker. However, for girls in secure care, the linking of their actions with their age confirmed to them that their lifestyle choices would be legitimate once they were old enough to 'decide for themselves'. As a consequence, participants reported that they longed to be 16 years of age so that they would not be targeted for interventions designed for vulnerable children (Ellis 2018).

Girls in secure accommodation were encased within a strict regime of behavioural regulation and therefore had limited space in which to challenge perceived vulnerabilities that were attached to them. While initially girls attempted to challenge pervasive understandings of vulnerability and to explain the rationality of decisions that they had made, they almost all reported that this strategy was ineffective and that staff did not take their views seriously. Rather than challenge the predominant stereotypes of vulnerability, and hence risk further intervention, the girls instead explained how they incorporated a 'display' of vulnerability, in order to convince the unit that therapy had been effective, and they had been healed and reformed and therefore allowed to return to their previous lifestyles (Ellis 2016). As Lola explains: "I just nod and agree with them... in a baby voice". This raises significant questions about the long-term effects of interventions in terms of addressing the difficulties that young people may experience, showing a deeply embedded resistance to their reforming nature on the part of some vulnerable girls.

Disrupting well-established understandings of vulnerability or telling alternative account of vulnerability can further risk women and girls being seen as undeserving beneficiaries of protection and services. For example, Smith (2015) found that some women sought asylum based on their political activities that lead to persecution. Whilst we acknowledge that much work has been done to ensure that gender-related persecutions are not simply viewed as private or domestic acts but are in themselves political acts (Crawley 2000; Freedman 2009), political activities have been long synonymised with male refugees (Guine and Moreno Fuentes 2007). Women have remained largely absent from contemporary debates about the ways in which refugees are made vulnerable for their political activism (Cheung and Phillimore 2017). Yet women told of organising oppositional activities that led to their persecution:

I love to fight for people (Precious);
... I was involved, especially with the woman's rights (Z);
I joined human rights work...I believed this was now where I belonged.
(Lucy)

Accounts of campaigning and organising demonstrations were not unusual as well as other activities that may not always be recognised as overtly political. Lucy told of how she had hidden people who the authorities were looking for and moved around the rural villages easily in her role as a health worker, distributing campaigning information and passing political messages between groups and individuals. In many of these asylum cases, authorities deciding on asylum may not recognise these types of activities as political actions and identify the associated vulnerabilities, and therefore vulnerabilities may be disregarded, trivialised and minimised (Crawley 2000; Muggeridge and Maman 2011).

For asylum-seeking women, being recognised as vulnerable as well as asserting political activities is fraught with risk. By identifying gender-based persecution and providing evidence of abuse and torture in intimate places on the female body, women risk being viewed as damaged and inevitably traumatised (Woodiwiss 2018). As such, women refugees may be dismissed as being *too* vulnerable and therefore unable to tell a coherent, credible account about their persecution (Herlihy, Scragg, and Turner 2002; Herlihy and Turner 2007); women may actually find themselves disentitled to protection, rights and resources because of their vulnerability (Smith and Waite 2018). Whilst an individual's asylum claim can strengthen the recognition of need for legal protection, the production and maintenance of a vulnerable status are central to the ways in which people are recognised as refugees or not (Tyler 2006; Kea and Roberts-Holmes 2013; Turner 2017). A vulnerable status reinforces the notion that "states exist.... to protect women and children" (Valji 2001, 31) and when women do not give accounts about their vulnerabilities, it may be deeply problematic not only for women seeking asylum but also for asylum decision-makers (and services) who understand vulnerability and respond to women refugees. Indeed, the lived experiences of political activities, as highlighted in Smith's research, may mean that women risk being removed from the category of refugee altogether.

Concluding comments

The lives of marginalised women and girls are structured by politically, economically and culturally rooted social divisions and material inequalities. Lived vulnerability is affected by the classification itself, which shapes how circumstances, needs and rights of women and girls are understood and responded to by policy-makers and service providers. They respond to such structural conditions and lived experiences in various ways, with varying strategies and resistances, which enable them to get by as best they can in difficult circumstances.

In this chapter, we have looked at the lived experience of vulnerable women and girls and suggested that although vulnerability is socially produced, contemporary understandings of vulnerability often fail to take into account the powerful social forces that exacerbate the difficulties of those living in the most difficult circumstances. Therefore, whilst some may make sense of their experiences through dominant understandings of vulnerability, in policy and practice, there is an urgent need to move beyond essentialised understandings of vulnerability to create a space where women and girls are able to draw on diverse experiences to make sense of their lives. We suggest that policy and practice need to make use of new understandings about what vulnerability is, which do not assume or simplistically categorise vulnerability and which recognise the "places we occupy on the many salient and changing axes of power that exist in any given time and place" (Williams 2018, 37).

In acknowledging that some marginalised women and girls do not give accounts of vulnerability, and even refute it, our concerns are not to deny structural gender inequalities and persecutions. We point instead to the risk of overlooking the lived experiences of women and girls who do not conform to rigid concepts of vulnerability and therefore may be disentitled to protection, rights and resources. Research, policy and practice must seek to appreciate the different ways in which women and girls understand their lived experiences, which may be extremely hard to tell (and hear) whilst they continue to be confronted with a concept of vulnerability which constructs them as vulnerable, weak, passive and traumatised. In order to forge better understandings of vulnerability, rather than seeking a definitive answer to what vulnerability is, we might contribute to a diversity of understandings of vulnerability. Whilst we have positioned lived experiences of vulnerability as of central importance, we would also argue that concepts of vulnerability should never be stripped from the socio-political context or their material constitution. It is only through bringing together structural and personal dimensions of vulnerability with its more discursive or narrative dimensions that we can stand the best chance of understanding how vulnerability is lived and experienced in contemporary society.

References

Bartkowiak-Théron, Isabelle, and Nicole L. Asquith. 2012. "The Extraordinary Intricacies of Policing Vulnerability." *Australasian Policing: A Journal of Professional Practice and Research* 4 (2): Summer, 43–49.

Brown, Kate. 2014. "Questioning the Vulnerability Zeitgeist: Care and Control Practices with 'Vulnerable' Young People." *Social Policy and Society* 13 (3): 371–387. doi:10.1017/S1474746413000535

Brown, Kate. 2015. *Vulnerability and Young People: Care and Social Control in Policy and Practice.* Bristol: Policy Press.

Brown, Kate. 2017. "The Governance of Vulnerability: Regulation, Support and Social Divisions in Action." *International Journal of Sociology and Social Policy* 37 (11–12): 667–682. doi:10.1108/IJSSP-04-2016-0049

Brown, Kate. 2019. "Vulnerability and Child Sexual Exploitation: Towards Understandings Grounded in Life Stories." *Critical Social Policy* 39 (4): 622–642. doi:10.1177/0261018318824480

Brown, Kate, Kathryn Ecclestone, and Nick Emmel. 2017. "The Many Faces of Vulnerability." *Social Policy and Society* 16 (3): 497–510. doi:10.1017/S1474746416000610

Butler, Judith. 2016. "Rethinking Vulnerability and Resistance." In *Vulnerability in Resistance*, edited by Judith Butler, Zeynep Gambetti, and Leticia Sabsay, 12–28. London: Duke University Press.

Cheung, Sin Yi, and Jenny Phillimore. 2017. "Gender and Refugee Integration: A Quantitative Analysis of Integration and Social Policy Outcomes." *Journal of Social Policy* 46 (2): 211–230. doi:10.1017/S0047279416000775

Cooper, Vickie, and David Whyte. 2017. *The Violence of Austerity.* London: Pluto Press.

Crawley, Heaven. 2000. "Engendering the State in Refugee Women's Claims for Asylum." In *States of Conflict: Gender, Violence and Resistance*, edited by Susie Jacobs, Ruth Jacobson, and Jennifer Marchban, 87–104. London: Zed Books.

Daniel, Brigid. 2010. "Concepts of Adversity, Risk, Vulnerability and Resilience: A Discussion in the Context of the 'Child Protection System'." *Social Policy and Society* 9 (2): 231–241. doi:10.1017/S1474746409990364

Dwyer, Peter. 2016. "Citizenship, Conduct and Conditionality: Sanction and Support in the 21st Century UK Welfare State." *Social Policy Review* 28: 41–62. Bristol: The Policy Press.

Ellis, Katie. 2016. "'He's Got Some Nasty Impression of Me He Has': Listening to Children in the Secure Estate." *British Journal of Social Work* 46 (6): 1553–1567. doi:10.1093/bjsw/bcv114

Ellis, Katie. 2018. "Contested Vulnerability: A Case Study of Girls in Secure Care." *Children and Youth Services Review* 88: 156–163. doi:10.1016/j.childyouth.2018.02.047

Ellis, Katie. 2020. "Blame and Culpability in Children's Narratives of Child Sexual Abuse." *Child Abuse Review* 28 (6): 405–417. doi:10.1002/car.2590

Flint, John. 2006. "Housing and the New Governance of Conduct." In *Housing, Urban Governance and Anti-Social Behaviour: Perspectives, Policy, Practice*, edited by John Flint, 19–36. Bristol: The Policy Press. doi:10.2307/j.ctt9qgs9f

Flint, John. 2019. "Encounters with the Centaur State: Advanced Urban Marginality and the Practices and Ethics of Welfare Sanctions Regimes." *Urban Studies* 56 (1): 249–265. doi:10.1177/0042098017750070

Fox Piven, Frances, and Richard Cloward. 1972. *Regulating the Poor: The Functions of Public Welfare.* London: Tavistock Publications.

Freedman, Jane. 2009. "Protecting Women Asylum Seekers and Refugees: From International Norms to National Protection?" *International Migration* 48 (1): 175–198. doi:10.1111/j.1468-2435.2009.00549.x

Frost, Liz, and Paul Hoggett. 2008. "Human Agency and Social Suffering." *Critical Social Policy* 28 (4): 438–460. doi:10.1177/0261018308095279

Grayson, John. 2017. *'Please Get Me Moved from Here!' Pregnant Woman in G4S Asylum Housing.* UK: Open Democracy.

Guine, Anouk, and Francisco Javier Moreno Fuentes. 2007. "Engendering Redistribution, Recognition and Representation: The Case of Female Genital Mutilation (FGM) in the United Kingdom and France." *Politics and Society* 35 (3): 477–519. doi:10.1177/0032329207304315

Harrison, Malcolm, and Laura Hemingway. 2014. "Social Policy and the New Behaviourism: Towards a More Excluding Society." In *Social Policies and Social Control: New Perspectives on the Not-so-Big Society,* edited by Malcolm Harrison, and Teela Sanders, 23–39. Bristol: Policy Press.

Harrison, Malcolm and Teela Sanders. 2014. *Social Policies and Social Control: New Perspectives on the Not-so-Big Society.* Bristol: Policy Press.

Hazel, Neal. 2008. *Cross-national Comparison of Youth Justice.* London: Youth Justice Board for England and Wales.

Herlihy Jane, Peter Scragg, and Stuart Turner. 2002. "Discrepancies in Autobiographical Memories – Implications for the Assessment of Asylum Seekers: Repeated Interviews Study." *BMJ* 324: 324–327. doi:10.1136/bmj.324.7333.324

Herlihy, Jane, and Stuart Turner. 2007. "Asylum Claims and Memory of Trauma: Sharing Our Knowledge." *The British Journal of Psychiatry* 191 (1): 3–4. doi:10.1192/bjp.bp.106.034439

Herman, Judith Lewis. 1981. *Father-daughter Incest.* Cambridge: Cambridge University Press.

Hunt, Alan. 1999. *Governing Morals: A Social History of Moral Regulation.* Cambridge: Cambridge University Press.

Jones, Ray. 2018. *In Whose Interest? The Privatisation of Child Protection and Social Work.* Bristol: Policy Press.

Kea, Pamela J., and Guy Roberts-Holmes. 2013. "Producing Victim Identities: Female Genital Mutilation and the Politics of Asylum Claims in the United Kingdom." *Identities: Global Studies in Culture and Power* 20 (1): 96–113. doi:10.1080/1070289X.2012.758586

Melrose, Margaret. 2013. "Twenty-First Century Party People: Young People and Sexual Exploitation in the New Millennium." *Child Abuse Review* 22 (3): 155–168.

Muggeridge, Helen, and Chen Maman. 2011. *Unsustainable: The Quality of Initial Decision-making in Women's Asylum Claims.* London: Asylum Aid.

Phipps, Alison. 2019. "'Every Woman Knows a Weinstein': Political Whiteness and White Woundedness in #MeToo and Public Feminisms Around Sexual Violence." *Feminist Formations* 31 (2): 1–25. doi:10.1353/ff.2019.0014

Phoenix, Joanna. 2002. "In the Name of Protection: Youth Prostitution Policy Reforms in England and Wales." *Critical Social Policy* 22 (2): 353–375. doi:10.1177/02610183020220020901

Phoenix, Joanna. 2008. "ASBOs and Working Women: A New Revolving Door?" In *ASBO Nation: The Criminalisation of Nuisance,* edited by Peter Squires, 289–303. Bristol: Policy Press.

Rogers, Hannah, Simone Fox, and Jane Herlihy. 2015. "The Importance of Looking Credible: the Impact of the Behavioural Sequelae of Post-traumatic Stress Disorder on the Credibility of Asylum Seekers." *Psychology, Crime and Law* 21 (2): 139–155. doi:10.1080/1068316X.2014.951643

Saphira, Miriam. 1981. *The Sexual Abuse of Children*. Auckland: Papers Inc.

Smith, Kate. 2015. "Stories Told by, for, and about Women Refugees: Engendering Resistance." *ACME: An International E-Journal for Critical Geographies* 14 (2): 461–469.

Smith, Kate. 2016. "Telling Stories of Resistance and Ruination: Women Seeking Asylum." *Journal of Resistance Studies* 2 (2): 33–64.

Smith, Kate. 2017. "Women, Asylum and Resistance: A Feminist Narrative Approach to Making Sense of Stories." In *Feminist Narrative Research: Challenges and Opportunities*, edited by Jo Woodiwiss, Kate Smith, and Kelly Lockwood, 179–206. Basingstoke: Palgrave Macmillan.

Smith, Kate and Kelly Lockwood. Forthcoming, 2020. "Narratives of Motherhood: Seeking Asylum." In: *Contemporary Perspectives on Migrant Families, Children and Youth*. Routledge.

Smith, Kate and Louise Waite. 2018. "New and Enduring Narratives of Vulnerability: Rethinking Stories about the Figure of the Refugee." *Journal of Ethnic and Migration Studies* 45 (13): 2289–2307 doi:10.1080/1369183X.2018.1496816

Turner, Lewis. 2017. "Who Will Resettle Single Syrian Men?" University of Oxford: *Forced Migration Review*, 54.

Tyler, Imogen. 2006. "Welcome to Britain: The Cultural Politics of Asylum." *European Journal of Cultural Studies* 9 (2): 185–202. doi:10.1177/1367549406063163

UNHCR. 2019. Ms. Pramila Patten Special Representative of the Secretary-General on Sexual Violence in Conflict. Women's rights and the 2030 Agenda: The CEDAW Convention and the 2030 Agenda for Sustainable Development, March 2019, United Nations Headquarters. Accessed February 13, 2020. https://www.un.org/sexualviolenceinconflict/statement/remarks-by-ms-pramila-patten-special-representative-of-the-secretary-general-on-sexual-violence-in-conflict-womens-rights-and-the-2030-agenda-the-cedaw-convention-and-the-2030-agenda-for-s/

Valji, Nahla. 2001. "Women and the Refugee Convention: Fifty Years of Seeking Visibility." *Refuge: Canada's Journal on Refugees* 19 (5): 25–35.

Wacquant, Loic. 2009. *Punishing the Poor: The Neoliberal Government of Social Insecurity*. London: Duke University Press.

Wacquant, Loic. 2013. "The Wedding of Workfare and Prisonfare in the 21st Century: Responses to Critics and Commentators." In *Criminalisation and Advanced Marginality: Critically Exploring the Work of Loic Wacquant*, edited by Peter Squires, and John Lea, 243–258. Bristol: Policy Press.

Williams, Fiona. 2018. "Intersectionality, Gender and Social Policy." In *Handbook on Gender and Social Policy*, edited by Sheila Shaver, 37–54. Cheltenham: Edward Elgar.

Women's Budget Group and Runnymead Trust. 2017. *Intersecting Inequalities: The Impact of Austerity on Black and Minority Ethnic Women in the UK*. London: Women's Budget Group and Runnymead Trust.

Woodiwiss, Jo. 2018. "From One Girl to 'Three Girls': the Importance of Separating Agency from Blame (and Harm from Wrongfulness) in Narratives of Childhood Sexual Abuse and Exploitation." *Pastoral Care in Education* 36 (2): 154–166. doi:10.1080/02643944.2018.1464593

3 Finnish welfare service system from the standpoint of women in vulnerable life situations

Elina Virokannas, Ulla Salovaara, Suvi Krok and Marjo Kuronen

Introduction

The Nordic welfare state has been described as a woman-friendly state (Hernes 1987). Historically, it has been an important ally for women, and their needs and interests have been taken into account in welfare policy-making and developing the service system. In Finland, woman-friendliness has primarily referred to the extensive public care services for children and older people, which have freed women from informal care responsibilities and given them access to the labour market and economic autonomy (Anttonen 1997).

However, the Finnish welfare service system itself is rather gender-blind. Its aim to treat service users equally has turned into sameness, where gender differences and the specific needs of women have been disregarded. For example, until recently, violence against women has been seen as 'family violence', and professionals in health care and social services have often failed to recognise it or found it difficult to intervene (Virkki et al. 2015; Virkki 2017). Furthermore, there are few women-specific services, and feminist social work has never properly arrived in Finland (Kuronen et al. 2004).

In this chapter, we analyse how the Finnish welfare service system, its different institutions and its professionals meet or fail to meet the needs of women in varying vulnerable life situations. In this study, they are women with severe substance abuse problems, women sentenced for committing a crime and poor lone mothers living on basic social benefits. What these women share are the problems they face with the welfare service system.

By using the concept of vulnerable life situations, instead of referring to these women as vulnerable individuals or groups, we want to turn the attention towards the society and its institutions, including the welfare service system, which compensate for, but possibly also generate and (re)produce vulnerability in these women's lives (Virokannas, Liuski and Kuronen 2020). We use institutional ethnography as our theoretical and methodological framework (Smith 1987, 2005). Within this framework, individual experiences are seen as being bound up in 'ruling relations' that organise these experiences and people's local actualities (Smith 1987, 157–158; Campbell

1998; Grahame 1998). By ruling relations, Smith (2004, 79) refers to the "internally coordinated complex of administrative, managerial, professional and discursive organization that regulates, organizes, governs and otherwise controls our societies". Institutional ethnography allows us to focus on the service system without losing the standpoint of women and the connection with their experiences as its service users (Kuronen 2020).

The data were collected mainly using ethnographic interviews. The interviews were not used to reveal informants' inner experiences but to investigate institutional processes (DeVault and McCoy 2006). The data concerning women with substance abuse problems come from seven group discussions and three individual meetings with 13 women aged 25–55. Participants had engaged in heavy drug use during some period of their lives, and most of them were still using drugs weekly or even daily. The data of women sentenced for committing a crime were gathered through interviews with 25 women, aged 23–55, who were in prison at the time or had been recently released. Women in both data sets had multiple problems in several areas of their lives and needed a range of medical, financial and social services. The third data set was gathered through face-to-face interviews with 16 low-income lone mothers aged 20–58. They were either unemployed, students or on maternity or child-care leave, while some of them had chronic diseases and were on sickness leave or pension. All of them had experiences of financial hardship and had applied for basic social benefits.

On the basis of our previous studies (Virokannas 2017, 2019; Salovaara 2019), the life situations of these women and the problems they face in their daily lives differ. In this chapter, however, we will focus on similarities in their experiences concerning encounters with the welfare service system and its professionals, in their access to and use of the services.[1] These experiences are positioned in a time and place where the Finnish welfare state and its service system have for some time been undergoing a process of major transformations.

The transforming Finnish welfare service system

In recent years, researchers in different countries have critically analysed changes in social policies and welfare service systems with terms such as neoliberalism, austerity measures, activation policies and increasing private responsibility (e.g. Martinelli, Anttonen and Mätzke 2017; Kamali, Jönsson and Alseth 2018). Finland is no exception to this trend.

Finland has been described as one of the Nordic welfare states, meaning that it features a universal social security system and extensive public social care services that provide support in and protection from social risks throughout an individual's life course and which reduce social inequalities (Anttonen 2002; Kangas and Palme 2009). Increasingly, however, these principles have been put into question. The transformation that the Finnish welfare state has undergone since the 1990s has reversed the emphasis

from expanding and improving the welfare state to tightening social spending and increasing individual responsibility for social risks (e.g. Kokkonen,
Närhi and Matthies 2018). The marketisation of public services is a strong
trend (Anttonen and Karsio 2017). The reform of the basic social assistance
system in 2017 has, since its inception, caused additional problems with financial security for many low-income people (Blomberg, Kroll and Kallio
2018; Blomgren and Saikkonen 2018; Chapter 8, Krok in this book). Overall,
services and benefits for people living in poverty have weakened, and food
bank lines have become a permanent phenomenon in Finnish society since
the 1990s (Silvasti 2015).

For more than ten years, several Finnish Governments have tried to
launch a massive social and health service reform, sometimes described as
the biggest reform ever in the world. The political parties in power have
had their own ambitions concerning the reform and have failed to find a
compromise to implement it. The original aim of the reform was to improve
the quality, regional availability and cost-effectiveness of the services by
restructuring local and national responsibilities in their funding and provision. It also aims at the integration of social and health care services to
provide better services for those using both, but the focus has strongly been
on health service reform (Saltman and Teperi 2016; Kangas and Kalliomaa-
Puha 2018). To date, all of these efforts have failed, most recently in spring
2019. Meanwhile, the local governments, which currently carry the main
responsibility for providing social and health services, have made their own
decisions in reforming and privatising services.

The reform project, but also other transformations in the service system,
has been criticised for ignoring the complicated needs of the most marginalised and 'heavy' service users (Hiilamo 2015; Hellman 2019). Service users
are increasingly seen as consumers who are expected to choose and purchase
the services and be aware of their legal rights (e.g. Rajavaara 2014; Toikko
2014). This requires knowledge, social and economic resources that people
in vulnerable situations often lack. These transformations might make the
access to, availability and use of the services even more difficult for women
in vulnerable life situations with multiple needs.

Women's welfare service experiences

The problems women in vulnerable life situations face when seeking services seem to be quite similar regardless of time and place (Taylor 2010;
Hines 2013; Lavee 2017; Virokannas 2019). Our findings also show that,
in certain aspects, women's experiences concerning encounters with welfare professionals and access to and use of the services have similarities.
Women with a criminal background, histories of drug use, as well as
low-income lone mothers described several barriers and problems. These
problems are related to the complexity of the service system, receiving
only limited support for basic needs combined with the experiences of

stigmatisation, and the lack of trust in and problems with face-to-face interaction with professionals.

Complexity of the welfare service system

The welfare service system is complex and fragmented, consisting of different institutions, services, professional groups and benefit forms. It requires knowledge and resources to determine where to obtain services and how to apply for social benefits. Women said that they would need more guidance and information in operating within the system. To them, it was hard to understand and looked like a jungle with arbitrary rules.

In the case of low-income lone mothers, the social assistance system felt complex and inflexible after its move to the National Social Insurance Institution (Kela). Previously, the social assistance was dealt with in the local social welfare office. The women were not only unfamiliar with the new system, but now many of them had to apply for financial support from several places. They first had to apply for the basic support from Kela. If that support failed to cover their needs or their application was rejected, they had to apply for additional assistance from the local social services. Maria describes how applying for income support is a difficult and confusing process.

> That's exactly what they said in the child welfare services that first you apply for this and then it comes back like a boomerang from the basic social assistance and not until then can you really apply for it. [laughs]
>
> After that, it goes to the municipality and then you might ask to meet a social worker. And now I should apply, but, I mean, it is the thing that I cannot take care of my business right now. That's why we made the supplementary application over a week ago. And I was supposed to check from Kela's website and everywhere those attachments when I am at home. And I have not done that yet. I mean, it takes several days to do that, you know, to be able to do that in my situation in which I have other things to worry about [—]... the supplementary benefit application, you should point out there that you want to meet the social worker. Well then, I suppose I must go there to make the third application about the same issue.
>
> (Maria)

Maria describes how the system that requires several applications with different documents for each benefit looks absurd from her standpoint. There are several steps in the application process, and the applicant can only wait and fear for the outcome. Maria finds her life situation as a mother who is solely responsible for her children burdensome enough without these bureaucratic procedures. It takes a lot of strength, and that is why she hasn't managed to complete the application, which means that she has to wait even longer and find other means to support herself and her children while waiting.

Women with a criminal background and a long history of substance abuse require help and guidance in many aspects of their everyday life. They were either unaware of where to get help or unable to get any. They discussed getting help as if it were like a stroke of luck. It was coincidental and occasional, not systematic or planned and rarely recognised their specific needs as women. Being released from prison is an extremely crucial moment when integration into society may or may not succeed. The most problematic issues are related to housing, coping with the authorities and substance abuse problems (Salovaara 2019; also Chapter 7, Salovaara in this book). Susanna describes the difficulties she had after being released from prison:

> And we know what it is. Like when you are released and you just have to take care of everything. Bills for example. And you just haven't paid anything. Like throwing them in garbage bin, if there are some. That just wasn't part of your everyday life then. Not to mention cooking, or doing laundry, cleaning. Those just were not part of your life before. Or socialising with people. You go to offices and try to solve your things … It's just impossible. Like filling out some forms. Just a simple form to fill out, you just can't understand it!
>
> (Susanna)

The contrast between controlled and structured life in prison and civilian life with freedom and responsibility to take care of ordinary daily tasks seems huge to Susanna. Along with everyday tasks she was not used to manage, she needed to deal with the welfare service system. Seeking help and filling out applications was the most difficult part because she did not understand what she was expected to do.

In the next extract, women with drug problems also discuss the difficulties they have had in understanding the requirements of the service system. Previously, women had discussed how hard it is to receive housing services while having drug problems.

PAULA: Well, you just wonder who do you want to or who you should please?

[The other women agree with Paula.]

ANNA: What should you be?

PAULA: You are not good enough for anyone.

KAISA: Do you have to be sober or do you have to relapse, use drugs? I mean, you never really know what they want.

PAULA: Yeah, that's what I was asking them, should I start right here to use something or, you know, mess around to get that dormitory room? Or… If I am in too good shape for them, my head is too clear, you know I guess I have to change my way of living totally. I mean, if I am not good enough like I am.

The women shared the experience that it is hard to know what the requirements to get the services they needed are. For them, it seemed that the decisions concerning their life were made somewhere in the system, and they were powerless to be involved in those processes. Furthermore, the rules might arbitrarily change. Occasionally, their problems seemed to be too serious to receive certain services, while at other times, those problems were defined as too minor to be entitled.

Limited support for basic needs and feelings of stigmatisation

In addition to the complexity of the system, women face other problems in availability of and access to the services, such as long distances, long queues and waiting times for decisions. Even if they managed to meet a social worker or another professional, they were often offered only minimal support without assessment of their life situation as a whole. Feelings of being stigmatised when seeking support for basic needs were common and might lead to withdrawing from the services entirely.

Women did not expect much from the authorities. For example, from social work, they usually only expected that their social benefits were correct and came on time. However, they reported several problems even in getting minimal support. In the next extract from the group of women with drug problems, Irene has just explained her situation after losing her apartment. Her social worker was supposed to support her with practical matters, but Irene felt that she did not receive any help.

IRENE: She [the social worker] was so bitchy. She did not take care of anything. I mean, all my business, I did not get a moving van, she just did not do anything, I mean, I got some 20 euros to my account and like this and I did not get anything.

[A few lines removed]

IRENE: But then there was an even worse bitch in the Asso [housing service]. I had to go there after, you know, I lost my stuff, all my stuff, because they did not give me any financial support, you know, any place to store my things.
JAANA: You mean a storage space
IRENE: Yeah, a storage space [changes her voice and imitates social worker's talk:] *it is not our duty,* not their duty and I wondered why they arrange storage for everyone else
JAANA: You would have the right to get it
IRENE: I lost everything. All my stuff was gone, you know. And then, they really can make your life like hell and I think I was on some black list for several years after that.

In Irene's story, basically quite a small neglect from the social worker led her life into chaos. From Irene's standpoint, the authorities limited their responsibility to the minimum, which caused her to lose not only her home but also all her belongings.

Women with a criminal background also have problems with housing. Especially women having severe problems with substance use and other difficult life situations are often released from prison and receive only minimal help with housing.

RESEARCHER: The last time you got released here you said that you didn't have a home. Did you have something already done here for you release, like an appointment at the social welfare office?

SANNA: I had the money in my bank account.

RESEARCHER: Well, that was that.

SANNA: I didn't have to go stealing as soon as I got out. But nothing much though, like I tried to get an apartment but didn't get it. Then I went and complained in the social welfare office. They seemed to have a picture of me that I'm a junkie and that's the only thing I'm going to be, so leave her be. Like I have no value in society anymore, not in any office or anywhere really. Like I have already screwed up my things. It's like really difficult to get back.

Just like Irene before, Sanna describes that she received no help with housing and she spoke about the stigma she felt as a service user. Integration back into society begins from having somewhere to live, a home, but Sanna felt the only safety net she had was some money in her bank account. She also combines her description of seeking support from the social welfare office with feelings of being stigmatised: from the authorities' viewpoint, she is not worth supporting because she has already screwed up her life. Feelings of stigmatisation were also present in the experiences of low-income lone mothers when applying for social benefits.

I applied for the income benefit last autumn and it was a shocking and a humiliating experience. I was there at Kela, I had a sort of officer who I visited and it went quite well. But then I began to receive those letters they sent, I mean requests for clarification. Those phrasings and how they express their requests were so awful, that I have not applied for income benefits since. And won't do it anymore.

(Sini)

For Sini, the face-to face encounter with Kela's official went fine, but she was confused about the clarification requests that came afterwards. She felt the expressions of Kela's letters were so humiliating that she gave up applying because she no longer trusted its procedures. Another mother felt that applying for income support was so stigmatising that she preferred standing in the food bank line instead (see also Linnavirta, Kroll and Blomberg 2019).

We are struggling financially. I experienced it as a salvation, when I realised that I would get food aid. After that day, during the last year, I have been applying from the church food bank line for bread and a bag of food.

(Miina)

In the Finnish welfare state, seeing the food bank line as 'salvation' cannot be anything else than a sign that the system has failed. Women described applying for basic social benefits as frustrating, 'soul destroying' and a 'shocking and humiliating experience'. The shame and stigma related to social assistance are deeply embedded in the history of classifying people into 'deserving' and 'undeserving' poor, and lone mothers still easily face moralistic blame. In the UK context, Mary Evans argues that in the current political climate, "pathologisation of those living in poverty increases the pressure on women to be 'respectable' employed citizens" (Evans 2016, 450).

Lack of trust – face-to-face interaction with professionals

Women reported difficulties in face-to-face interaction with the professionals. They were tired of explaining their situation to changing authorities and felt that nobody was interested in their life situation as a whole. These assumptions were based on their previous experiences. In the social benefit office, the encounters were experienced as rather bureaucratic and neutral, but in the case of women with drug problems and a criminal background, there was deep distrust and negative experiences.

In the next extract, three women with drug use history share their experiences of the encounters where they had trusted the authorities and been honest about their substance use. Previously, Niina's therapy had been ended as soon as she told the therapist about her occasional recreational drug use. She describes how she was again honest and once more did not receive help:

NIINA: And then I went to the XX's emergency treatment because I did not feel well and, and then they started to ask if I have used any drugs, you know. I wondered if I should this time lie but then I thought that no, I will be honest and once more also there it felt, kind of, well, you have to first go to the drug tests and you must do this and that before you can come back to these. I mean, to the mental health services

[A few lines removed]

IRENE: It is just like you said, I have been punished so many times for being honest [Irene tells about her friend who has have similar experiences.]
KAISA: Yeah, it does not help anyway, or it might help but then you start to doubt you know. Would it still be better to lie, just tell huge lies.

All three women had experiences that it is better not to trust authorities. Talking honestly about one's drug use in one service created barriers to receiving other services. In Niina's case, she was bothered by mental health problems while her drug use was a minor issue. However, giving clean drug tests was set as a condition for receiving any services.

Women also described how social workers' or health professionals' behaviour changed in face-to-face interaction as soon as their drug use was revealed. Women with criminal background had similar experiences. Next, Laura describes how a social worker was suspicious and even scared of her and her husband as they tried to seek support from social welfare office after their release.

LAURA: We went there once, got in, it was the only time. And then there was a young girl, you know. Goddamn she was so scared when we told her that we have been in prison. She was like panicking in the room. You know, I felt kinda bad. I felt a bit sorry for her. But we weren't. All our history and every detail were in our papers. That we are loud, that when we get nervous in the office we might get loud. Well of course she had read all the papers, so that's why she was even more scared. There was the security guard all the time walking in the background. Like they had gotten the information about what we might be like.

RESEARCHER: How did it feel?

LAURA: It felt kind of stupid and like a bit weird. I kind of got the feeling like I'm not a normal citizen anymore, because I've been to some prison for nine or eleven months. Like does that make me a really violent person immediately?

Laura begins by emphasising that she has visited the social welfare office only once and will not go again. She and her husband had been in prison for violent crimes, which could be seen in their files. The young social worker had obviously read the files and that was the reason for her reactions and security arrangements. Laura felt that she was treated as a violent and dangerous woman who was not able to get any support. It was widely shared among women with criminal backgrounds that the encounters with social workers were stressful and frightening. Social workers have the power to support or reject their requests, and face-to-face encounters contained significant tension.

Social work is expected to take an ethical stand and empower as well as advocate for people in marginalised and powerless positions within society. In particular, feminist social work practice emphasises recognition of women's specific needs and an equal relationship between social workers and their female clients (Dominelli 2002). Instead, the women in our study would rather avoid social workers and other professionals. They do not trust the Finnish social welfare system and want to reveal their personal life to the authorities.

Conclusion

From the standpoint of the women in this study, the Finnish welfare service system presents itself as a complex and complicated entity with arbitrary rules that are difficult to understand and predict. Encounters with the system and its professionals often left these women with feelings of frustration, stigmatisation and even anger for being treated and categorised as poor, drug-using or criminal, even violent women. Thus, they felt that the service system and its professionals cannot be trusted, and it is even wiser to avoid it if possible and seek help from other sources.

Women's expectations of the service system and its authorities were modest. They expected support mainly in basic needs related to their poor financial situation as well as housing and health problems, but even in these, they were often disappointed. Especially living without a home due to a lack of support and services was fatal. Having a home means a return to society for women released from prison. It provides privacy and safety from violence that homeless and drug-using women face on the streets. It also provides a place where one can look after one's hygiene and clothing in order to feel more like a woman. For those women who are mothers, it also offers better chances to have their children returned to them from foster care (Salovaara 2019).

Women's experiences of the service system were often personified by certain professionals, most of them women as well, whom they blamed for not understanding their situation and rejecting their requests for benefits or services. These experiences often have negative concrete consequences in women's lives, worsening their already vulnerable situations. However, both service users and professionals are embedded within the same relations of ruling (Smith 1987, 3) of the welfare service system and are part of its organisational order (Hicks 2009; Høgsbro 2017; Kuronen 2020). These include national policies and legislation, local procedures and organisational guidelines as well as practices structuring the welfare service provision. Due to tightening economic conditions and the changes in the Finnish welfare state, professionals have been shown to suffer from 'moral distress', with an accompanying emotional burden, when they are not able to behave according to their professional code of ethics (Mänttäri-van der Kuip 2016). Thus, instead of focusing on the actions or attitudes of individual professionals, it is important to ask how the welfare system should be developed to better meet the needs of these women and whether more women-specific services and interventions would be needed.

At least in principle, these women would benefit from better integration of different parts of the welfare service system, including social benefits, because they often have multiple needs and would require strong and long-lasting support to improve their situation. This is one of the original aims of the Finnish social and health service reform in progress, but there are doubts whether the system will be developed according to the requirements of those needing it most. Instead, the service system, especially after the changes it has undergone, is increasingly built for those who are capable of making their voice heard, searching for and demanding services, and knowing their rights; in other words, for those who work within the system as expected.

The welfare system does not consider women's situation and their specific needs as women, but it also seems that women rarely mention these needs in their encounters with professionals. The guiding principle of the Finnish welfare service system, as well as the whole society, is gender equality or neutrality rather than a feminist or gender-sensitive approach. Women-specific welfare services are rare. They are something 'additional', available only occasionally and locally as specific fixed-term projects, often organised by NGOs (Haahtela 2014). There is still a moral stigma on these women, who have failed both as 'active citizens' and as 'decent women'. They are aware of this status and have to cope with it in their daily lives unless they receive the professional help and services that take their needs seriously and treat them respectfully as women.

Note

1 The chapter is based on the findings of the project 'Transforming welfare service system from the standpoint of women in vulnerable life situations' funded by the Academy of Finland (2016–2020, project no 294407).

References

Anttonen, Anneli. 1997. *Feminismi ja sosiaalipolitiikka.* Tampere: Tampere University Press.

Anttonen, Anneli. 2002. "Universalism and Social Policy: A Nordic-Feminist Revaluation." *Nora: Nordic Journal of Women's Studies* 10 (2): 71–80. doi: 10.1080/080387402760262168

Anttonen, Anneli, and Olli Karsio. 2017. "How Marketisation Is Changing the Nordic Model of Care for Older People." In *Social Services Disrupted. Changes, Challenges and Policy Implications for Europe in Times of Austerity*, edited by Flavia Martinelli, Anneli Anttonen and Margitta Mätzke, 219–238. Cheltenham: Edward Elgar Publishing.

Blomberg, Helena, Christian Kroll, and Johanna Kallio. 2018. "On the Changing Frontline of Welfare Delivery: Views on Social Assistance Recipients among Finnish Frontline Workers." *Journal of Poverty and Social Justice* 26 (2): 263–280. doi:10.1332/175982718X15232796966637

Blomgren, Sanna, and Paula Saikkonen. 2018. *Viimesijaisen turvan palveluissa vielä parannettavaa: toimeentulotukiuudistuksen kuntakyselyn tuloksia.* THL Tutkimuksesta tiiviisti: 2018_012. http://urn.fi/URN:ISBN:978-952-343-116-4

Campbell, Marie. 1998. "Institutional Ethnography and Experience as Data". *Qualitative Sociology* 21 (1): 55–73.

DeVault, Marjorie. L., and Liza McCoy. 2006. "Institutional Ethnography: Using Interviews to Investigate Ruling Relations." In *Handbook of Interview Research:*

Context and Method, edited by Jaber F. Gubrium and James A. Holstein, 751–776. Thousand Oaks, CA: Sage Publications.

Dominelli, Lena. 2002. *Feminist Social Work Theory and Practice*. Basingstoke and New York: Palgrave.

Evans, Mary. 2016. "Women and the Politics of Austerity: New Forms of Respectability." *British Politics* 11 (4): 438–451. doi:10.1057/s41293-016-0037-1

Grahame, Peter R. 1998. "Ethnography, Institutions, and the Problematic of the Everyday World." *Human Studies* 21 (4): 347–360.

Haahtela, Riikka. 2014. "Homeless Women's Interpretations of Women-Specific Social Work among the Homeless People." *Nordic Social Work Research* 4 (1): 5–21. doi:10.1080/2156857X.2013.778210

Hellman, Matilda. 2019. "Social and Healthcare Reforms and Vulnerable Groups." *Nordic Studies on Alcohol and Drugs* 36 (1): 3–5. doi:10.1177/1455072 519829392

Hernes, Helga. 1987. *Welfare State and Woman Power: Essays in State Feminism*. London: Norwegian University Press.

Hicks, Stephen. 2009. "Sexuality and the 'Relations of Ruling': Using Institutional Ethnography to Research Lesbian and Gay Foster Care and Adoption." *Social Work & Society* 7 (2): 234–245.

Hiilamo, Heikki. 2015. *Hyvinvoinnin vakuutusyhtiö – Mistä sote-uudistuksessa on kysymys?* Helsinki: Into.

Hines, Lisa. 2013."The Treatment Views and Recommendations of Substance Abusing Women: A Meta-Synthesis." *Qualitative Social Work* 12 (4): 473–489. doi:10.1177/1473325011432776

Høgsbro, Kjeld. 2017. "Institutional Ethnography for People in a Vulnerable and Oppressed Situation." In *Social Work and Research in Advanced Welfare States*, edited by Kjeld Høgsbro and Ian Shaw, 117–130. London and New York: Routledge.

Kamali, Masoud, Jessica H. Jönsson, and Ann Kristin Alseth, eds. 2018. *Neoliberalism, Nordic Welfare States and Social Work: Current and Future Challenges*. London and New York: Routledge.

Kangas, Olli, and Joakim Palme. 2009. "Making Social Policy Work for Economic Development: The Nordic Experience." *International Journal of Social Welfare* 18 (s1): S62–S72. doi:10.1111/j.1468-2397.2009.00627.x

Kangas, Olli, and Laura Kalliomaa-Puha. 2018. *Finland: The Government's Social and Healthcare Reform Is Facing Problems*. ESPN Flash Report 2018/2. European Social Policy Network. https://ec.europa.eu/social/main.jsp?catId=1135&langId=en

Kokkonen, Tuomo, Kati Närhi, and Aila-Leena Matthies. 2018. "Transformation of the Finnish Welfare State." In *Neoliberalism, Nordic Welfare States and Social Work: Current and Future Challenges*, edited by Masoud Kamali, Jessica H. Jönsson, and Ann Kristin Alseth, 35–45. London and New York: Routledge.

Kuronen, Marjo. 2020. "Institutional Ethnography as a Feminist Approach for Social Work Research". In *Institutional Ethnography in the Nordic Region*, edited by Rebecca W.B. Lund and Ann Christin E. Nilsen, 117–127. London and New York: Routledge.

Kuronen, Marjo, Riitta Granfelt, Leo Nyqvist, and Päivi Petrelius, eds. 2004. *Sukupuoli ja sosiaalityö*. Jyväskylä: PS-kustannus.

Lavee, Einat. 2017. "Low-Income Women's Encounters with Social Services: Negotiation over Power, Knowledge and Respectability." *British Journal of Social Work* 47 (5): 1554–1571. doi:10.1093/bjsw/bcw131

Linnavirta, Suvi, Christians Kroll, and Helena Blomberg. 2019. "The Perceived Legitimacy of a Basic Income among Finnish Food Aid Recipients." *International Journal of Social Welfare* 28 (3): 271–281. doi:10.1111/ijsw.12362

Martinelli, Flavia, Anneli Anttonen, and Margitta Mätzke, eds. 2017. *Social Services Disrupted. Changes, Challenges and Policy Implications for Europe in Times of Austerity.* Cheltenham: Edward Elgar Publishing.

Mänttäri-van der Kuip, Maija. 2016. "Moral Distress among Social Workers: The Role of Insufficient Resources." *International Journal of Social Welfare* 25 (1): 86–97. doi:10.1111/ijsw.12163

Rajavaara, Marketta. 2014. "Yksilöllisestä henkilökohtaiseksi? Henkilökohtaistaminen hyvinvointipolitiikan uudistusideana." In *Sosiaalihuollon tila ja tulevaisuus*, edited by Riitta Haverinen, Marjo Kuronen and Tarja Pösö, 141–160. Vastapaino: Tampere.

Salovaara, Ulla. 2019. *Rikoksista tuomitut naiset: Yhteisöstä erottaminen ja takaisinliittämisen mahdollisuudet.* Acta Poenologica 1/2019, Rikosseuraamusalan koulutuskeskus.

Saltman, Richard B., and Juha Teperi. 2016. "Health Reform in Finland: Current Proposals and Unresolved Challenges." *Health Economics, Policy and Law* 11 (3): 303–319. doi:10.1017/S1744133116000013

Silvasti, Tiina. 2015. "Food Aid – Normalising the Abnormal in Finland." *Social Policy & Society* 14 (3): 471–482. doi:10.1017/S1474746415000123

Smith, Dorothy E. 1987. *The Everyday World as Problematic. A Feminist Sociology.* Oxford: Open University Press/Milton Keynes.

Smith, Dorothy E. 2004. "Ideology, Science and Social Relations: A Reinterpretation of Marx's Epistemology." *European Journal of Social Theory* 7 (4): 445–462.

Smith, Dorothy E. 2005. *Institutional Ethnography. A Sociology for People.* Lanham, MD and Oxford: AltaMira Press.

Taylor, Ozietta D. 2010. "Barriers to Treatment for Women with Substance Use Disorders." *Journal of Human Behavior in the Social Environment* 20 (3): 393–409. doi:10.1080/10911351003673310

Toikko, Timo. 2014."Vastuullisen asiakkuuden paradigma". In *Sosiaalihuollon tila ja tulevaisuus*, edited by Riitta Haverinen, Marjo Kuronen and Tarja Pösö, 161–157. Vastapaino: Tampere.

Virkki, Tuija. 2017. "Development of Finnish Policies against Domestic Violence in Terms of Gender Equality." *Social Sciences* 6 (1): 31. doi:10.3390/socsci6010031

Virkki, Tuija, Marita Husso, Marianne Notko, Juha Holma, Aarno Laitila, and Mikko Mäntysaari. 2015. "Possibilities for Intervention in Domestic Violence: Frame Analysis of Health Care Professionals' Attitudes." *Journal of Social Service Research* 41 (1): 6–24. doi:10.1080/01488376.2014.917449

Virokannas, Elina. 2017. "Eriarvoisuuden kokemuksia ja hallinnan suhteita hyvinvointipalvelujärjestelmässä: Huumeita käyttävien naisten "standpoint"". *Yhteiskuntapolitiikka* 82 (3): 274–283. http://urn.fi/URN:NBN:fi-fe2017102350239

Virokannas, Elina. 2019. "Treatment Barriers to Social and Health Care Services from the Standpoint of Female Substance Users in Finland." *Journal of Social Research* Advance online publication. doi:10.1080/01488376.2019.1598532

Virokannas, Elina, Suvi Liuski, and Marjo Kuronen. 2020. "The Contested Concept of Vulnerability – A Literature Review." *European Journal of Social Work* 23 (2): 32–7339. doi:10.1080/13691457.2018.1508001

4 Interpreting vulnerabilities facing women in urban life

A case study in Madrid, Spain

M. Victoria Gómez and Marjo Kuronen

Introduction

Every spring, since 2018, massive demonstrations against male violence have been organised all over Spain, the biggest ones being in Madrid. These demonstrations indicate increased awareness of the inequalities, social problems and vulnerabilities that women face in their daily lives. The political leadership that governed the City of Madrid from 2015 until spring 2019 was actively promoting gender equality policies and even announced Madrid to be a feminist city. The local leadership has since changed and is currently even hostile towards feminism, but this still makes the city an interesting case to study the vulnerabilities facing women in urban life and local actions to counter them. In this chapter, we ask how these vulnerabilities are interpreted and encountered in local policymaking and welfare services, and how they actualise in women's daily lives, presenting a case study from Madrid,[1] the capital city of Spain.

Gender influences all aspects of our being, our relationships and the society and culture we live in (Järviluoma, Moisala, and Vilkko 2011). Gender intersects with other distinctions and inequalities related to age, ethnicity, class, economic situation and so on. Even if violence against women has been the most visible topic in many countries recently, all over the world, there are other vulnerabilities facing women, related to poverty and economic hardship, poor housing and even homelessness, insecurity, loneliness and lack of social support, drug problems and so on. Many of these intensify in urban environments (e.g. Wratten 1995; Laparra and Pérez 2008; Fundación Foessa 2019).

Big cities harbour a significant part of the social problems that characterise contemporary urban societies. Even if often seen in terms of economic prosperity or employment hubs, they are also spaces where inequality, poverty, social segregation and isolation cumulate, in addition to enormous environmental problems. The most common sociological description of urban life reflects a weakening of local ties, individualisation and a sense of uprooting (Putnam 2000; Ascher 2010). Such a problem-oriented portrait of cities dominates sociological discussion, but there are also other interpretations of urban life emphasising belonging and social action in local contexts (Kuurne and Gómez 2019).

Feminist scholars have shown that urban life has a gender dimension, which is most often discussed in terms of gendered use of urban space and city planning (e.g. McDowell 1983; Fenster 2005; Álvarez 2017). Conceptions, experiences and daily life differ depending on gender, which leads to different ways of using the city (McDowell 1983; Durán 2017). Women suffer from spatial constraints related to the gendered division of public and private spheres (Harding and Blokland 2014). Many authors have also pointed out the dangers that cities pose for women (e.g. Wesely and Gaarder 2004; Sweet and Ortiz 2015; Pernas and Román 2017). Women limit their use of urban space due to their dedication to care tasks, but also because of their awareness of insecurity and the risk of sexual attacks and other forms of violence. In addition to gendered urban space, it is important to study local welfare policymaking and how it influences women (Kutsar and Kuronen 2015). Several feminist scholars have also called for an everyday life perspective in studying gendered urban life (e.g. Vaiou and Lykogianni 2006; Sánchez de Madariaga 2013; Beebeejaun 2017).

In analysing how vulnerabilities facing women are interpreted in different contexts, we use three different datasets collected between 2016 and 2018. We have first analysed policy documents to find out whether and how vulnerable situations of women are recognised and addressed in the local policymaking of the city of Madrid. These documents were collected from the former local government website and were chosen based on their focus on equality, human rights and social and health issues. We analysed more carefully those parts of the documents where women and vulnerabilities were explicitly mentioned. Second, one of the authors has interviewed women living in one of Madrid's central neighbourhoods about their daily life, their sense of belonging to the local environment and their coping after the severe economic crisis that hit many European countries and had a particularly severe impact in Spain. Third, we have interviewed professionals from the local welfare services and NGOs working with people facing severe vulnerable life situations, including homelessness, violence, mental health and drug problems. These three datasets provide different perspectives on and interpretations of the vulnerabilities faced by women in a large city.

Local policies recognising the vulnerable life situations of women

Local governments have an important role in making urban welfare policy, even if their mandate differs from country to country. Spain has a multilevel governance system, divided into different territorial tiers and characterised by the strong role of the regions (Kuronen and Caillaud 2015). The City of Madrid makes its own policy, but it has limited powers and resources for it. In recent years, there was a political commitment on gender equality and even feminist politics due to its former socialist-oriented local Government and the Major Manuela Carmena (2015–2019). Jesus M. Gonzalez Perez, Rubén C. Lois González and María José Piñeira Mantiñán (2016), in their comparison of urban policies in Barcelona and Madrid, conclude that social issues were the priority of the former local government in Madrid, with special attention given to disadvantaged groups and vulnerable neighbourhoods. Their analysis shows that local political priorities depend on the parties in power and can change quite rapidly.

The City of Madrid presents its local policy priorities in different documents. For our analysis, the most important document is the gender equality plan 2018–2020 (Plan Estratégico para la Igualdad de Género de la Ciudad de Madrid). Other documents are the operational plan concerning human trafficking and prostitution (Plan Operativo contra la Trata de Mujeres y Otros Abusos de Derechos Humanos en Contextos de Prostitución) and the Madrid addiction plan 2017–2021 (Plan de Adicciones de la Ciudad de Madrid). We also analysed the City of Madrid's annual report from 2017 (Cuenta General Ayuntamiento de Madrid[2]) where the City Council described, among other things, its actions to tackle vulnerable situations of women and its financial contribution to these actions.

Under the former local government, the City set up the gender equality plan, which included four main goals: integrate gender perspective into all local policies, make Madrid a city free of gender violence, promote 'sustainability of life' related to gender division of care as formal and informal work and increase the political and social participation of women. The plan first identified the major 'gender gaps' in Madrid, stating that the population is highly feminised and the gap increases in the oldest age groups. It mentions the high percentage of older women living alone as well as the high number of single-parent households headed by a woman. The plan further recognises women's position in the labour market, their lower participation rate and higher share of part-time contracts relative to men. The majority of the city's residents of non-Spanish nationality are also said to be women, and these residents' insecure social position is specifically mentioned. Many of these identified gender gaps are related to economic vulnerabilities and the high risk for poverty among women.

> In our city, many people suffer from inequality, poverty and exclusion that hinder the full exercise of their rights and affect women in a specific way. On the one hand, the feminisation of poverty punishes many women and their dependents with living conditions below basic standards, limiting their access to basic goods and resources. And on the other, gender violence in all its manifestations deprives basic rights of many women, such as the right to life, security and freedom, and represents the most common violation of human rights in the entire world.
> (Gender equality plan, 22)[3]

In the quotation, poverty and violence against women are linked and strongly defined in terms of human rights violations. It also refers to the feminisation of poverty, which has become a widely used academic and policy concept, but which has also been criticised for its conceptual and methodological weaknesses (Chant 2006) and for disregarding important issues in the understanding of vulnerability processes (Anderson 2003). Even so, many authors see the connection between poverty and gender as an incontestable fact (e.g. Laparra and Pérez 2008). In this policy document, the feminisation of poverty is not analysed further in the local context, but it simply refers to the high poverty risk of women.

Eliminating gender violence was raised as one of the four main aims of the plan:

> The municipal obligation is to prevent and detect violence early, and to guarantee sufficient, accessible and quality resources to assure integral attention and recovery to the victims. ... priority will be given to actions with older women, migrants, disabled people, homeless women and girls.
>
> (Gender equality plan, 29)

The plan recognises social responsibility and the obligation of the local government to prevent gender violence and help the victims by, for example, offering psychological and social services and legal advice. This statement is in line with the way in which the American legal theorist Martha Fineman (2010) is calling for the responsibility of the state to reduce the risks of vulnerability.

Male violence against women and services for the victims receive special attention in all of the policy documents. They report that there are special services for the women in prostitution and the victims of trafficking, such as a mobile unit and a shelter (Gender equality plan, 29–30; Operational plan against trafficking of women ... 2018–2020). The Madrid addiction plan recognises the specific problems that women face in obtaining addiction services but also the likelihood of violence:

> The most relevant differential characteristics observed were that women encounter greater difficulties in access, treatment and social integration, that they have greater delays in demanding treatment, tend to suffer family burdens and are more likely to suffer gender-based violence.
>
> (Madrid addiction plan, 75)

Furthermore, the City of Madrid's annual report states that, for example, new housing programmes were carried out for the groups at risk of social exclusion. One of them was the programme for attention to women in vulnerable situations, where the objective was to temporarily provide housing for and improve the living conditions of single mothers and their children, especially those who are recovering from abuse (Annual report 2017, 110).

The policy documents also describe other welfare services and discuss women as service users. The annual report says that the percentage of women served in the local social services was significantly higher than that of men in 2017, representing 72.7% of the service users. It is explained that women are more likely to seek support not only for themselves but also for the whole family. A higher number of women among older people also means higher care service needs (Annual report 2017, 153). The report also describes the activities of Samur Social, the local social emergency service, which runs mobile units and emergency centres, provides a telephone helpline, intervenes in social emergency situations and attends especially to homeless people and the immigrant population on the streets of Madrid. No specific services for women are mentioned but the amounts of service users are presented by gender.

The policy documents not only describe the actions taken by the City Council but also those of other local actors. NGOs have an important role in Spain in complementing public welfare services, and in raising public awareness and campaigning for improvements (Muñoz 2016). A vast majority of the NGOs receive public funding (Besteiro de la Fuente 2016). The annual report shows that this is the case also in Madrid. The local government is making contracts with and financially supporting the work of various NGOs in their specific fields (poverty, Roma population, LGTBI persons, homeless people and so on) which complement the actions of the local government. There are also national NGOs, such as the Spanish Red Cross, which is working with people in vulnerable situations across Spain and has also published a series of reports on social vulnerability. Two of these reports are specifically on women (Cruz Roja Española 2015, 2017). Many of these NGOs are described as having specific services or activities for women such as shelters or emergency housing, group activities or training to improve their employability.

Analysis of these documents shows that in the local policymaking under the previous local government, the vulnerabilities faced by women, the analysis of their causes and actions to tackle them received wide attention. The main focus, in line with the feminist campaigning, was on gender violence, along with economic vulnerabilities and the poverty risk of women, especially of specific groups, such as lone mothers, older women living alone or migrant women. However, there is no assessment in these policy documents whether and to what extent these local policy statements have been transformed into concrete action that have an impact which improves women's lives.

Economic vulnerabilities in women's daily lives

The central neighbourhood of Madrid where we carried out 29 interviews with women is inhabited by a social mix of working-class residents, students, older people, artists, academics and other professionals. Most women reported especially about their economic hardship after the financial crisis in 2008 and its consequences in their daily life. They had lived a rather ordinary life before, but it changed dramatically and resulted in an economically vulnerable situation where they were struggling to cope, with great impact on their social life and relations.

One of our interviewees, Amparo, a cook who was looking for a better job because her current one was part-time with a very low salary, explained her total lack of a social life and the need to reduce her expenses after the economic crisis:

> Social life, going out, I already told you that since the crisis started, nothing, nothing. My husband got ill, so nothing. After that, because the economy went down, I was out of work, now I only work a few hours. I'm cutting back, cutting back. In the past I used to go to the gym nearby. I also had to give that up, I'm cutting back on things.
>
> (Amparo, 54 years)

Amparo describes the vicious circle leading to an even more vulnerable situation: unemployment and illness making things worse, giving up hobbies and social life, thereby limiting social connections with other people, which leads to a life where everything is just about 'cutting back'.

Another interviewee, Isabel, was working in the field of the performing arts, organising personal development and empowerment workshops using theatrical dynamics. Until recently, her work had been funded by public institutions. Yet those institutions had begun to make financial cuts and other social programmes were being reduced. As a result, she was facing serious economic problems:

> I share the flat. I live sharing because I have to, I mean, at the beginning when I bought this flat – I'm still paying the bank – the idea was … I did not want to share the flat, but well, things got very ugly with the crisis and in the end … I also like living with people, although I have almost always lived alone, now I like it. And now I'm still having to share the flat, that is, I live with two other people, usually women.
>
> (Isabel, 48 years)

In Isabel's case, problems coping with her housing costs eventually led to a positive solution, sharing her apartment with other women, even if she was forced into it in the first place. However, Isabel's situation demonstrates the problem affecting the entire city of Madrid and many other Spanish cities, namely, difficulties in accessing affordable housing. The shortage of social housing in Spain together with the low level of wages has given rise to a large problem that increases the economic vulnerability of the population (Rodríguez López 2018).

Mónica, who has moved to Madrid from Paraguay, is a documented migrant but as many women who arrived in Spain looking for a better life, she has faced many problems:

> But as I say, I have three children and my intention was that they came here to study. That was my intention. And I do not know, it was a dream at the same time too, right? Time passed, time passed, and in the end when you do not have work here, you are not anyone, because of course, you have to pay for everything. For us who do not have a flat on our own, it is very expensive, the rent ... And when you do not have a job in two, three months, all the money is gone. And here, being here, you have to send for your children, for your family.
>
> (Mónica, 49 years)

Mónica had a dream to bring her family to Spain so that her children could receive an education and a better life. Instead, she ended up living on her own in a precarious employment situation and struggling with the high cost of housing. Previous studies have shown that the position of migrant women is weak and vulnerable, especially for those who, unlike Mónica, are undocumented migrants. Their employment situation is unprotected, and they do not have rights even for basic social and health services (Caballé-Climent 2018), which is not a unique situation in Madrid or in Spain.

Some of the women shared how they are supporting their family members who have economic problems, which makes their own situation even worse. An older lady, Maruja, describes how she financially supports both her adult son and grandson:

> I have been helping him, my son [50 years old], who does not work anymore. He does not work because he is unemployed and does not receive the unemployment benefit because of his bad head, and I have been helping him. But I already told him that I could not because the repairs in the building where I live are very expensive and every Monday and Tuesday you have to be fixing something. [...] My grandson [19 years old] comes to my flat to eat on a Saturday, and the next Saturday my son comes.
>
> (Maruja, 85 years)

Maruja's way of acting is an example of the articulation of strong family ties in Spain (Tobío et al. 2010). Her situation shows the devastating impact of unemployment due to the economic crisis and the dependence of several family generations, in this case, Maruja's son and grandson, on aid from the poor pensions of the elderly.

The vulnerable situations that these women from different social backgrounds reported were primarily caused by their economic situation but it influenced their entire life in many ways: their housing conditions, family and other social relations, social life and activities in the urban environment where they were living. They were searching for solutions to cope but often did not see a way out. They did not mention any welfare services where to seek help. Instead, coping on their own and even helping others was their strategy of survival (also Chapter 12, Virokannas in this book).

Professional perceptions of women's vulnerable situations

We also interviewed managers and professionals in different welfare services to get their views on vulnerable situations of women, their needs as service users and the provision of specific services for women. These professionals were from the local social emergency services (Samur Social), addiction services and the Red Cross. We asked them whom they considered to be women in the most vulnerable situation and why. They reflected on this question from the perspective of their specific field of expertise, which is different and more concrete than the one in the local policy documents, but it also differs from the daily life experiences of the women we interviewed.

The representative from the social emergency services mainly spoke about homeless people, which is one of the main groups they work with:

> I believe that they are mentally ill women, not because they are worse than other women, who are already very bad off, but because there are fewer resources for mental health cases. As there is less coverage, they are more vulnerable, they have less protection .... But [homeless] women are in general very bad, very bad.
>
> (Interview in Samur Social)

The professional working in the Red Cross mentioned two groups of women, victims of violence and lone mothers without support from the child's father:

> Women in situations of great vulnerability are those who suffer violence because up to the moment when they receive a response in economic or legal terms, a time occurs in which this situation makes them feel very unprotected. They do not have money to pay the rent, electricity is cut off, and what about the children? Another situation that we address here has to do with non-shared responsibility, mothers with children whose father does not participate in their care and attention.
>
> (Interview in Spanish Red Cross)

Both of these professionals stated that vulnerability is not an individual characteristic but the consequence of a complex combination of a lack of services, economic resources and protection. It is interesting to see how they are aware of and emphasising the social and structural causes of vulnerabilities. These female professionals had a good sense of the concrete problems women face in their daily lives and how those are connected with the gendered structures of Spanish society. Representatives from the addiction services described the connection between addiction and women's experiences of violence:

> Gender violence is quite common, unfortunately. First of all, gender-based violence may be the cause of women entering into substance abuse, that is, it can be used as a way to relieve the suffering. ... And then, the women who are substance users normally find themselves in situations of violence much more frequently, they are more vulnerable, they lose the defence signals, the signals at a certain moment that can warn you that you are getting into a problematic situation, in many cases you lose them completely. In addition, normally the woman enters the consumption of substances through her partner. That is very common. It is a common thing that they suffer violence in those relationships.
>
> (Interview in the Addiction Services)

In the quotation above, the professional is describing the complex connections of violent intimate relationships and addiction problems. Violence against women is seen to intertwine with other problems women face. Other professionals also discussed violence at homes, on the streets and even in the centres where women seek help and protection. Gender violence has received a lot of attention in local policies, as was shown in the analysis of the policy documents.

Professionals further emphasised the significance of family networks. A lack of social support from the family get women to search for help from the social emergency services as a last resort.

> Mothers with limited resources usually have a more or less stable network: friends, parents, family, but [migrant] women who are currently in Spain in an irregular situation are those who came from their country of origin, built a family here, the man has disappeared and that leaves them in a situation of very high defencelessness because until they get the regularisation of their administrative situation, they spend a period of time that is usually about three years or so and that does not allow them to find a job, take an offer, and that does not allow them to get into a stable situation.
>
> (Interview in Red Cross)

> Previously there was greater protection, greater solidarity with women than with men in cases of need. That's why women also took it longer ... [they are usually] less sick, less affected by problems, less damaged, with more capabilities, while... because the environment protects women more. The other women in the family, above all.
>
> (Interview in Samur Social)

The professionals were talking about the situations where family protection fails or is lacking, and how solidarity between women has declined. Jupp (2014) argues that women are expected to recreate and strengthen weakened community solidarity, especially in disadvantaged communities. In a similar sense, the professionals pointed out how family, and especially female family members, protect women in vulnerable situations. They also stated that because of their family role and responsibilities, women try to cope even in extremely difficult situations. Family connections are strong in Spain, and with the low level of public social security, extended family even provides financial support for its members (as we saw earlier in Maruja's interview). Carrascosa (2015) argues that family is more important than the welfare state in Spain in protecting its members and that the economic crisis has even increased the importance of family solidarity. Moreover, Tobío et al. (2010) conclude that in difficult times, kinship relationships, especially the vertical ones, become more important. When this 'safety net' is missing, as in the case of migrant women or lone homeless women living on the streets, they end up in extremely vulnerable situations economically, psychically and mentally (also Chapter 11, de Miguel-Calvo in this book).

In terms of family support, male partners were actually excluded from this concept; they were seen as a source of financial security but more often as a problem for women when violent and abusive. Despite the threatening situation, women often remain in violent relationships to avoid homelessness (Laparra and Pérez 2008). Men might provide a sort of 'protection' for women from other men, but at the same time that relationship can be very abusive, as our next interviewee describes:

> ... some homeless women, and I believe with home too, they feel more protected with a man next to them. It is true that there may be a man who abuses them but if not, there might be abuses by many more men. This is what happens with the pimps and prostitutes that, indeed, there is a man who abuses them but they are protected from the rest of the men, and this phenomenon I have seen it, this happens a lot.
>
> (Interview in Samur Social)

Professionals defined the vulnerabilities women face from their specific field of expertise but what they shared was the connection they made between economic problems, violence and various other vulnerable situations, and how they saw the lack of family support and protection causing or worsening women's situation. Professionals actually discussed very little how vulnerabilities facing women are tackled in the services they provided. They recognised the need for specific services for women but also the lack of them. One of our interviewees emphasised that the action should be taken at different levels: at the individual level by empowering women and helping them to improve their life, at the community level by creating supportive social networks and at the societal level with gender equality work, prevention and by raising public awareness.

Conclusion

In this chapter, we have analysed vulnerable situations that women face in urban life from the perspectives of local policymaking, professionals in the welfare services and as experienced by women themselves. These three contexts provide different interpretations of vulnerabilities, but there are also some similarities. Local policy documents remain at the general level in defining vulnerabilities and some specific groups of women at greater risk. Even if the gender inequalities of the society are recognised, policy documents are institutional texts that have no connection with the actualities of women's daily life and their experiences (Smith 2005, 183–201). The interviewed women, but also welfare service professionals, reflected more concretely on how vulnerabilities actualise in women's daily lives. Such an everyday perspective is important, as some feminist urban sociologists have argued (Vaiou and Lykogianni 2006; Beebeejaun 2017). It is important to take the standpoint of women's local actualities and their material conditions when analysing the wider social and economic processes that generate vulnerable situations (Smith 2005, 54–57).

However, it is worth noting that in the interviews with professionals and women themselves as well as in local policy documents, vulnerabilities were connected with social structures and economic conditions. They were not interpreted as individual failures or characteristics, a tendency that has recently been criticised by many academics (see Virokannas, Liuski, and Kuronen 2020). It is also evident that vulnerable life situations were seen as a combination of various problems and processes influencing women's lives simultaneously. Professionals often discussed how living in an abusive and violent relationship is combined in complex ways with other problems, such as economic hardship, substance abuse or housing problems. Both women and professionals stated how economic problems are connected with the lack of social relations and activities, influencing one's whole wellbeing. The cumulative nature of vulnerabilities requires further research. The limited scope of the welfare services also deserves deeper scrutiny. The professionals simultaneously recognised the need for specific services for women and their absence. To this should be added the fact that women did not even mention such services when they described their daily difficulties.

Initially, we wanted to study the vulnerabilities that women face in a large city as urban vulnerabilities. However, the question remains as to what extent these vulnerabilities are specifically urban. For example, vulnerable situations related to gender-based violence are not only an urban phenomenon but also permeate entire societies, whereas vulnerabilities that women face in the Madrid neighbourhood are related to the local urban environment, unemployment and the excessive costs of housing. Some problems such as homelessness or drug abuse are more wide-ranging in cities, but are not specifically urban problems. However, the idea of modern urban life characterised by the weakening of local ties, individualisation and the sense of lost community is somewhat questioned in our findings, which emphasise the importance of (female) family relations and social support, but also other social ties protecting women from and in vulnerable life situations. In order to answer this question, there is a need to deepen the promising intersection of research on vulnerabilities and social welfare with sociological research on urban life and urban environments.

Notes

1 Unless mentioned otherwise, we refer here to the city of Madrid, not the Region (Autonomous Community), which is also called Madrid.
2 2017 was the most recent year where the annual report was available at the time of the data collection.
3 Translated by the authors from Spanish into English. All the policy documents and interviews are originally in Spanish. Madrid addiction plan is translated in English, and we have used its English version. For the sake of clarity, English translations of the names of these documents are used in this chapter.

References

Álvarez, Nuria. 2017. "El espacio urbano como condición social. La experiencia de la mujer en la ciudad contemporánea". In *Género y política urbana. Arquitectura y urbanismo desde la perspectiva de género*, edited by Begoña Serrano, Carolina Mateo, and Alberto Rubio. 159–176. Valencia: Instituto Valenciano de la Edificación.

Anderson, Jeannine. 2003. "Desafíos conceptuales de la pobreza desde una perspectiva de género". A paper presented in the Seminar of Experts on Poverty and Gender *CEPAL – OIT.* Santiago de Chile, 12–13 August, 2003.

Annual Report of the Madrid City Council 2017. No date. [Cuenta General Ayuntamiento de Madrid 2017] Memoria de cumplimiento de objetivos. Volumen I. Accessed April 13 2019. https://www.madrid.es/UnidadesDescentralizadas/Presupuestos/EjecucionPresupuestaria/Cuentas_aprobadas/FicherosCuentas/CUENTA_AYTO_2017_WEB.pdf

Ascher, François. 2010. *Los nuevos principios del urbanismo.* Madrid: Alianza.

Beebeejaun, Yasminah. 2017. "Gender, Urban Space, and the Right to Everyday Life." *Journal of Urban Affairs* 39 (3): 323–334. doi:10.1080/07352166.2016.1255526

Besteiro de la Fuente, Yolanda. 2016. "El tercer sector como expresión de ciudadanía". In *Trabajo Social Madrid. Trabajo social hoy: una profesión, múltiples ámbitos*, 37–41. A Report of a Social Work seminar in Madrid, 16–17 March 2016. Colegio Oficial de Diplomados en Trabajo Social y Asistentes Sociales de Madrid.

Caballé-Climent, Laura. 2018. "Undocumented Migrant Mothers and Health Cuts in Madrid: A Gendered Process of Exclusion." *European Journal of Women's Studies* 25 (1): 28–40. doi:10.1177/1350506816665232

Carrascosa Lorenzo, Laura. 2015. "Ageing Population and Family Support in Spain." *Journal of Comparative Family Studies* XLVI (4): 499–516. doi: 10.3138/jcfs.46.4.499

Chant, Sylvia H. 2006. "Re-thinking the "Feminization of Poverty" in Relation to Aggregate Gender Indices." *Journal of Human Development* 7 (2): 201–220. doi: 10.1080/14649880600768538

Cruz Roja Española. 2015. "Vulnerabilidad Social de las mujeres atendidas por Cruz Roja". *Boletín sobre vulnerabilidad social* Numero 10. Cruz Roja Española. Departamento de estudios innovación social.

Cruz Roja Española. 2017. "Las mujeres víctimas de violencia de género, atendidas en el servicio ATENPRO". *Boletín sobre vulnerabilidad social* Número 14. Cruz Roja Española. Departamento de estudios innovación social.

Durán, María-Angeles. 2017. "La ciudad compartida: urbanismo y movimientos sociales". In *Género y política urbana. Arquitectura y urbanismo desde la perspectiva de género*, edited by Begoña Serrano, Carolina Mateo, and Alberto Rubio, 33–58. Valencia: Instituto Valenciano De La Edificación.

Fenster, Tovi. 2005. "The Right to the Gendered City: Different Formations of Belonging in Everyday Life." *Journal of Gender Studies* 14 (3): 217–231. doi:10.1080/09589230500264109

Fineman, Martha A. 2010. "The Vulnerable Subject and the Responsive State." Emory Public Law Research Paper No. 10–130. *Emory Law Journal* 60 (2): 251–275.

Fundación Foessa. 2019. *Resumen 2019. VIII Informe sobre exclusión y desarrollo social en España*. Madrid: Fundación Foessa.

Gender equality plan 2018–2020 No date. [Plan Estratégico para la Igualdad de Género de la ciudad de Madrid 2018–2020]. The City of Madrid. Accessed April 13 2018. https://www.madrid.es/UnidadesDescentralizadas/IgualdadDeOportunida des/Publicaciones/Plan%20Estrat%C3%A9gico%20para%20la%20igualdad %202018-2020/ficheros/PlanEstrategicoIgualdadGenero2018_20.pdf

González Pérez, Jesús M., Rubén C. Lois González, and María José Piñeira Mantiñán. 2016. "The Economic Crisis and Vulnerability in the Spanish Cities: Urban Governance Challenges." *Procedia – Social and Behavioral Sciences* 223: 160 –166. doi:10.1016/j.sbspro.2016.05.339

Harding, Alan, and Talja Blokland. 2014. *Urban Theory: A Critical Introduction to Power, Cities and Urbanism in the 21st Century*. London: Sage.

Järviluoma, Helmi, Pirkko Moisala, and Anni Vilkko. 2011. *Gender and Qualitative Methods*. London: SAGE. doi:10.4135/9781849209199

Jupp, Eleanor. 2014. "Women, Communities, Neighbourhoods: Approaching Gender and Feminism within UK Urban Policy." *Antipode* 46 (5): 1304–1322. doi:10. 1111/anti.12088

Kuronen, Marjo, and Pascal Caillaud. 2015. "Vertical Governance, National Regulation and Autonomy of Local Policy Making." In *Local Welfare Policy Making in European Cities*, edited by Dagmar Kutsar and Marjo Kuronen, 71–85. Switzerland: Springer.

Kutsar, Dagmar, and Marjo Kuronen, eds. 2015. *Local Welfare Policy Making in European Cities*. Switzerland: Springer.

Kuurne, Kaisa and M. Victoria Gómez. 2019. "Feeling at Home in the Neighbourhood: Belonging, the House and the Plaza in Helsinki and Madrid." *City and Community* 18 (1): 213–237. doi:10.1111/cico.12368

Laparra, Miguel and Begoña Pérez. Coord. 2008. *Exclusión social en España. Un espacio diverso y disperso en intensa transformación*. Madrid: Fundación Foessa.

Madrid addiction plan 2017–2021. No date. Madrid City Council. Government Area of Health, Safety and Emergencies. Addiction Institute from City of Madrid.

Accessed February 6 2020. https://www.madrid.es/UnidadesDescentralizadas/Salud/Adicciones/PlandeAdicciones/ficheros/MadridAddictionPlan2017-2021.pdf

McDowell, Linda. 1983 "Towards an Understanding of the Gender Division of Urban Space." *Environment and Planning D: Society and Space* 1 (1): 59–72. doi:10.1068/d010059

Muñoz, Luz M. 2016. "El impacto de la regulación estatal en las ong de desarrollo en España." *Revista de Estudios Políticos* 171: 193–222. doi:10.18042/cepc/rep.171.07

Operational Plan against Trafficking of Women and Abuse of Human Rights in the Context of Prostitution 2018–2020. No date. [Plan Operativo contra la trata de mujeres y otros abusos de derechos humanos en contextos de prostitución 2018–2020.]. Accessed April 13 2018. https://www.madrid.es/UnidadesDescentralizadas/IgualdadDeOportunidades/Publicaciones/Publicaciones%202018/ficheros/plantrataweb.pdf

Pernas, Begoña, and Marta Román. 2017. *Ciudades igualitarias. Guía práctica de urbanismo y género.* Madrid: Área de Gobierno de Desarrollo Urbano Sostenible del Ayuntamiento de Madrid.

Putnam, Robert. D. 2000. *Bowling Alone: The Collapse and Revival of American Community.* New York: Simon & Schuster.

Rodríguez López, Julio. 2018. *¿Se aplicarán las propuestas socialistas en materia de vivienda?* Economistas Frente a la Crisis. Accessed November 27 2019. https://economistasfrentealacrisis.com/se-aplicaran-las-propuestas-socialistas-en-materia-de-vivienda/.

Sánchez de Madariaga, Inés. 2013. "From Women in Transport to Gender in Transport: Challenging Conceptual Frameworks for Improved Policymaking." *Journal of International Affairs* 67 (1): 43–65. https://www.jstor.org/stable/24461671

Smith, Dorothy E. 2005. *Institutional Ethnography. A Sociology for People.* Lanham, MD and Oxford: AltaMira Press.

Sweet, Elizabeth S., and Sara Ortiz Escalante. 2015. "Bringing Bodies into Planning: Visceral Methods, Fear and Gender Violence." *Urban Studies* 52 (10): 1826–1845. doi: 0042098014541157

Tobío, Constanza, M. Silveria Agulló, M. Victoria Gómez and M. Teresa Martín. 2010. *Caring for Others a Challenge for the 21st Century.* Madrid: La Caixa Foundation. Social Studies Collection No. 28. Accessed August 10 2019. http://envejecimiento.csic.es/documentos/documentos/tobio-caring-01.pdf

Vaiou, Dina, and Rouli Lykogianni. 2006. "Women, Neighbourhoods and Everyday Life." *Urban Studies* 43 (4): 731–743. doi: 10.1080/00420980600597434

Virokannas, Elina, Suvi Liuski, and Marjo Kuronen. 2020. "The Contested Concept of Vulnerability – A Literature Review." *European Journal of Social Work* 23 (2): 327–339. doi:10.1080/13691457.2018.1508001

Wesely, Jennifer K., and Emily Gaarder. 2004. "The Gendered "Nature" of the Urban Outdoors: Women Negotiating Fear of Violence." *Gender & Society* 18 (5): 645–663. doi:10.1177/0891243204268127

Wratten, Ellen. 1995. "Conceptualizing Urban Poverty." *Environment & Urbanization* 7 (1): 11–33. doi:10.1177/095624789500700118

5   Risky mothers

State–family relations, risk and the gendered reproduction of vulnerability in Canadian child welfare

Mandi Veenstra

Introduction

This chapter takes a bold look at the interplay between mothering and the state. Despite the promotion of gender equality throughout developed nations, caregiving remains the chief responsibility of women. From the promotion of breastfeeding infants to carrying the mental load of scheduling, gathering groceries and organising extra-curricular activities, women remain disproportionately involved in child rearing; this involvement and the breadth of responsibilities associated with mothering continue to rise (O'Reilly 2004; Brown 2006; Nelson 2012). Even in the Nordic countries where welfare states encourage the redistribution of childcare within the family through targeted family policies such as father-specific parental leave, in everyday practice, mothers remain constrained by cultural demands of good mothering (Lammi-Taskula 2006; Leira 2006; Gislason and Simonardóttir 2018). In Canada, mothers are enveloped by these cultural demands. Although sites of resistance exist, throughout the nation, there is persistent pressure to perform a precise definition of mothering.

Expectations of mothers to excel in raising children, often alongside maintaining paid labour in the public domain, is defined by sociologist Sharon Hays (1996, 2003) as the ideological imperative of intensive mothering. Intensive mothering identifies culturally appropriate child rearing in Western societies as "child-centred, expert-guided, emotionally absorbing, labor-intensive, and financially expensive" (Hays 1996, 8). This ideology permeates all social relations including family policy and social work practice.

This chapter explores the nuanced relationship between maternity, vulnerability and risk within state-sanctioned child welfare services in Ontario, Canada and aims to identify how gender interacts with vulnerability. With specific reference to understanding how mothers become identified and reproduced as 'risky' and requiring reform, this chapter situates Canada's international reputation as a friendly and gender-progressive nation together with the entrenchment of intensive mothering to reveal how the individuation of risk reproduces a gendered situational vulnerability. In this case,

Canadian child welfare is an integral site for examining how contemporary cultural contradictions of mothering unfold.

Drawing on findings from a collective ethnographic case study (Veenstra, forthcoming), this chapter uses a thematic analysis of qualitative data. This data includes the collection of observations, discussions with mothers and professionals involved with child welfare and available policy and program documents; the analysis in this chapter is primarily informed by policy and program documents. A critical ethnographic approach to research understands the role of social science in critiquing the political and historical entanglement of contemporary issues (O'Reilly 2009). This critique entails approaching national child welfare systems with knowledge surrounding the instrumental roles welfare states play in shaping expectations of child rearing. For Canada, in addition to the moral policing of women (Little 1998; Hallgrimsdottir, Benoit, and Phillips 2013), this knowledge must include a historical understanding of the enduring legacy of colonialisation and the persistent overrepresentation of Aboriginal families involved with child welfare services (Cull 2006; Lonne et al. 2009).

Addressing the entanglement of gender, vulnerability and risk

Teasing apart the entanglement of gender, vulnerability and risk, how they function and interact, exposes a preoccupation with female individuation – where surveillance, rationale and attributed blame is directed towards the female body (McRobbie 2009). The increasing individuation of risk reproduces a gendered situational vulnerability. While the concept of vulnerability is contested in academia (see Virokannas, Liuski, and Kuronen 2020), it nonetheless remains operational in policy and everyday practice. According to Martha Fineman (2010), the concept of vulnerability is complex and does not fit a diagnostic set of principles. Rather, the elasticity of the concept extends beyond labelling individuals and groups and permits a focus on the social processes involved in its (re)generation. It is this regeneration or the reproduction of vulnerability that is taken up here. More intently, the use of the concept of situational vulnerability references the social conditions, both materially and relationally, that interact in defining who is identified as vulnerable as a result of their social location. In social services, vulnerability often refers to deprivation or victimhood. In the context of child welfare services, however, involved mothers are more accurately identified as risky rather than vulnerable; their social conditions are not recognised as distinct from their body.

The application of a material feminist perspective addresses how the female body becomes the site of surveillance and scrutiny (McRobbie 2009). With relevance to child welfare services, it is of particular interest to question how the female body in relation to mothering becomes identified and reproduced as risky. How a nation defines adequate mothering, and values motherhood in relation to citizenship, impacts how women are seen as service users. When involvement with state services is gendered, as is the case with Canadian child welfare, it is necessary to critically analyse how expectations of maternity function to reproduce involvement.

Cultural expectations of what constitutes adequate care for children continue to rise. While scholars argue that intensive mothering is the dominant ideology of child rearing in Canada today, not all enjoy the same socioeconomic support to achieve such expectations (Hays 1996, 2003; Taylor 2011; Romagnoli and Wall 2012). To mother intensively requires women to have access to high degrees of economic, social, cultural and symbolic capital (Veenstra 2015). Mothers experiencing strained access to capital have a more difficult time fulfilling the tenets of intensive mothering. A failure to perform intensive mothering and to demonstrate engagement in its properties is interpreted as a deviation from normative expectations. In turn, this deviation generates increased surveillance. In the same way, the ideology of intensive mothering arguably serves to (re)produce classed hierarchies, manufactured social constructions of risk serve a similar function. Understanding what and who is considered risky is an integral component in addressing the interplay between constructed social policy and its subsequent impact on families' lives.

The socio-historical context of Canadian child welfare

Models of child welfare differ internationally. The family service model in the Nordic countries, for example, frames child welfare as a collective of preventative measures and family support. This model emphasises the child's rights in conjunction with offering practical assistance to the entire family. Contrary to Canada's legal-judicial model, in the Nordic nations, there is an abrupt difference between 'child welfare', an umbrella of provisions to foster a child's wellbeing, and 'child protection', specific provisions for a child experiencing or at risk of experiencing maltreatment. In this way, child welfare is understood as proactive rather than reactive. This research echoes Walmsley and Tessier's (2015) findings that child welfare in the Nordic nations, provided by the state together with non-government organisations (NGOs), encompasses a range of proactive services. These services include extensive health care, internationally renowned education systems, state-sponsored childcare, generous parental leave policies, financial transfers to families, mother–child health clinics, social workers and nurses in local schools, hot lunches during the school day and an abundance of community playgrounds to promote physical activity.

Characteristic of Anglo-American countries, Canada adopts a legal-judicial model of child welfare. This model is captured by investigations and responses to claims of child maltreatment for potential court presentation where decisions surround the need for state protection (Swift and Parada 2004; Walmsley and Tessier 2015). In contrast to the family service model in the Nordic countries, the distinction between 'child welfare' services and 'child protection' services in Canada's legal-judicial model is blurred. The terms child welfare and child protection are used interchangeably to reference the state's mandate to intervene and provide responsive services in situations where child maltreatment either is at risk of occurring or already substantiated. Framed within this premise, child welfare in Canada is reactive rather than proactive and carries the same fears and stigmas associated with child protection.

In Canada, ten provincial and three territorial governments are responsible for funding and the delivery of child welfare services, with the exception of Aboriginal peoples living on reserve. Although provinces and territories vary in their implementation of legislation and policies, the overarching calls for improvements are shared. Alongside six other provinces and territories, Ontario uses the *Child and Family Services Act* (2018) as governing legislation. This *Act* was revised in 2018 after calls in the media and by the provincial government of Ontario for its reform (Contenta, Monsebraaten, and Rankin 2014; Ministry of Children and Youth Services 2015).

Historically, the passing of *The Children's Act* in 1893, and subsequently to follow, the establishment of Children's Aid Societies in Ontario, witnessed child protective services move from the umbrella and delivery of charitable organisations to government-mandated provisions. Margaret Little explains how this *Act* "opened the door for greater state involvement in the regulation of moral behaviour" (1998, 6). Particularly, the regulation of low-income mothers.

Although child welfare services became state-sanctioned, what remains to this day, is the framing of child welfare as a humanitarian endeavour of 'bettering' specific populations, this includes working class and immigrant women (Hill Collins 2001; Hallgrimsdottir, Benoit, and Phillips 2013). In this way, specific groups of mothers rather than situational contexts were deemed vulnerable. Early philanthropic initiatives entailed mostly financial transfers in conjunction with the Ontario Mother's Allowance in the early twentieth century to avoid single mothers and widows from entering the workforce and leaving their children alone in the home (Little 1998). Child welfare services rapidly transpired into the close moral supervision of mothers receiving financial assistance from the state. Similar to the landscape of employed social workers today, child welfare professionals were predominantly white, middle-class women. As representatives of the state, these moral reformers promoted gendered, classed and racialised ideologies of mothering that are arguably still perpetuated (Little 1998; Hill Collins 2001; Hallgrimsdottir, Benoit, and Phillips 2013).

Canada's international reputation as a friendly and diverse nation is overshadowed by the tragic racialised treatment of Aboriginal peoples (Blackstock, Trocmé, and Bennett 2004; Cull 2006). Together, the enforcement of residential school attendance (enacted from 1940 to 1994) and what's known as the Sixties Scoop (an era in the 1960s where children were literally 'scooped' from their families without just cause and placed for adoption) are disturbing examples of the state's mass removal of Aboriginal children from their families in efforts to inflict assimilation. All this was done in the name of 'child welfare' (Cull 2006; Veenstra and Keenan 2017). Against this racialised backdrop, we begin to see how maternity, situational vulnerability and risk interact in Canada. Cultural disjoints in caregiving expectations and the failure to adequately address situational vulnerabilities, including poor living conditions and substance abuse, see the overrepresentation of Aboriginal families involved with child welfare services persist (Blackstock, Trocmé, and Bennett 2004). Whether it is the establishment of legislation or addressing subsequent modern-day revisions, the following section questions how policy reproduces ideological assumptions of mothering and furthers gender inequality.

Rendering gender invisible: ideological assumptions of Ontario child welfare policy

One tool used to exercise state expectations of women is the implementation of family policy. In Canada, family policy generally references policies that affect families with dependent children such as parental leave and means-tested financial transfers (*The Canadian Child Tax Benefit* for example). Although classified as universal family policy, in practice, child welfare legislation affects mostly marginalised families (Veenstra 2015). Similar to the national average, 90% of caregivers involved with Ontario child welfare are biological mothers (Canadian Incidence Study of Reported Child Abuse and Neglect (CIS) 2008; Ontario Incidence Study (OIS) 2015). This landscape of involvement is undeniably gendered. What's more, this gendered landscape is taken-for-granted; it is assumed that mother is the initial and primary contact (Brown 2006; OACAS 2015).

In 2018, the *Child and Family Services Act* (CFSA) was revised to include gender-neutral language. Part III of the CFSA titled Child Protection interprets who is considered a parent by law and references when a child requires state protection as a result of the parent's failure to adequately care. In this version of the *Act*, 'mother' is replaced with the gender-neutral language of 'parent' or 'person having charge'. The CFSA description of who constitutes a parent is linguistically convoluted and immediately references the 'Rules of Parentage' in another policy, *The Children's Law Reform Act*. Below is an excerpt from the updated CFSA, which captures the new language:

1   ...'parent', when used in reference to a child, means each of the following persons, but does not include a foster parent:

   1   A parent of the child under Sections 6, 8, 9, 10, 11 or 13 of the *Children's Law Reform Act*.
   2   In the case of a child conceived through sexual intercourse, an individual described in one of paragraphs 1–5 of subsection 7 (2) of

the *Children's Law Reform Act*, unless it is proved on a balance of probabilities that the sperm used to conceive the child did not come from the individual.

3   An individual who has been found or recognised by a court of competent jurisdiction outside Ontario to be a parent of the child ...

2   A child is in need of protection where

a   the child has suffered physical harm, inflicted by the person having charge of the child or caused by or resulting from that person's

i   failure to adequately care for, provide for, supervise or protect the child or

ii   pattern of neglect in caring for, providing for, supervising or protecting the child ... (2018, Part III 37: 1–2).

Responding to changing family forms is not contested here. Figuring out how to be inclusive of change while not ignoring the landscape of who policies primarily serve in everyday practice is integral. While the linguistic reforms to the CFSA embrace diversity, they do not reflect the reality that women in Canada remain disproportionately responsible for child rearing. It is this absence of recognition in policy rather than the revision of the language itself that is of concern.

The adoption of gender-neutral language is not coupled alongside gender-specific support services such as services for victims of domestic violence or increased access to affordable housing and childcare that reflect the needs of involved mothers. In their research on Canada's welfare state and its failure to provide a national childcare policy, Hallgrimsdottir, Benoit and Phillips (2013) reveal how Canada's blind spot in social welfare spending includes a lack of services for families and children. This absence of material support is part of a much larger issue of gender equality where "the individualization and privatization of social care" predominantly affects women who remain culturally responsible for child rearing (Hallgrimsdottir, Benoit, and Phillips 2013, 28). Policy, and resistance to policy that supports gender-specific provisions, is an important mechanism for ensuring the agendas of welfare states.

Policy must not ignore the current climate of women's over-involvement with child welfare services. In the case of Ontario, this ignorance denies attention to gendered social problems that require material resources. The assumption that all genders participate equally in child rearing is just not the reality (OIS 2015). Masked in the discourse of equality, the presumed gender neutrality of the caregiver in Ontario legislation denies women the visibility required to make significant reforms – reforms that address vulnerable situations where quality support from the state would positively impact the entire family. An example of this is the prevalence of neglect as substantiated child maltreatment in low-income families. In Ontario, neglect constitutes 24% of all substantiated child maltreatment investigations (OIS 2015).

Patterns of neglect could entail a failure to provide secure housing, safe drinking water, proper clothing and healthy food. While these are serious concerns, since its introduction to policy in 2000, substantiated neglect has become co-opted with policing the poor (Swift and Parada 2004).

The reproduction of gendered situational vulnerability

Together with the fact that the vast majority of caregivers involved with child welfare services are biological mothers, most woman involved with Ontario child welfare are situationally vulnerable (Hazen et al. 2007; Black et al. 2008; Eljdupovic 2013). This means that most mothers experience identified vulnerability because of their social conditions. In child welfare, where the safety of the child is paramount, the mother's need for help often corresponds with her being understood as risky. For example, if the mother is a victim of intimate partner violence, her social conditions construct her as a risk to her children. Here, situational vulnerability and risk become synonymous in their application. What makes the mother situationally vulnerable also makes her risky.

The Ontario Incidence Study of Reported Child Abuse and Neglect (2015) captures a snapshot of child protection across the province and details primary caregiver risk factors in child maltreatment investigations. In this report, primary caregiver risk factors are defined as: being a victim of intimate partner violence (49%); having few social supports (34%); mental health issues (27%); alcohol or drug abuse (19%); being the perpetrator of domestic violence (16%); physical health issues (8%); a history of foster care/group home (5%) and cognitive impairment (5%) (OIS 2015). In all investigations, 76% of primary caregivers exhibited at least one factor considered risky (OIS 2015).

It is necessary to position child maltreatment alongside what defines a caregiver as risky. In doing so, a pattern of involvement emerges where women in particular social situations have a greater risk of being involved with child welfare services (Swift and Callahan 2009). These particular contexts detailed above, being a victim of intimate partner violence and having few social supports for example, capture the interplay between gender, situational vulnerability and risk. As a mother, asking for help is liable to expose a vulnerable context that identifies some sort of risk. In this way, distance from needing the state's assistance supresses surveillance and the identification of risk.

In 2013, nearly half (49%) of all substantiated child maltreatment cases were the result of the child(ren) being exposed to domestic violence – experiencing the emotional harm of seeing their caregiver abused (OIS 2015). It is important to juxtapose this knowledge of involvement alongside duty-to-report obligations where women's shelters, for example, are mandated to report suspected intimate partner violence (Swift and Parada 2004). A woman's negotiation to report or flee an abusive situation is further complicated when few supportive resources exist (Black et al. 2008).

In Canada, the individual mother involved with child welfare is labelled as a woman who has made a series of poor life choices. Nico Trocmé, Director of the School of Social Work at McGill University in Montreal, Canada, comments on the relationship between problematic categories of maltreatment, such as neglect, and female individuation stating:

> ... the term 'neglect' itself is an unfortunate, in fact, problematic term. It's a term we inherited through the history of development of child welfare in North America that appears in our child protection legislation as a category of maltreatment. But it is not a particularly helpful term. It's inaccurate, it's mother-blaming, it lumps together very different situations that do not fit a coherent set of diagnostic principles.
>
> (OACAS 2017)

There is a co-option between classified child neglect and experienced poverty in Ontario (Swift and Parada 2004). As expectations of mothers intensify financially, an appropriation between neglect and poverty must be recognised as a social problem (Swift and Callahan 2009). This social problem requires prevention, practical directives and material resources rather than solely reaction through risk management. Mothers cannot be expected to uphold ideologies of intensive mothering without quality support from the state (Featherstone and Fraser 2012). A current tension exists between mothers expressing what they actually need and the risk of being deemed inadequate as a result of that need.

Risk assessment in child welfare

The introduction of risk reforms to Ontario child welfare legislation in 2000 represents a fundamental shift in social policy that emphasises the increasing surveillance of parenting practices. Vandenbeld Giles states that within

> the hegemonic neoliberal ethos, the social concept of risk and the economic concept of speculation collude to provide a powerful self-reinforcing and self-justifying political framework that is only gaining in ascendency
>
> (Vandenbeld Giles 2012, 113–114)

Social policy is increasingly preoccupied with safety and mitigating future risk rather than meeting the material and practical needs of families. Vandenbeld Giles (2012) characterises this as a move from the material to the arbitrary. This shift is evident in the adoption of risk assessment tools in state-sanctioned child welfare services. According to Turnell and Edwards (1999), Australian founders of the Signs and Safety approach used across Ontario child welfare agencies, and risk assessment tools serve to document decisions already subjectively determined by social work professionals.

Swift and Callahan further comment that risk is "widely cited as a concept that makes the 'incalculable, calculable'" (2009, 20).

The identification of risk is positioned alongside the rising status of the child. Child welfare services in Ontario are foremost positioned to protect the child with policies reflecting this primacy. Swift and Parada (2004, 6) comment, "the principle of supporting the family unit is now considered secondary to the safety and protection of the child". Although Ontario child welfare legislation in 2006 mandated family reunification as the desired result, caregivers are not offered quality support to achieve such expectations. Divorced from the material reality of marginalised families, constructions of risk within child welfare policy fundamentally impact social work practice (Brown 2006; Romagnoli and Wall 2012; Vandenbeld Giles 2014). Vandenbeld Giles states, "it becomes advantageous for the state to offload social reproduction onto the shoulders of mothers while simultaneously creating a 'feminist' contradictory narrative of emancipation through 'choice'" (2014, 417). It is precisely this paradox – the perception of choice within the constraints of social structure – that furthers risk adverse social policies (Gardner 2009). These structural constraints play out in child welfare policy where the presumed neutrality of the caregiver's gender denies recognition of the care work women continue to perform.

As discussed earlier, women in vulnerable situations experience liability in being identified as risky mothers by the state. When the province removes itself from the responsibility of helping caregivers to achieve adopted parenting standards, vulnerable contexts such as experienced poverty are more likely to be reproduced. Without material assistance and quality support, the durability of domestic violence, neglect and substance abuse persists. Knowledge of this persistence is far from novel as social work professionals are well aware of the cyclical construction of clientele's involvement.

Risky mothers fail to perform adequate caregiving skills. Alongside intensive mothering, the entrenchment of medical and psychology disciplines in Ontario child welfare is evident in the focus on determining the competency of the mother. The competency of the mother is evaluated in assessed interactions with the child. For example, the PICCOLO™ (2013) assessment is one tool used to examine and determine the mother's behaviours. Measures of affection, responsiveness, encouragement and teaching are numerically assessed during observations. The mother's tone, enthusiasm, use of affectionate nicknames, attention, interest, patience, smile, engagement and willingness to pretend play with the child are examples of scored observations. In this way, maternal–child attachment is 'objectively' evaluated and determined with checklists using a score of 0–2. The measures assessed in the PICCOLO™ tool mirror rising expectations of mothers and do not reflect the reality of daily life as a parent. Furthermore, to expect a women experiencing intimate partner violence, by example, to be enthusiastic and pretend play with her child in a clinical environment where she is being surveyed is unrealistic.

Education on adequate parenting strategies is also offered through child welfare agencies in Ontario. These programs are primarily offered to parents *after* their involvement with child welfare and focus on broad-based interventions through learned routines and child development. The premise being, that if mothers can learn to parent more effectively – based on 'accepted expert knowledge' – their involvement with child welfare can be mitigated (Brown 2006). The Parenting Enrichment Program (P.E.P.) offered at one child welfare agency in Ontario is an example of this transfer of expert knowledge. The P.E.P. at this agency features three different components: *Triple P* focuses on instruction surrounding the behaviours of children and their development; *Home Stability* focuses on generating a 'broad level of understanding' in the areas of home maintenance and nutrition for example; and *0–18 Months* focuses on educational support around feeding, safety and community services. Administration of this enrichment program varies according to provincial funding and the availability of local staff. It is important to highlight that the content of the P.E.P. is created by third-party sources with little reference to the cultural landscapes they serve. The program is detached from both the expertise of local social workers and their clientele. Social workers express frustration with this gap as they see first-hand the disjoint between the standardised programs and their clients' lives.

Focusing on the competency of the mother further positions the material body as the site of analysis and perpetuates child welfare as an individual rather than a social problem. While it is in fact necessary to provide tailored service to service users on a case-by-case basis, the distance between focusing on the mother's competency versus understanding how their social locations shape involvement is alarming.

Conclusion

The Ontario child welfare system focuses their energies on managing risk. As a legal-judicial system, risk adverse policies saturate the framework of child protection in Ontario. Although recent linguistic revisions to legislation embrace gender diversity, the landscape of caregivers involved with child welfare remains gendered. In this way, the invisibility of care work persists alongside the management of mothers.

Mothers identified as risky experience situational vulnerability. These contexts are reproduced when the state fails to address how gendered social problems contribute to involvement with child welfare. Instead, the expectations of mothers continue to rise. Mothers experiencing situational vulnerability are expected to perform intensive mothering despite strained access to the capital required to achieve such demands; this includes demonstrating adequate caregiver competency and performing an acceptable level of maternal–child attachment.

A failure to recognise the extent to which families – children *and* their caregivers, not either-or – are situationally vulnerable is evidenced in the lack of material resources addressing domestic violence and neglect – two prevalent categories of child maltreatment. Positioning individual mothers as the site of scrutiny perpetuates the individuation of risk and reproduces the situational contexts that could in fact mitigate involvement if they were addressed. The ongoing failure to recognise the extent to which mothers experience situational vulnerability perpetuates the gross need for a child welfare system that primarily responds to allegations of child maltreatment rather than prevents them. Martha Fineman states that:

> Increasingly, government is unresponsive to those who are disadvantaged, blaming individuals for their situation and ignoring the inequities woven into the systems in which we all are mired.
>
> (Fineman 2010, 257)

A step towards reimagining Canada's child welfare paradigm is embracing Fineman's call for a more responsive state. Part of this response must include partnering with mothers and not just policing them. It is time to halt the mother-blame-game and start living up to our reputation as a gender-progressive nation.

References

Black, Tara, Nico Trocme, Barbara Fallon, and Bruce MacLaurin. 2008. "The Canadian Child Welfare Response to Domestic Violence Investigations." *Child Abuse & Neglect* 32 (3): 393–404. doi:10.1016/j.chiabu.2007.10.002

Blackstock, Cindy, Nico Trocme, and Marilyn Bennet. 2004. "Child Maltreatment Investigations among Aboriginal and Non-Aboriginal Families in Canada." *Violence against Women* 10 (8): 901–916.

Brown, Debra J. 2006. "Working the System: Re-Thinking the Institutionally Organized Role of Mothers and the Reduction of "Risk" in Child Protection Work." *Social Problems* 53 (3): 352–370. doi:10.1525/sp.2006.53.3.352

Canadian Incidence Study of Reported Child Abuse and Neglect (CIS) 2008: Major Findings. Public Health Agency of Canada. Ottawa: ON, 2010. Accessed 26 April 2019. http://www.phacaspc.gc.ca/cm-vee/public-eng.php

Child and Family Services Act. 2018. RSO 1990, c C.11. Accessed 17 May 2019. https://www.ontario.ca/laws/statute/90c11#BK177

Contenta, Sandra, Laurie Monsebraaten, and Jim Rankin. 2014. "Why Are So Many Black Children in Foster Care and Group Homes?" *Toronto Star*, December 11, 2014.

Cull, Randi. 2006. "Aboriginal Mothering under the State's Gaze." In *"Until Our Hearts Are On the Ground": Aboriginal Mothering, Oppression, Resistance, and Rebirth*, edited by Memee Lavell-Harvard and Jeanette Corbiere Lavell, 141–156. Toronto: Demeter Press.

Eljdupovic, Gordana. 2013. "'I Wanted to Be, I Tried to Be, I Will Be a Good Mother': Incarcerated Mothers' Construal of the Mother-Role." In *Incarcerated Mothers: Oppression and Resistance*, edited by Gordana Eljdupovic, and Rebecca Jaremko Bromwich, 173–184. Brantford: Demeter Press.

Featherstone, Brid, and Claire Fraser. 2012. "'I'm Just a Mother. I'm Nothing Special, They're all Professionals': Parental Advocacy as an Aid to Parental Engagement." *Child & Family Social Work* 17 (2): 244–253. doi:10.1111/j.1365–2206.2012.00839.x

Fineman, Martha. 2010. "The Vulnerable Subject and the Responsive State." *Emory Law Journal* 60 (2): 251–275.

Gardner, Dan. 2009. *Risk: The Science and Politics of Fear.* London: Virgin Books, Kindle Edition.

Gislason, Ingólfur V., and Sunna Simonardóttir. 2018. "Mothering and Gender Equality in Iceland: Irreconcilable Opposites?" *Social Policy and Society* 17 (3): 457–466. doi:10.1017/S1474746417000525

Hallgrimsdottir, Helga, Cecilia Benoit, and Rachel Phillips. 2013. "The Mother-Citizen and the Working Girl: First-Wave Feminist Citizenship Claims in Canada and Discursive Opportunities for Twenty-First Century Childcare Policy." *Canadian Review of Sociology* 50 (1): 27–51. doi:10.1111/cars.12001

Hays, Sharon. 1996. *The Cultural Contradictions of Motherhood.* New Haven, CT: Yale University Press.

Hays, Sharon. 2003. *Flat Broke with Children: Women in the Age of Welfare Reform.* Oxford: Oxford University Press.

Hazen, Andrea, Cynthia Connelly, Kelly Kelleher, John Landsverk, and Richard Barth. 2007. "Intimate Partner Violence in the Child Welfare System: Findings from the National Survey of Child and Adolescent Well-Being." In *Child Protection: Using Research to Improve Policy and Practice*, edited by Ron Haskins, Fred Wulczyn, and Mary Bruce Webb, 44–61. Washington, DC: Brookings Institution Press.

Hill Collins, Patricia. 2001. "Like One of the Family: Race, Ethnicity, and the Paradox of US National Identity." *Ethnic and Racial Studies* 24 (1): 3–28. doi:10.1080/014198701750052479

Lammi-Taskula, Johanna. 2006. "Nordic Men on Parental Leave: Can the Welfare State Change Gender Relations?" In *Politicizing Parenthood in Scandinavia: Gender Relations in WelfareStates*, edited by Anne Lise Ellingsæter, and Arnlaug Leira, 79–99. Bristol: The Policy Press.

Leira, Arnlaug. 2006. "Parenthood Change and Policy Reform in Scandinavia, 1970s–2000s" In *Politicizing Parenthood in Scandinavia: Gender Relations in Welfare States*, edited by Anne Lise Ellingsæter and Arnlaug Leira, 27–51. Bristol: The Policy Press.

Little, Margaret. 1998. *'No Car, No Radio, No Liquor Permit:' The Moral Regulation of Single Mothers in Ontario, 1920–1997.* Don Mills: Oxford University Press.

Lonne, Bob, Nigel Parton, Jane Thomson, and Maria Harries. 2009. *Reforming Child Protection.* New York: Routledge Press.

McRobbie, Angela. 2009. *The Aftermath of Feminism.* London: Sage Publications.

Ministry of Children and Youth Services. 2015. *Report on the 2015 Review of the Child and Family Services Act – Executive Summary.*1–6.

Nelson, Margaret K. 2012. "What Mothers Need for Parenting to Get Under Control." In *What Do Mothers Need? Motherhood Activists and Scholars Speak Out on Maternal Empowerment for the 21st Century*, edited by Andrea O'Reilly, 44–52. Bradford: Demeter Press.

Ontario Association of Children's Aid Societies (OACAS). 2015. "Children Exposed to Domestic Violence Represent Almost 50% of Substantiated Investigations by Ontario Children's Aid Societies." https://www.oacas.org/2015/12/children-exposed-to-domestic-violence-almost-50-of-substantiated-investigations-by-ontario-childrens-aid-societies/

Ontario Association of Children's Aid Societies (OACAS). 2017. "Nico Trocmé of McGill University Discusses Why Identifying and Treating Child Neglect Can Be So Challenging." https://www.oacas.org/2017/10/nico-trocme-discusses-why-identifying-and-treating-child-neglect-can-be-so-challenging/

Ontario Incidence Study of Reported Child Abuse and Neglect-2013. (OIS) 2015. Child Welfare Research Portal, 2015. Accessed 6 March 2019. http://cwrp.ca/publications/OIS-2013

O'Reilly, Andrea. 2004. "Introduction." In *From Motherhood to Mothering: The Legacy of Adrienne Rich's of Woman Born*, edited by Andrea O'Reilly, 1–23. Albany: State University of New York Press.

O'Reilly, Karen. 2009. *Key Concepts in Ethnography*. London: Sage Publications.

PICCOLO^{TM} Tool—Parenting Interactions with Children: Checklist of Observations Linked to Outcomes. 2013. Lori Roggman, Gina Cook, Mark Innocenti, Vonda Jump Norman, and Katie Christiansen. Baltimore, MD: Paul Brookes Publishing Co., Inc.

Romagnoli, Amy, and Glenda Wall. 2012. "'I Know I'm a Good Mom': Young, Low-Income Mothers' Experiences with Risk Perception, Intensive Parenting Ideology and Parenting Education Programmes." *Health, Risk & Society* 14 (3): 273–289. doi:10.1080/13698575.2012.662634

Swift, Karen, and Henry Parada. 2004. "Child Welfare Reform: Protecting Children or Policing the Poor?" *Journal of Law and Social Policy* 19: 1–17.

Swift, Karen, and Marilyn Callahan. 2009. *At Risk: Social Justice in Child Welfare and Other Human Services*. Toronto: University of Toronto Press.

Taylor, Tiffany. 2011. "Re-examining Cultural Contradictions: Mothering Ideology and the Intersections of Class, Gender, and Race." *Sociology Compass* 5 (10): 898–907. doi:10.1111/j.1751–9020.2011.00415.x

Turnell, Andrew, and Steve Edwards. 1999. *Signs of Safety: A Solution and Safety Oriented Approach to Child Protection*. New York: W.W. Norton & Company.

Vandenbeld Giles, Melinda. 2012. "From "Need" to "Risk": The Neoliberal Construction of the "Bad" Mother." *Journal of the Motherhood Initiative for Research and Community Involvement* 3 (1): 112–133.

Vandenbeld Giles, Melinda. 2014. "Mothers of the World Unite: Gender Inequality and Poverty Under the Neo-Liberal State." *Society for International Development* 57 (3): 416–422. doi:10.1057/dev.2015.8

Veenstra, Mandi. 2015. "Manufacturing Ideologies of the "Bad" Mother in Ontario Child Welfare." Master's thesis, Queen's University.

Veenstra, Mandi. Forthcoming. "Re-imagining Canada's Child Welfare Paradigm: A Collective Ethnographic Case Study of Canadian and Finnish Child Welfare Systems." PhD diss., Queen's University.

Veenstra, Mandi, and Marlee Keenan. 2017. "Manufacturing Ideologies of the "Bad" Mother: Aboriginal Mothering, "Neglectful" Caregiving, and Symbolic Violence in the Ontario Child Welfare System." In *Bad Mothers: Regulations, Representation, and Resistance*, edited by Michelle Hughes Miller, Tamar Hagar, and Rebecca Jaremko Bromwich, 48–72. Brandford: Demeter Press.

Virokannas, Elina, Suvi Liuski, and Marjo Kuronen. 2020. "The Contested Concept of Vulnerability: A Literature Review." *European Journal of Social Work* 23 (2): 327–339. doi:10.1080/13691457.2018.1508001

Walmsley, Christopher, and Lise Tessier. 2015. "A Comparison of Nordic and Canadian Approaches." *Canadian Centre for Policy Alternatives Monitor*. December 2014/January 2015, 21 (7): 30–34. *See* https://www.policyalternatives.ca/sites/default/files/uploads/publications/National%20Office/2014/12/Monitor_Dec2014-Jan2015.pdf

Part II

Women's encounters with the welfare service system

6 The right to have a child

An institutional response to
the motherhood of drug users
in Slovenia

Vesna Mejak and Vesna Leskošek

Introduction

Women are an invisible category in the majority of studies on substance abuse. Feminist researchers in particular have been pointing out that in epidemiological and clinical research studies, female drug users are often presented as a pathological and problematic group unable to fulfil the expectations about their gender roles (Lupton 2012). Substance abuse among women is still perceived as a gender failure, moral breakdown and the social and psychological inability to perform and maintain normative female roles (Anderson 2008; Campbell and Ettore 2011).

Researchers have shown (Benoit et al. 2015) that drug-using mothers often experience a punitive attitude and the lack of understanding and support from professionals. Prejudice and stereotypes only aggravate their vulnerable position because of increased stigma. Consequently, drug-using mothers experience less empathy and understanding (McCreaddie et al. 2010). Research on the use of illicit drugs in Slovenia concentrates primarily on the risks associated with substance abuse among men, while gender differences were not addressed (Flaker 2002; Kvaternik 2006). Women drug users therefore remain overlooked and invisible.

Statistical information concerning pregnant drug-using women and mothers in Slovenia are scarce. In 2013, maternity clinics in Slovenia included the question of substance abuse in the questionnaires for pregnant women, and in 2014, there were 58 pregnant women with the history of substance abuse, and 48 women were using drugs at the time when they gave birth. The data found from the National perinatal database showed that in 2017, of the 19,706 women who gave birth, 42 had drug addiction recorded in their health card and 29 of those were using drugs during pregnancy (NIJZ 2019). The data collected by the Centres for the prevention and treatment of drug addiction show that in 2009, there were 166 drug-using mothers among their service users (Mejak 2009, 103). This figure is much higher than official numbers, but still not inclusive enough to be estimated accurately. There is no information on what is the use of services in non-governmental organisations or other social services and how many pregnant drug-using women do not use services at all and do not report to health services on drug use.

This chapter focuses on the experiences of mothers on their journey through health care and social welfare services in Slovenia. Our aim is to show how institutional practices within health care and social welfare institutions add to or even generate stigma and vulnerable situations experienced by drug-using mothers. The chapter is based on a qualitative research, which was conducted in 2014. The main approach used is institutional ethnography, as conceptualised by Dorothy E. Smith (2005), who explores the social relations that structure people's everyday lives by looking at how the external institutional environment interacts with human behaviour. Empirical material was collected through semi-structured in-depth interviews with 40 drug-using mothers and 22 practitioners (social workers, psychologists, sociologists and health care workers from social services, drug treatment clinic, maternity hospital, low-threshold and high-threshold treatment programmes). The interviewed mothers who volunteered to participate were either undergoing drug-addiction treatment programmes at the time of interviews or they had been included in such programmes at some point in the past. We rely on quotes from professionals and mothers simultaneously to illustrate the difference in their understanding of situations and to emphasise how institutional practices, acts and opinions influence women lives and the relationship with their children.

Motherhood of drug-using women

Motherhood is one of the most socially constructed women's roles, which importantly influences their public status, access to paid work and terms of livelihood. Ideal-type mothers are constructed as healthy, devoted to their mission, capable of and willing to subordinate their own ambitions to the duty of social reproduction and capable of harmonising housework and motherhood obligations. The good mother loves and controls her children, spends time with her child and is patient and supportive. The good mother sets an example for her child and for other women (Perälä-Littunen 2004, 184–190).

By contrast, bad, risky mothers (see also Chapter 5, Veenstra in this book) are constructed as those who cause harm to their children, are bad role models and fail to raise their children to be good citizens. In this way, they pose a threat not only to their children but also to the nation as a whole as well (Albanese 2006). Drug-using mothers with low socioeconomic status and those with various family problems are more exposed to institutional control than drug users with higher socioeconomic status who have at their disposal sufficient financial means what makes them less visible within the support system because they do not claim social benefits and they can pay for services (Leppo 2012). Mulia (2002) connects this with multiple identities of being drug users, women, mothers and poor. Drug-using poor women face a degree of scepticism, disdain and suspicion on the part of service providers. Therefore, they

are strictly supervised by institutions, condemned and their children are often taken away from them (Stone 2015). Instead of being attentive to poverty,
violence and homelessness, practitioners focus on drug addiction.

Given the prevailing stance that drug-using women should not be mothers, they are often criticised for allowing themselves to become pregnant
(Baker and Carson 1999, 348). All women who lack the ability to control
themselves are believed to pose a danger to their children, so they need to be
supervised, punished and disciplined (Lupton 1992) because they are seen
as deviant and pathological (Virokannas 2011; Hughes, Chau, and Vokrri
2016). Even though there is an evidence that substance use cause harm to
children, which may be related to unsafe environment, long-standing stress
and non-adequate responding to the child's needs (Raitasalo and Holmila
2017), it is problematic to ascribe lack of care and control to all drug-using
mothers. Radcliffe (2011) argues that once a woman is labelled 'drug user',
she is often perceived as an inconsiderate, incapable parent unworthy of
trust even if she manages to abstain from drugs and change her lifestyle.
Faced with the prospect of stigma and other adverse consequences, they opt
not to ask for help although they need it. They want to remain invisible as
long as possible and avoid institutions. This has far-reaching and fatal consequences and increases the vulnerability of women drug users.

Slovenian healthcare and social welfare services for drug-using mothers

Drug-using mothers in Slovenia come in contact with the healthcare services
during pregnancy, when giving birth and after birth. Healthcare services
include gynaecological outpatient clinics in local health centres, maternity
clinics, outpatient clinics providing low-threshold and high-threshold health
services as replacement and maintenance therapies, as well as the Centres
for prevention and treatment of drug addiction, which operate under the
auspices of local health centres, 20 of them over the country. In the capital
Ljubljana, there is the Centre for Treatment of Drug Addicts, which is a
unit of the University Psychiatric Hospital. They provide detoxification programmes and hospital treatment that lasts 14 weeks and also offer follow-up
programmes like support groups, day centre and counselling.

Social welfare organisations do not provide specific services to drug users, and they usually come into play when family issues need to be addressed
or in cases of unemployment, homelessness or poverty. Main organisations
here are state social services, 63 of them over the country. A number of
NGOs also offer services to drug users such as counselling services for drug
users and their relatives, day centres, therapeutic groups (several-years rehabilitation and reintegration programmes) and field work such as mobile
teams at musical concerts.

Only two drug treatment programmes include drug-using mothers
and pregnant women: the Centre for Treatment of Drug Addicts and the

Therapeutic Community at the Association Project Human. The latter programme lasts at least two years, 24 hours a day, so parents and their children
live in the community. In addition to social rehabilitation and treatment of
addiction, the programme also focuses on strengthening parenting skills.
The Centre for Treatment of Drug Addicts in Ljubljana provides counselling for drug-using women during pregnancy, childbirth and post-natal period. It provides guidance and counselling, opioid substitution therapy and
other medicament therapies. Drug-using mothers that cannot obtain care
for their children during treatment can live in a special apartment along
with children. Due to the lack of available space, most mothers during therapy obtain care for their children – it is usually grandparents who step in
and rarely their partners. This causes problems that need to be addressed in
the future if services for drug-using mothers are to be improved. The most
problematic is the lack of cooperation both within health and social services
and with NGOs.

In the next sections, we are presenting findings of our research divided
into three periods of motherhood: pregnancy, childbirth and period after
birth.

Pregnancy

The journey of drug-using women through institutions in Slovenia starts
during their pregnancy. Some come in contact with institutions even before
pregnancy because of variety of reasons such as attending rehabilitation
programmes, receiving opioid substitution therapy, receiving social benefits, being homeless or have problematic family life or partnership. Once
they are pregnant, their contacts with institutions become more regular because pregnant women are entitled to health checks while social services
become more vigilant of the context of pregnancy.

Young, Boles and Otero (2012) drew attention to the fact that health care
practitioners often describe the use of drugs during pregnancy as deviant
behaviour and hold that abstinence is the only appropriate choice for a
pregnant woman, while merely reducing harm is a less-desired option, since
drug-taking is associated with damage caused to the foetus (Paltrow 2006).
Substance use is perceived as an abuse of the child. Mothers are personally
responsible for their children's health, which is a priority that justifies institutional supervision (Radcliffe 2011).

Our research showed that within healthcare and social protection systems, pregnancy and motherhood of drug-using women are predominantly
understood as an abuse of unborn child caused by the emotional numbness
of the drug user, their lack of empathy and inability to establish emotional
ties with the child.

> It [drug use] definitely belongs in the child abuse category. I understand
> that they [drug-using women] realize quite late that they're pregnant,

because although they miss the period they don't know it. But even when they realize it, they continue to take drugs.

(Practitioner 14)[1]

The research of Silva et al. (2013) on the sample of 24 drug-addicted mothers show that pregnancy is often an unexpected condition due to menstrual irregularity or even an absence of menstruation for years, so they think that they cannot be pregnant. Consequently, late-detected pregnancy is increasing the insecurity feelings. Women cannot prepare physically and psychologically to become mothers what affects an inadequacy or failure of the prenatal medical care. Drug-use is often a strategy how to cope with conflicts or traumatic experiences, and drug-using women need time and strength to change it. The emphasis of professionals in our research on the lack of awareness of pregnancy aims at pointing to the emotional detachment from feelings that is ascribed to drug-using mothers and results in the opinion that they cannot bond with their child:

> She is in fifth month and it [pregnancy] came out only two weeks ago, because she hides it. She does not know even who the father is, it is difficult to help her, because she is personally immature, she does not want any information, lives her own life without any responsibilities. [...]. She did not visit gynaecologist yet even though we encourage her to go. She is very pathological.

(Practitioner 9)

Mulia (2002) points to the fact that social identity of drug-using mothers is shaped by stereotypes about their deviant sexuality what can be seen from the quote. They are pregnant because of their promiscuity. Interviewed mothers in our research pointed to the insecurity they felt about themselves and doubts they developed about their pregnancy because of the judgements and condemnation they experience from professionals. Their feelings also point to the process of stigma internalisation. Drug-using women internalise the conviction that, as drug users, they should not opt for motherhood, which often leads them to refuse to acknowledge the signs of pregnancy or they are hiding or covering up their addiction. Concealment starts during pregnancy, when mother's behaviour becomes more supervised and medicalised. Some of the mothers managed to keep hidden their substance use throughout pregnancy. The main reason is to avoid pressure placed on them to change the behaviour and quit on drugs. Those who were identified as addicts gave false information about the extent of substance abuse to avoid pressure.

> I was ascribed that label, that I'm cold as a prisoner in a prison who gets the number.

(Mother 17)

It's not right to label you right from the start. They don't want to hear that you want a child, it's simply something you cannot do to the child. You [drug-using women] shouldn't have children at all. And then you really start to think that you really did something terribly wrong.

(Mother 20)

Many practitioners believed that abortion is a much better option. They blamed pregnant drug-using women for failing to identify signs of pregnancy because had they done that, it would be responsible and socially acceptable to have an abortion. In this way, they would have prevented potential consequences for the child and would not incur costs for society. Their decision to have a child is perceived as egoistic.

I encourage them to do it [have an abortion], since they take high dosage of drugs [...].

(Practitioner 19)

What professions define as encouraging women to choose better option, women perceive as suppressing and violent practice that aims at labelling them as incapable to raise a child.

She told me to have an abortion. How are you going to take care of it, you aren't capable of it! It was horrible to hear something like that.

(Mother 1)

Murphy and Rosenbaum (1999) claim that the attempts of mothers to avoid institutional attention reflect their personal dilemma about pregnancy. As long as it is not visible, they can avoid gynaecological checks and do not need to take decisions related to drug-use. Silva et al. (2013, 362) state that:

Pregnancy and motherhood is characterized by a strong ambivalence between addiction and parenting. Contradictory feelings and thoughts tend to arise: on one hand deep feelings of despair, anguish and anxiety emerge, on the other hand, pregnancy and motherhood are simultaneously moments of hope, in which mothers stop to think, and begin to see their child as a salvation.

Once they accept pregnancy, this can motivate change. Most drug-using mothers in our research, and especially those who were undergoing a treatment programme, changed their lifestyles during pregnancy, primarily reducing the drug intake. Most of them went for the opioid substitution therapy or they regulated their use of drugs and took better care of themselves.

Childbirth

While it is possible for drug-using women to avoid regular gynaecological checks, giving birth in the maternity ward is almost unavoidable. A maternity ward is an institutional environment where it becomes obvious how a woman took care of her body and the baby, which, for the practitioners, is an indication of how good a mother she will be. Here, they confront the strongest stigma and discrimination coming from practitioners.

> [...] Everything was 'cool' until I told them that I was addicted, everything normal, and nobody really found out because I had long sleeves, everything was fine. When they started to ask I told them the truth, that I was undergoing a treatment. And then a complete change, right away the worst approach you can imagine. Indeed, how badly they reject people who are addicted.
>
> (Mother 14)

> Even though she was clean and nicely dressed, she came to the maternity clinic and had a crisis. [...]. One can ask what kind of mother is she to opt for a child.
>
> (Practitioner 10)

The situation that almost invariably triggers negative attitude in practitioners is when mothers are confronted with the fact that the baby is experiencing the neonatal abstinence crisis. With the focus being on mother's responsibility for her child's health, the body of a pregnant drug user becomes a dangerous environment calling for child's protection. They are exposed to criticism, and their choices are condemned (Campbell and Ettore 2011), what is also shown in our research.

> I asked if something was wrong, and she [the doctor] said, "of course, what do you think it is. You know what you did to her [her daughter]". It's slapping you in the face with your guilt. Of course I know that it's my fault.
>
> (Mother 3)

> At the birth midwife loudly said that how dare such people have a child.
>
> (Practitioner 18)

Mothers infected with hepatitis C were most likely to experience stigmatisation in the maternity ward. They were isolated and put in a separate room to prevent infection, which made them feel anomalous and set them even more apart from other mothers. Childbirth is therefore the point at which an institution separates drug-using women from other women and relegates them the status of the 'Other'.

They put that yellow sign on the door and anyone who went by knew that there was a chance of hepatitis or AIDS infection. And there was the sign on my daughter's bracelet too. When I saw it, I went mad; they cannot treat my child like that.

(Mother 28)

Mothers' narratives reveal how institutions transfer the stigma attached to mothers to newly born children. Paradoxically, the wellbeing of a child is the priority within healthcare, but right after birth, that same child is stigmatised as problematic, different and as a potential addict. The ambivalence between care for the child and its potential addiction or behavioural difficulties is reflected in healthcare and social services attitude towards mothers.

Period after the birth

Even during the mother's stay in the maternity ward, healthcare services establish contact with social services regarding further monitoring of the mother. Assessment of the child's best interest is a priority, but it rests on stereotypes and prejudices towards drug-using mothers, so they do not have many chances of keeping the child and receiving adequate support. Their greatest fear is that their children will be taken away from them, so they often choose to remain invisible within the support system, although this is risky, since it leaves them without needed support. Practitioners rarely consider if the reason for drug users' reluctance to ask for help is precisely their own inappropriate approach and treatment.

I thought that they'd immediately take my child away if I tell the social workers that I couldn't take care of it.

(Mother 15)

Mothers avoid asking for help because they are afraid of institutional control and potential negative consequences:

There's always that feeling that someone is watching you, overseeing you, that you're not alone with the child. I too do not trust anyone, not even professionals. Personally I'd rather be alone, without help, I mean.

(Mother 3)

There is a stereotype among practitioners that mothers do not ask for help because they want to continue taking drugs and motherhood means nothing to them. Bruland Selseng (2017) claims that these are socially circulating stories about clients with substance-use problems that also serve as a cultural resource for welfare workers. Many mothers therefore attempted to present to them an ideal image of themselves as mothers. Their children were smartly dressed, tidy, had many toys or they were saying that they were not heavily addicted and could take good care of the child although they were taking drugs.

> In the beginning, before we came to the issue [in a conversation] of how difficult it was sometimes and how they couldn't cope, everything was perfect and nice. Because they wanted it to be so. She said that if she admitted [that she was taking drugs], she would've been regarded as a bad mother who cannot take care of her child.
>
> (Practitioner 10)

Some mothers compared themselves to other drug-addicted mothers, emphasising that they were different. They did not stick around places where drugs were present, and they did not take drugs in front of children. Those survival strategies were more often used by mothers who were still taking drugs and were more burdened by the fear of consequences and the possibility of losing the child. Copes (2016) claims that individuals who may be perceived as being stigmatised, users create perceptual divisions between themselves as functional and others as dysfunctional. They do this by creating symbolic boundaries if they wish to avoid having low-status labels attached to them. They use socially circulating stories as yardsticks to evaluate their own experience of other users. Copes (2016) emphasises that gender roles have a strong impact on the nature of boundary making. This is most apparent in the way motherhood act as a key boundary.

One of the mothers in our research managed to evade all institutions until her daughter was seven, despite the fact that the family experienced a lot of problems, domestic violence and substance abuse by the partner.

> I didn't take my daughter to the doctor, they invited me to health checks, I went for a year and then stopped. So I evaded everyone. Nobody knew.
>
> (Mother 2)

Once the drug-use is recognised, mothers face various restrictions and conditions imposed by institutions, and some of them cannot follow requirements. Twenty-seven percent of respondents in our research had their children in foster care[2] at the time of the interview, mainly because they could not provide adequate care for them. The interviewed mothers had difficulties talking about this issue and felt guilty. Some of them think that foster care was a better solution for their children.

> An early placement in foster care would be the most favourable option. In my opinion the postponement by social services and other institutions is the biggest problem.
>
> (Practitioner 6)

Although practitioners in healthcare and social welfare institutions encourage foster care as a more adequate option ensuring better protection of children, mothers are accused of letting their children being taken away by opting for drugs rather than motherhood. As Virokannas (2011) says, the drug-using mothers are perceived by institutions as responsible mothers only when they come for help on their own initiative, but if the child is taken away from them or they lose the right to care for the child, it is much more difficult, what is also confirmed in our research. One of the mothers said:

> Then I completely gave in. Once my daughter left, I started taking more drugs.
>
> (Mother 40)

Placing the child in foster care is a stress and trauma for mothers. It makes them feel powerless because they also lose the identity of the mother (Skyes 2011). Children of drug-using mothers placed in foster care spend long time there, move from one foster family to another and are less often returned to their family of origin (Skyes 2011). The period of foster care is therefore the time during which drug-using mothers need to make many changes to meet the requirements of professional services. Often, the means they have at their disposal to make such changes are inadequate, so they retreat, shut out the child and sink even deeper into addiction.

> I got so drugged after my son left that I don't even know what I'm talking about, I constantly forget things or I mostly take tablets too, whole months in a row, my memory is full of holes. The last three years.
>
> (Mother 9)

One consequence is that mothers gradually lose contacts with their children because they cannot meet the demanding requirements within a very short time given, and their chances of getting the child back diminish as the times passes.

> If the child is placed in foster care, we include in the agreement the obligations or conditions under which the child could be returned: get clean from drugs, arrange the apartment, find a job, suitable living conditions, then regarding the partnership, if we find out that it is burdening. And if they want to be together, we send them to relationship counsellors, and if she has some other problems, we send them to the psychiatrist, and when she fulfils all those requirements, there is no reason not to send the child back.
>
> (Practitioner 13)

Only one of the mothers in our study was waiting for the child to be returned to her from foster care because she and her partner fulfilled the requirements. Even when the mothers meet all the conditions in the agreement, practitioners continue to have doubts as to whether the child is still attached to the mother.

> If they didn't have contacts for a long time and the child carries the image of the addict, of someone who was strange according to their criteria, and now, if the parent put itself into order, the child must go through a different experience with him, must store into its memory a different parent.
>
> (Practitioner 10)

Practitioners also sometimes provide dubious information by presenting foster care as a temporary measure although at the time of placing the child in foster care, they already believe that the chances of returning the child to the mother are minimal. An important role here is also played by the discourse of relapse or of 'chronic disease', implying that a relapse can occur at any time, which in drug users raises doubts that they will ever be able to live without drugs.

> It is also important how long the abstinence lasted, because we know that addiction is a long-lasting and chronic disease. Relapses are frequent and some time must pass and several relapses must be dealt with before we can trust the mother.
>
> (Practitioner 12)

> That labelling, 'once a junkie, always a junkie.' Even if you have been clean for 20 years, they'll still see you as a junkie.
>
> (Mother 3)

This reinforces apprehensions of practitioners too, as to whether a drug-addicted mother will ever be able to fulfil the role of the 'adequate parent'. In such cases, mothers are ready to do many things to keep the child. They voluntarily accept increased control by the institutions, and sometimes, they understand conditioning as positive, as it helps them to keep clean in order to keep the child.

> I'm fine with conditions, someone have to force you, there is no other way, because you will not do it yourself. You love your child but to give up drugs, I do not know anyone to be capable of it.
>
> (Mother 17)

Conclusion

In this chapter, based on our empirical findings, we have shown that practitioners juxtapose pregnancy and motherhood of drug-using mothers next to child abuse, since the mothers do not match the ideal of a good mother espoused by the discourse of idealised motherhood within the hegemonic gender order. Drug-using mothers often faced condemnation from practitioners, which only increased their stigma and vulnerability. The main attitude to them is negative, and they have been labelled as pathological and stigmatised as unfit to raise a child.

Stone (2015) writes that the transgression of the moral code of motherhood, doing wrong things as a mother, is controversial and harmful to women and to children. To avoid the consequences of stigmatisation and discrimination, mothers refrained from asking for help when they needed it. Stigma is one of the biggest obstacles preventing women from accessing help (Baker and Carson 1999; Benoit et al. 2015). It causes social, material and psychological marginalisation, which has an impact on both mothers and children, since once the woman is labelled as 'drug user', she is often perceived as incapable parent who cannot be trusted, with the stigma carrying on even when she stops using drugs and makes other changes in her life. The stereotypical perception and the identity of the drug user become irreversible.

Although practitioners acknowledge the importance of an early identification of the problem and help to the family, in Slovenia, there are no adequate programmes to support drug-using mothers and their children. As long as women are perceived by society as 'satisfactory mothers' who fulfil the role ascribed to them in the social reproduction system, their needs are de-politicised and are deemed as unimportant in the sense of social support, since those mothers who are drug-addicts are not worthy of public support (Ettore 2010). We further concluded that when dealing with the negligence of children, practitioners mainly focus on the mother's guilt and scrutinise her inadequacies rather than her potentials and efforts to do the best she can.

Krane and Davis (2000) hold that practitioners should accept that what is best for the child is not contrary to what is best for the mother, so the support process should be based on the positive resources within the family. Drug-using women are more willing to make changes during pregnancy than during other stages in life. It is also necessary to learn and understand how the mother is equipped for life, what skills she possess, which traumatic factors affect her and how much help and support she receive from her social network.

Results of our research also point to a negative effect of non-cooperation among health care and social welfare services. What is missing is a holistic approach; leaving services fragmented and dispersed is what affects the accessibility and responsiveness to the needs of drug-using mothers. Each of the institutions creates their own expectations towards drug-using mothers and demands certain actions and behaviour from them in order to keep their child. Quite often, expectations and demands are contradictory, and the consequence is an inability of mothers to fulfil conditions and follow expectations that can have fatal consequences. As Virokannas states (2011), social and health care professionals should make an effort to overcome the negative perception of drug-using mothers. More interaction among them would be needed so that they can help drug-using mothers acquire skills and improve contact with the child. Cooperation between practitioners within and between different sectors would also prevent different perspectives and priorities (advocacy for the rights of drug users or child's rights and benefits, understanding of addiction as a disease or behaviour, professional blindness, etc.), enable consistent policy planning and provide space for improvements.

Notes

1 We use serial numbers to denote the number of the interviewed practitioner or the mother participants (e.g. Mother 1, Mother 2, Practitioner 1, Practitioner 2 etc.).
2 In Slovenia, children are placed into foster families by social services. Foster families are usually heterosexual couples with children. Traditionally, these were village families, but their number has been decreasing steadily. Foster care is regulated by a special law and social services are authorised to organise it.

References

Albanese, Patricia. 2006. *Mothers of the Nation: Women, Families, and Nationalism in Twentieth-Century Europe*. Toronto: University of Toronto Press.

Anderson, L. Tammy. 2008. *Neither Villain nor Victim. Empowerment and Agency among Women Substance Abusers*. New Brunswick, NJ: Rutgers University Press.

Baker, L. Phyllis, and Amy Carson. 1999. ""I Take Care of My Kids". Mothering Practices of Substance-abusing Women." *Gender and Society* 13 (3): 347–363. doi:10.1177/089124399013003005

Benoit, Cecilia, Samantha Magnus, Rachel Phillips, Lenora Marcellus, and Sinéad Charbonneau. 2015. "Complicating the Dominant Morality Discourse: Mothers and Fathers Constructions of Substance Use during Pregnancy and Early Parenthood." *International Journal Equity Health* 14 (72): 72–83. doi:10.1186/s12939-015-0206-7

Bruland Selseng, Lilian. 2017. "Formula Stories of the "Substance-Using Client": Addicted, Unreliable, Deteriorating, and Stigmatised." *Contemporary Drug Problems* 44 (2): 87–104. doi:10.1177/0091450917698963

Campbell, D. Nancy, and Elizabeth Ettore. 2011. *Gendering Addiction. The Politics of Drug Treatment in a Neurochemical World*. New York: Palgrave Macmillan.

Copes, Heith. 2016. "A Narrative Approach to Studying Symbolic Boundaries among Drug Users: A Qualitative Meta-Synthesis." *Crime Media Culture* 12 (2): 193–213. doi:10.1177/1741659016641720

Ettore, Elizabeth. 2010. "Bodies, Drugs and Reproductive Regimes." In *Culture, Bodies and the Sociology of Health*, edited by Elizabeth Ettore, 153–172. Farnham: Ashgate.

Flaker, Vito. 2002. *Živeti s heroinom 1. Družbena konstrukcija uživalca v Sloveniji*. Ljubljana: Založba.

Hughes, Judy, Shirley Chau, and Lisa Vokrri. 2016. "Mothers' Narratives of Their Involvement with Child Welfare Services." *Affilia: Journal of Women and Social Work* 31 (3): 344–358. doi:10.1177/0886109915574579

Krane, Julia, and Linda Davis. 2000. "Mothering and Child Protection Practise. Rethinking Risk Assessment." *Child and Family Social Work* 5 (1): 35–45. doi:10.1046/j.1365-2206.2000.00142.x

Kvaternik, Ines. 2006. *Politika drog, Pogledi uporabnikov in uporabnic.* Ljubljana: BOEX.

Leppo, Anna. 2012. Precarious Pregnancies: *Alcohol, drugs and the regulation of risks.* PhD diss., University of Helsinki. http://urn.fi/URN:ISBN:978-952-10-6711-2.

Lupton, Deborah. 1992. "Discourse Analysis: A New Methodology for Understanding the Ideologies of Health and Illness." *Australian Journal of Public Health* 16 (2): 145–150. doi:10.1111/j.1753–6405.1992.tb00043.x

Lupton, Deborah. 2012. "Precious Cargo. Foetal Subjects, Risk and Productive Citizenship." *Critical Public Health* 22 (3): 329–340. doi:10.1080/09581596.2012.657612

McCreaddie, May, Imogen Lyons, Debbie Watt, Elspeth Ewing, Jeanette Croft, Marion Smith, and Jeniffer Tocher. 2010. "Routines and Rituals. A Grounded Theory of the Pain Management of Drug Users in Acute Care Settings." *Journal of Clinical Nursing* 19 (20): 2730–2740. doi:10.1111/j.1365–2702.2010.03284.x

Mejak, Vesna. 2009. "Doživljanje materinstva in potrebe po pomoči pri ženskah, odvisnih od prepovedanih drog. Master theses. University of Ljubljana.

Mulia, Nina. 2002. "Ironies in the Pursuit of Well-Being: The Perspectives of Low-income, Substance-using Women on Service Institutions." *Contemporary Drug Problems* 29 (4): 711–748. doi:10.1177/009145090202900404

Murphy, Sheigla and Marsha Rosenbaum. 1999. *Pregnant Women on Drugs: Combating Stereotypes and Stigma.* New Brunswick, NJ: Rutgers University Press.

National Institute of Public Health (NIJZ). 2019. *Data from Perinatal Information System* (IVZ 17). PERIS: Health Care Data Centre.

Paltrow, M. Lynn. 2006. *Punishing Women for Their Behaviour during Pregnancy. An Approach That Undermines the Health of Women and Children.* New York: National advocates for pregnant women. Accessed 10 April 2019. http://advocates forpregnantwomen.org/file/Punishing%20Women%20During%20Pregnancy_Paltrow.pdf

Perälä-Littunen, Satu. 2004. *Cultural Images of a Good Mother and a Good Father in Three Generations.* PhD diss., Jyväskylä studies in education, psychology and social research, University of Jyväskylä. http://urn.fi/URN:ISBN:951-39-1779-7

Radcliffe, Polly. 2011. "Motherhood, Pregnancy, and Negotiation of Identity: The Moral Career of Drug Treatment." *Social Science Medicine* 72 (6), 984–991. doi:10.1016/j.socscimed.2011.01.017

Raitasalo, Kirsimarja and Marja Holmila. 2017. "Parental Substance Abuse and Risks to Children's Safety, Health and Psychological Development." *Drugs: Education, Prevention and Policy* 24 (1): 17–22. doi:10.1080/09687637.2016.1232371

Silva, A. Sofia, António P. Pires, Cristina Guerreiro, and Antónia Cardoso. 2013. "Balancing Motherhood and Drug Addiction: The Transition to Parenthood of Addicted Mothers." *Journal of Health Psychology* 18 (3): 359–367. doi:10.1177/1359105312443399

Skyes, Jennier. 2011. "Negotiating Stigma. Understanding Mothers Responses to Accusations of Child Neglect." *Children and Youth Services Review* 33 (3): 448–456. doi:10.1016/j.childyouth.2010.06.015

Smith, E. Dorothy. 2005. *Institutional Ethnography: A Sociology for People.* London: Altamira Press.

Stone, Rebecca. 2015. "Pregnant Women and Substance Use: Fear, Stigma and Barriers to Care." *Health and Justice* 3 (2): 1–15. doi:10.1186/s40352-015-0015-5

Virokannas, Elina. 2011. "Identity Categorisation of Motherhood in the Context of Drug Abuse and Child Welfere System." *Qualitative Social Work* 10 (3): 329–345. doi:10.1177/1473325011408480

Young, K. Nancy, Sharon M. Boles, and Cathleen Otero. 2012. "Parental Substance Use Disorders and Child Maltreatment. Overlap Gaps and Opportunities." *Child Maltreatment* 12 (2): 137–149. doi:10.1177/1077559507300322

7 Incarcerated women, welfare services and the process of re-entering society in Finland

Ulla Salovaara

Introduction

The pathways in and out of crime differ according to gender, people's life histories, social situations and networks. Before being sentenced, many women have been living in vulnerable and traumatic life situations and violent intimate relationships. Substance abuse often plays a crucial role in committing crimes. These circumstances are likely to have an influence in their entry into crime and substance abuse. There might have also been destructive relationships before the sentence. Being in a relationship often prevents men from committing crimes, but, conversely, they can expose women to criminality. Many studies have shown that supportive relationships and social bonds have a significant influence on female desistance as well as on their assimilation and incorporation back into society (Lynch, Fritch and Heath 2012; Fleetwood 2014; Leverentz 2014; Kruttschitt and Kang 2019).

Women are also more likely to be carers to children. Their relationships with their children play a huge role while they are in prison and after their release. Children motivate their mother to refrain from crime and substance use. Children of incarcerated women are often taken into custody, while their mothers are left without any appropriate support for their feelings of sorrow and shame. In many studies, it has been shown how complex and diverse women's needs for support are (Devlin 1998; Chesney-Lind 2006; Estrada and Nilsson 2012; Virokannas 2017a, 2017b).

Being released from prison and re-entering society is a process that requires women's own motivation to desist along with help and support from society. Women with criminal backgrounds live in vulnerable situations, but I do not take women's vulnerable life situations for granted. The vulnerability is often the result of living in communities in which crime and substance abuse is pervasive and which have male-dominated social networks where violence is prevalent. After these women are released from prison, vulnerability emerges in their interactions with society (see Virokannas, Liuski and Kuronen 2020).

In this chapter, I focus on how women narrate and describe their experiences after being released from prison, especially how they report the ways in which the welfare system responds to their needs. Women discussed their needs for support and the provision of social services, how they viewed the logic of the system providing the services and whether and how they managed to get the services they needed. The data used in this chapter consist of narrative interviews with 31 Finnish women who were either in prison at the time of the interview or recently released from prison. The first set of 18 interviews was gathered in 2009–2010 for my dissertation (Salovaara 2019b). The second set consists of 13 interviews with women between 2017 and 2019.

Women and imprisonment

Incarcerated women are a diverse group. However, women are typically imprisoned less frequently and for shorter periods than men are (Hypén 2004, 43; Gelsthorpe and Wright 2015). Women are also more motivated and willing to change their life situations after release. They take more responsibility for their actions and crimes and are more likely to recognise their impacts (Lempert 2016, 241–243).

In Finland, the number of female prisoners is much higher than that in other Nordic countries (Statistical Yearbook 2018 of the Criminal Sanctions Agency, 28; Kristoffersen 2019, 31–35). Moreover, a larger proportion of women are sentenced for violent crimes than in any other European country. In 2015, this accounted for 51% of all women sentenced. In 2018, the number had fallen to 44%. In Finland, the committing of violent crimes is equally common for women and for men and is also the most common reason for a prison sentence (KOS 2018; Statistical Yearbook 2018 of the Criminal Sanctions Agency, 33; Kristoffersen 2019). There is a strong correlation for a woman being a victim of intimate partner violence and for her committing violent acts. The linkage devices from the violent culture that induces individuals to be violent and is also a response to being a victim (Lattu 2016; Venäläinen 2017; Hautala et al. 2019; Salovaara 2019b).

Despite these figures, the proportion of women sentenced to prison terms remains scarce. Their deviation from the male standard creates an illusion whereby women may be treated as challenging and exceptional cases in terms of imprisonment. Imprisoned women remain on the margins of prison culture. After arriving in prison, women become 'invisible' along with their specific needs (Devlin 1998, vii). That may lead to a lack of women-specific services and suitable rehabilitation (Chesney-Lind 2006; Lynch, Fritch and Heath 2012; Salovaara 2019a). After release, they remain in the same position, as the narratives of the interviewed women show.

Women's needs after release

The circumstances that led to the imprisonment of women were challenging and being released does not make these problems disappear. On the contrary, changing these circumstances is a long and demanding process. Before incarceration, women might have been living in subcultures favourable to substance abuse and crime as well as in harmful and violent intimate relationships. There is always a risk they would return to the same situation. While in prison, there was the opportunity to make plans and dream about how to change their lives. Incarceration was experienced as a halt and a pause: a time to concentrate, think and learn about themselves. After release, it was necessary for the women to change their former lifestyles and social networks, especially when their plan was to re-integrate back into society. The most relevant issue is women's own willingness to change and their motivation to do so. However, in order to make this change, there is also a need for support and open-mindedness from the local welfare service system and authorities as well as from fellow citizens. The combination of women's own motivation together with social support and adequate services was necessary for the successful integration and re-entry. Women talked about the needs they had for welfare services in the area of housing and rehabilitation (Salovaara 2019b). One of the basic steps to this integration is having an apartment of one's own:

> ... But the thing that everything is all right, when you get out of here. Like that you have a home. A home is crucial, because then you have your own place where you can just be. So that if you don't have your own place, then you have nothing of your own. But if you have that place where you can be, it carries you far, like really far. I noticed that last time.
>
> (Sanna)

Sanna explains the meaning of an apartment as home, which is more than just walls and a roof over one's head; it also means privacy, safety and one's own space. Moreover, it also symbolises belonging and acceptance, being part of society. Housing and permanent residency are essential when trying to end a criminal life and substance use. Without a proper and stable home, the ability and motivation to change one's lifestyle is severely restricted. In Finland, one-third of all the prisoners released in 2018 were released without an apartment (Ara 2019). Being released from prison without a place to live means living with friends, relatives or in a shelter or other institutions. In Finland, the homeless do not commonly live on the streets, and therefore homelessness is more invisible than it is in other countries (Ara 2019). In the following excerpt, Emmi talks about her long-term homelessness:

> Well, I had an apartment of my own for five years, like my own flat. So, it wasn't a boyfriend's or anybody else's. Like five years of my life. Otherwise, I have always been homeless, but then I have been living with my boyfriends... I was mentally in a bad shape, so I did a runaway from my own home. Sounds weird to say, 'from my own home'. When he [last boyfriend] went somewhere, he told me that 'there is someone watching over you here'. And there was nobody in the flat. I was so messed up...

Then one day I left there and went to my mother's place. And so, I did get rid of that bloke. I had a psychosis and went into a mental hospital for three months. I trusted no one, and I didn't let the doctors examine me. I was in bad shape 'cause I had been using stuff for so long. Then we got some distance between us. Before that we were together all the time.

(Emmi)

Emmi discussed being without her own apartment for ten years, living with boyfriends in abusive relationships, and finally, how she had managed to leave the last and most traumatic of these relationships. The situation of not having any apartment or a safe place to live is one of the major causes of women-specific vulnerability. The homeless women are relatively more invisible than homeless men are. Women are more likely to live with their ex-partners or in harmful relationships than in shelters. Homelessness exposes women to being dependent on people, mostly men, who have an apartment. Being homeless also exposes them to harmful situations, violence and abusive relationships (see also Chapter 10, Lavee in this book). The necessity of having an apartment or some place to live leads to dependence on those who are able to provide such a place. That may lead to women becoming dependent on a man for the housing, drugs, money and shelter they can provide. Living on one's own enables non-violent and non-abusive living conditions (e.g. Sallmann 2010; Lewison, Thomas and White 2014; Granfelt 2016). There is also a high demand for women-specific services as well as a clear need to understand the traumatic and abusive life course. But having an apartment is not always enough, there is still a need for support.

And if you have got to arrange things with specific dates and time limits, there is always a fear of how it will end. How am I supposed to arrange everything then? Then you'll make some 'quick-fix' and you are in a panic. And when you are in a panic, you don't think reasonably. You can't think straight, and you waste a lot of energy. They are saying 'first things first'. But how in the hell are you supposed to know which is the first when you have dozens of those things to do? You are not able to say which is the most important, because all of them seem to be that. It leads to a situation when you just can't explain and arrange your own issues. You don't know what you think about those. And when you don't know, you just can't even phone someone. Hell, I don't know how to stay sober and without drugs and cope with my life. These are the most important issues, and I don't know how to solve them. But I know that you can't do it by yourself.

(Helena)

Helena is describing her needs in everyday living. It seems as if she is trying to control her life and manage with chaotic issues in a problematic phase in her life. Helena talked about 'issues with specific dates and time limits'. These issues referred to the different official forms and applications and also to dealing with the authorities and the whole welfare system. These issues seem to be hard to handle, and there is an obvious need for counselling, which includes support with housing, coping with the authorities and society in general. To Helena and several other women, living without substance use is not something that can be taken for granted. In particular, when problems come along, substances might be the old and familiar way of solving problems. After a year of being sober, Helena still has to consider how to stay without the use of substances in situations where she really requires counselling on many issues, and her own ability to manage on the whole is poor. Old habits are easy to fall back on when there are financial hardships, and the possibilities of a 'quick-fix' include selling drugs to solve financial problems. In the manner which Helena described this 'quick-fix', one can see that she is worried about her own situation.

Women explained that they had problems and challenges in taking care of and filling in different forms and applications, which may be the result of long-term marginalisation. Furthermore, society's digitalisation may cause digital marginalisation (Eubanks 2011). As running errands and providing services increasingly moves online, the lack of digital skills are denying the unskilled from the services they are entitled to. Helena and several other women told about the need for 'interpreters' because they required someone to explain to the authorities what they really meant and needed. There is also a need for an 'interpreter' to explain to the authorities the life situations and challenges women have. In Finland, there are some non-governmental organisations (NGOs) that provide interpreters who work with ex-prisoners and know their everyday lives.

Women's challenges in receiving services in the welfare system

Being released from prison and having a background with substance abuse, violence, criminality and even homelessness leads women to a situation that challenges the welfare system's ability to help them. As a result, they are seen as a service user with demanding needs. The welfare service system could not always respond to the needs of released women. In some cases, the structure of the service system seems to be system-oriented instead of service-user-oriented, and there might be diversion or expulsion (Määttä 2012; Metteri 2012). Anu describes her experiences:

> My prison counsellor phoned to Kela[1] and there was this very lovely person. She said that I have plenty of opportunities although I am on a disability pension. If you first go and see a doctor, you could go to the work try-out. You can also study when you are on a pension. So, when the probationary freedom ends, I go to the doctor. And then I got myself an appointment at Kela. There the clerk said that I couldn't go to a work try-out. He was a young bloke. Then I said that we just called you guys with my counsellor from prison. The bloke replied that no

one could have said anything like that because there is no record here that you had called. I said that my counsellor made the call. He again replied: 'It is not possible because there isn't any record of any phone calls'. Then I asked him: 'Are you saying that she didn't make the call?' 'Yes', he replied, 'because there is no record of the phone call'. He decided that I couldn't do any work.

(Anu)

The service system seems to be so complex that even those working in it could not help service users and even they did not have enough knowledge of the services as a whole. Anu described her experiences with the National Insurance Institution Kela and the conflicting advice offered about its services. Preparation for her release was done in prison. The preparation included getting familiar with the service system and the different kinds of offices. Both Anu, other women and the professionals working with them reported that opportunities for face-to-face contacts with authorities were scarce and weak. Many services are available online and require filling in an application form or participating in a written online chat. There is an urgent need for contacting and starting the cooperation between prisoners and the authorities already during the incarceration period. But unfortunately the authorities both outside and inside prison find it hard to contact each other. From the perspective of the prisoner being released, the role of the social worker and other authorities is rather limited. In addition, authorities seemed to be acting as gatekeepers who have the right to provide or deny the service (Lipsky 1980; Kallio and Saarinen 2013; Blomberg, Kallio and Kroll 2016). Women's experiences of being marginalised with regard to services increase their feelings as outsiders in the society. In the following extract, Maria describe failing to get a pre-arranged treatment:

Sometimes you won't get any service even though you ask for it. I was having a terrible psychosis, like I hadn't taken any drugs for many days. My sister didn't know what else to do, so she and my mother had decided to take me for treatment. I was there for a few days. Then they called from the hospital to the clinic. They put me in a taxi in the morning and told me 'go to the addiction clinic where there is a place for you. Take a voucher with you to pay for the ride'. Well, I did go to the clinic and then I was knocking at the door saying 'there should be a place for me in there'. Then there comes a guy to the door and says 'what, there's no place here for you'. I was like 'what the fuck'. You know, I was still in psychosis then. I was like 'where should I go? I don't have any flat, I don't have anything'. The answer was like, 'it's not our business'. And they had called from the hospital that I was coming! And they gave me a voucher for the taxi! I still don't get that... After that I walked to social services and told them the situation. They told me to go to the shelter for homeless people.

(Maria)

Maria failed to receive the services that had been arranged for her. The experience of being left on the streets in the middle of a psychosis and withdrawal symptoms had a considerable effect on Maria's trust and self-esteem. After experiences of the authorities' neglect, Maria and other women thought that it was much easier not to ask anyone more favours. In this narrative, it is significant that Maria felt that nobody had taken responsibility for her case after all. These kinds of narratives of rejection share features of randomness and feelings of 'almost getting the service'.

> I remember one time, when I went to the social office and I felt kind of shitty. I had thought that I wouldn't take another hit [of amphetamine], so that I could sort my things. The social worker was there, [turning up her nose] for real! I went to my car; our drugs were there. I took a huge hit and went back inside to shout and rage. Like I did that on purpose, like if you really want to … if you treat me like a junkie, then you'll get the fucking junkie. I get this, like, stupid rage. It feels bad, especially if you go there sober. Then the other one looks at you like you had syphilis or some other contagious disease.
>
> (Maria)

Maria told about her feelings of frustration and rage after her meeting with a social worker did not go as she had planned. In her narrative, Maria was not very pleased with her own 'stupid rage'. When having contact with authorities, Maria and other women had many expectations of getting help and counselling from them. For that reason, these contacts were also fulfilled with many emotions. Women described their dealings with authorities as being demanding and sometimes even shocking. They described situations where the authorities did not understand their problems and their circumstances. Women also pointed out that they felt that authorities were ignoring their needs or providing insufficient services.

Strategies to obtain suitable services

The welfare system in Finland is based on legislation and universal rights based on nationality or residence, but municipalities can decide how services are provided. For this reason, the services which are provided for people with multiple problems can sometimes be fragmentary. That may lead to insufficient or even wrong services for service users. Because of these gaps in the encounters that users have with services, there is also an under-use of certain services. A lack of proper encounters also influences cooperation between different authorities. In the next excerpt, Anu shares her feelings of being a former prisoner and now a service user:

> Because you have been in prison for years where you could never argue against anything in there or to have your own opinion, so you accept

everything as it is because you think that it is the correct way, and you think that is the way it goes, and this is what I have to deal with.

(Anu)

Like Anu, other women talked about how they feel the need to have a humble attitude when getting services. They also talked about having to tolerate inappropriate or even humiliating behaviour. Daring to contact authorities and asking for help or advice could be challenging and stressful for women released from prison. In addition, the governing and operative codes of behaviour might be different or even strange. There was also confusion about correct procedures. After being released, the feelings of shame and guilt could be so strong that they became a barrier against asking for any services (Virokannas 2019). Laura was in a desperate situation in her search for an apartment. In this excerpt, she describes her experiences with the authorities:

That was a surprise, when we came here to the city because we weren't in the books here and we had come from prison [laughter]. And I as a woman couldn't imagine that they would look at me in that way. I said, 'I came from prison and I've been there for that long and now I have to live somewhere'. 'You can't get a home here just like that! You have to be a resident in the city first'. It was difficult in the end to get an apartment from here. We had to get an apartment from a private renter because both of our credit ratings had gone. Both my husband and I had to go back to the group of drunks and use some stuff because, of course, it seemed that life won't go on from there. Then we heard from those drunks that there is this guy named Heikki. From him we got the apartment in a suburb. If we hadn't heard that there is this guy, I don't know where we would have gone from there. Probably back to the prison.

(Laura)

Laura shared how she and her husband did not get help until they were back on the streets after being released. She said they wanted a fresh start in their new city of official residence. In Finland, people have the right to get services from the municipality where they have their official residence. After release, several women talked about their interest in moving somewhere besides their old city of official residence, as Laura above did. They had the idea of starting over without the shame and stigma of being former prison inmates. Moving to another locality also contributes to building social relations. When returning to one's former city of residence, there are old substance-use-oriented friends, and the opportunities to desist are scarce. Women's motivations and reasons to move to another town are not visible or understandable to the authorities. Laura and her husband found their apartment by using unofficial help and peer support (Chapter 12, Virokannas in this book). Next, Elina describes her way out of addiction.

I decided I wouldn't use any drugs there [in prison]. Then I held on to that. Yes, there were all kind of drugs even in a closed prison. I would have had many opportunities to use them. Then I had the possibility of going to the drug-free section. I thought that I would try. There was an interview and after that, they told me I could come. Then they asked me to apply to the open prison's rehabilitation course and I got the place! There were many applicants and I was one who got in. So, I had to be happy. There I completed the course and the rest of my sentence. There was a counsellor for substance abusers, and she suggested I apply to rehabilitation for the rest my sentence. And I got in. Then I got three months extra time for rehabilitation. That time gave me tools and encouraged me to try a different way of living. And the possibility to stay in this town. And then there was also a housing subsidy for a year after rehabilitation. During the rehabilitation I thought I could check this all the way. If being sober didn't suit me, I could always go back to the old way.

(Elina)

The ability to get a place from the open prison means that the inmate met the requirements for managing her substance use. The prison system therefore endorses and supports those who have better equipped to follow the rules. This system categorises prisoners according to their addiction and their ability to handle it. In closed prisons, the services are inadequate and to get decent service requires demanding it. What is common and remarkable in women's narratives both in prison and after release is the lack of social work services. The services are arranged in prisons, and after release, the services are provided by the NGOs.

Being released from prison could be a step forward and an opportunity to change one's life course. Sometimes, this transition also means the need to change one's whole social network: both friends and one's city of residence. Re-entry into society is a long and demanding process. The path from addict to non-addict, from criminality to the ability to get by on little money depends on having suitable professionals around. It was startling to hear women say that they had 'good luck' when they have encountered an understanding official and received appropriate services. The women's narratives all had in common the way they described their path to re-entry: successful re-entry requires suitable services, good encounters and experiences with the professionals and the service system and sufficient self-motivation to move towards integration.

Conclusion

Being released from prison exposes women to those vulnerable life situations they had experienced before their sentencing. They are living in vulnerable life situations because they exist at the margins of the welfare system. Being at the margins means that the welfare service system lacks the ability to offer them women-specific services and support, but also the services are fragile, and there is an absence of empowering social work. As a result, the women wander around the margins lacking decent services. They are denied access to the services or are viewed as not suitable to receive them. Without adequate provision of timely, women-specific services, their needs will not be met. In addition, these women also require women-specific understanding of the traumas they face and the trauma-based behaviour they exhibit, which has been caused by living in a drug- and crime-related culture and by experiencing abusive relationships (Chapter 9, Karttunen in this book).

The needs the women described were basic ones: having an apartment and getting help in keeping it. However, these are the very things that are essential for successful re-entry into society. The means and strategies to obtain services and meet their needs included having a humble attitude. Moreover, there seems to be a lack or at least a low profile of social work in the narratives of these women. It seems that the current provision of social work with adults is not able to answer the needs of women after they are released from prison. In the Finnish welfare service system, the role of social work is to act as an advocate for clients' rights. This feature seems lacking in the women's narratives about social work. The service providers are not able to understand the needs of these women on being released from prison nor do they comprehend what it means to be a woman with a criminal background. Inappropriate services lead to the invisibility of social work in their lives. When services are not able to meet people's needs, the welfare system looks fragile.

The services and support planned for and provided to released women should include a women-specific orientation. Here, 'women-specific' means an understanding of vulnerable life situations and the consequences these may have. It means understanding violence, traumas and substance abuse. The services women require seem to be available through peer support and from NGOs. However, the funding of such organisations in Finland is based on project funding and is therefore short, fragile and uncertain. Moreover, they operate regionally and so cannot provide services across the nation.

The logic of the welfare system and its services seems to be vague, hit-and-miss and incoherent. In their narratives, the women attempted to describe their understanding of it as well as their abilities to adapt to it and operate within it. The women knew their rights as citizens of the welfare state, but they did not know which services were available or how to obtain them. On the other hand, they were aware of their repute as former prisoners. However, they required more face-to-face contacts and interactive services. Instead, the procedures of the authorities and the service system were unfamiliar and incoherent for them. They said that getting services depended on good luck. As a whole, the welfare system in Finland seems to offer sufficient services. When the service user needs multiple and concurrent services, however, the provision of an appropriate combination of these can be challenging.

Note

1 National Social Insurance Institution. See Chapter 8, Krok, and Chapter 3, Virokannas, Salovaara, Krok and Kuronen in this book.

References

Ara 2019. *Asunnottomat 2018.* Accessed 7 March 2019. https://www.ara.fi/fi-FI/Tietopankki/Tilastot_ja_selvitykset/Asunnottomuus/Asunnottomat2018(49593)

Blomberg, Helena, Johanna Kallio, and Christian Kroll. 2016. "Häpeää ja laiskuutta: Asiakkaiden, muiden kansalaisten sekä katutason työntekijäryhmien käsitykset toimeentulotukiasiakkuudesta." *Yhteiskuntapolitiikka* 81 (3): 301–312.

Chesney-Lind, Meda. 2006. "Patriarchy, Crime and Justice; Feminist Criminology in an Era of Backflash." *Feminist Criminology* 1 (1): 6–26. doi:10.1177/1557085105282893

Devlin, Angela. 1998. *Invisible Women: What's Wrong with Women Prisons?* Winchester: Waterside Press.

Estrada, Felipe, and Anders Nilsson. 2012. "Does It Cost More to Be a Female Offender? A Life-Course Study of Childhood Circumstances, Crime, Drug Abuse, and Living Conditions." *Feminist Criminology* 7 (3): 196–219. doi:10.1177/1557085111429783

Eubanks, Virginia. 2011. *Digital Dead End: Fighting for Social Justice in the Information Age.* Gambridge, MA: MIT Press.

Fleetwood, Jennifer. 2014. "Keeping Out of Trouble: Female Crack Cocaine Dealers in England." *European Journal of Criminology* 11 (1): 91–109. doi:10.1177/1477370813491177

Gelsthorpe, Loraine, and Serena Wright. 2015. "The Context: Women as Lawbreakers." In *Women and Criminal Justice: From the Corston Report to Transforming Rehabilitation*, edited by Jill Annison, Jo Brayford, and John Deering, 39–58. Bristol: Policy Press.

Granfelt, Riitta. 2016. "Vankilasta desistanssipolun kautta kotiin." In *Siirtymät ja valinnat asumispolulla*, edited by Kirsi Juhila and Teppo Kröger, 215–229. Jyväskylä: SoPhi.

Hautala, Sanna, Pekka Hakkarainen, Kristiina Kuussaari, Kati Kataja, and Saila Kailanto. 2019. "Violence as a Part of the Drug Scene." *Nordic Journal of Criminology* 1, 1–18. doi:10.1080/14043858.2019.1572943

Hypén, Kimmo. 2004. *Vankilasta vuosina 1993–2001 vapautuneet ja vankilaan uudestaan palanneet.* Rikosseuraamusviraston julkaisuja 1/2004. Rikosseuraamusvirasto: Helsinki.

Kallio, Johanna, and Arttu Saarinen. 2013. "Katutason byrokraattien käsitykset työttömistä ja työttömyysturvasta." *Työelämän tutkimus* 11 (3): 192–208.

KOS 2018. *Kriminalvård och statistic.* Accessed 6 October 2019. https://www.kriminalvarden.se/globalassets/publikationer/kartlaggningar-och-utvarderingar/kos-2018.pdf

Kristoffersen, Ragnar. 2019. *Correctional Statistics of Denmark, Finland, Iceland, Norway and Sweden 2013–2017.* Lillestrøm: University College of Norwegian Correctional Service.

Kruttschnitt, Candace, and Timothy Kang. 2019. "Do Intersectional Variations Shape Prisoners' Understanding of Their Past Lives? An Examination of the

Stock Narratives of Persistent Offenders." *Justice Quarterly* 36: 1–28. doi:10.1080/07418825.2019.1575456

Lattu, Emmi. 2016. *Naisten tekemä väkivalta.* Tampere: Tampereen yliopisto.

Lempert, Lora Bex. 2016. *Women Doing Life.* New York: New York University Press.

Leverentz, Andrea M. 2014. *Ex-Prisoner's Dilemma: How Women Negotiate Competing Narratives of Reentry and Desistance.* New Brunswick, NJ: Rutgers University Press.

Lewison, Terri, Lori M. Thomas, and Shaneureka White. 2014. "Traumatic Transitions: Homeless Women's Narratives of Abuse, Loss and Fear." *Affilia: Journal of Women and Social Work* 29 (2): 192–205. doi: 10.1177/0886109913516449

Lipsky, Michael. 1980/2010. *Street-Level Bureaucracy: Dilemmas of the Individual in Public Services.* New York: Russell Sage Foundation.

Lynch, Shannon M., April Fritch, and Nicole M. Heath. 2012. "Looking Beneath the Surface: The Nature of Incarcerated Women's Experiences of Interpersonal Violence. Treatment Needs, and Mental Health." *Feminist Criminology* 7 (4): 381–400. doi:10.1177/1557085112439224

Määttä, Anne. 2012. *Perusturva ja poiskäännyttäminen.* Helsinki: Diakonia-ammattikorkeakoulu.

Metteri, Anna. 2012. *Hyvinvoinnin lupaukset, kohtuuttomat tapaukset ja sosiaalityö.* Acta Universitatis Tamperensis 1778. Tampere: Tampereen yliopisto.

Sallmann, Jolanda. 2010. "Living with Stigma: Women's Experiences of Prostitution and Substance Use." *Affilia: Journal of Women and Social Work* 25 (2): 146–159. doi:10.1177/0886109910364362

Salovaara, Ulla. 2019a. "Päihteet ja naiserityisyys." *Haaste* 4/2019: 24–25.

Salovaara, Ulla. 2019b. *Rikoksista tuomitut naiset – yhteiskunnasta erottaminen ja takaisinliittymisen mahdollisuudet.* Acta Poenolociga 1/2019. Helsinki: Rikosseuraamusalan koulutuskeskus.

Statistical Yearbook 2018 of the Criminal Sanctions Agency. Accessed 23 April 2019 https://www.rikosseuraamus.fi/material/attachments/rise/julkaisut-tilastollinenvuosikirja/xZlsnncf1/RISE_Statistical_Yearbook2018.WWW2.pdf

Venäläinen, Satu. 2017. *Women as Perpetrators of Violence: Meanings of Gender and Violence in the Tabloid Press and in the Narratives of Women Imprisoned for Violent Crimes.* Publications of the Faculty of Social Sciences 62/2017. Helsinki: Helsingin yliopisto.

Virokannas, Elina. 2017a. "Eriarvoisuuden kokemuksia ja hallinnan suhteita hyvinvointipalvelujärjestelmässä: Huumeita käyttävien naisten "standpoint"." *Yhteiskuntapolitiikka* 82 (3): 274–283.

Virokannas, Elina. 2017b. "Rajoitettuja avunsaannin kokemuksia ja hallinnan suhteita huumeita käyttävien naisten keskusteluissa hyvinvointipalvelujärjestelmässä." *Janus* 25 (2): 111–126.

Virokannas, Elina. 2019. "Treatment Barriers to Social and Health Care Services from the Standpoint of Female Substance Users in Finland." *Journal of Social Service Research.* doi:10.1080/01488376.2019.1598532

Virokannas, Elina, Suvi Liuski, and Marjo Kuronen. 2020. "The Contested Concept of Vulnerability – A Literature Review." *European Journal of Social Work* 23 (2): 327–339. doi:10.1080/13691457.2018.1508001

8 The reform of the Finnish income benefit system from the standpoint of lone mothers

Suvi Krok

Introduction

In many countries, families headed by lone mothers are at the centre of debates on rising social inequality. The inequalities between different family forms are intertwined with gendered inequality (Nieuwenhuis and Maldano 2018). Lone-parent families, most often headed by the mother, are at a bigger risk of being poor than two-parent families are. Lone mothers have a double role as the breadwinner and primary carer in the family, and the combination of these two roles can easily put lone mothers in an economically vulnerable life situation. Because of their financial situation, lone mothers often need to turn to the social security system for social benefits.

This chapter presents a critical analysis of the Finnish income benefit system from the standpoint of lone mothers after the system was transferred from municipal social work to the National Social Insurance Institution (Kela) in 2017. When financial difficulties arise, lone mothers have to apply for financial support first from the universal social security system and then from the means-tested income benefit system as a last resort.

There have been assessments of how the reform has affected the income of economically vulnerable people (Perusturvan riittävyyden III arviointityöryhmä 2019), but less is known about poor people's views and experiences of the reform. Poverty is often defined in terms of flows of income and consumption, but economically vulnerable people themselves have different criteria of wellbeing and deprivation. In addition to food or housing, the poor have other priorities. Unemployment and waiting for benefits means economic insecurity. Vulnerable people's wants and needs are complex, and they are concerned with issues related to independence, social and income mobility, security and self-respect. Governments often wrongly assume that poor people do not stay poor and that income mobility is considerable (Chambers 1989; Shildrick et al. 2012, 12–26).

The critical analysis is based on institutional ethnography, which means analysing how lone mothers experience their everyday world to be organised by the income benefit system and to make this organisation visible and help to understand 'how it actually works'. That means a commitment to beginning the inquiry from the standpoint of lone mothers (Smith 1987, 2005).

The data were gathered through phenomenological interviews with 16 lone mothers between summer 2017 and autumn 2018. The interviewees were selected for the interviews through the social workers of one city, an association for single parents and a Facebook group for lone mothers. The phenomenological interviews were by nature open and inductive, much like a conversation, and proceeded dialogically (see Warren 2002). The lone mothers had experiences of financial hardship, and they had tried to solve their financial problems by applying for the income benefit or other social benefits. Otherwise, the interviewed lone mothers were a diverse group, ranging in age from 20 to 58. For them, lone motherhood had been the result of different life events such as divorce, separation or the death of a partner. Some of them had never lived with the father of their child. In this dataset, lone mothers had from one to three children varying in age from infants to teenagers over 17 years. The status of lone mother varies across the life course and is usually not permanent.

The Finnish social security system and means-tested income benefit as a last resort

Finland is a Nordic country with a universal welfare system. The Nordic social security system is based on universal benefits aimed at providing protection for everyone who faces certain social risks, ill-health or unemployment. In Finland, there are two types of social protection: earnings-related social security benefits and universal basic social security benefits available to all permanent residents (Blomberg, Kroll and Kallio 2018). However, as Susan Kuivalainen and Mikko Niemelä (2010) have shown, the idea of selectivism has increasingly crept into the Finnish social benefit system, leading to the use of means-testing to determine who is qualified for the benefits. Yet the Finnish welfare system secures for all permanent residents at least the most basic means for living and taking active part in society. The welfare system rests on the assumption that citizens have the moral duty to work and thus finance the welfare system (Kettunen 2001). In the Nordic countries, social protection systems vary considerably, but multi-tiered safety nets are common in all the countries. In the case of loss of earnings, citizens are primarily expected to apply for the national and centrally governed social insurance benefits. The last safety net is the income benefit, which is usually governed locally by municipal social services and provides means-tested benefits to poor citizens (Blomberg, Kroll and Kallio 2018; Minas et al. 2018).

The Social Assistance Act (1980) guarantees every Finnish resident a minimum income through the income benefit system. The income benefit is strictly means and needs tested. The means-tested income benefit should ensure the subsistence of the claimant and the claimant's family when they are not able to earn their living with their work or with other social security benefits and to promote the ability of the individual to cope independently (Niemelä and Salminen 2006). In the history of the income benefit, it has been strongly connected with the Poor Relief Act (1923), and it still carries the burden of the idea that there are deserving and undeserving poor, and of poor people as scroungers eager to take advantage of state benefits. Applying for the income benefit can still create a stigmatised position (Blomberg, Kroll and Kallio 2018).

Until recently, income benefit was provided by the municipal social workers' combining financial support with other forms of non-financial support, including counselling and support in practicing control over one's personal life. After the economic recession of the early 1990s, the nature of the income benefit has changed because the number of claimants multiplied. Today, approximately 7% of Finnish residents receive means-tested social assistance. Nowadays, the income benefit is a supplement to other forms of benefits, and it is the form of last resort for income security (Blomberg, Kroll and Kallio 2018).

In 2017, the income benefit system was reformed in Finland. Nordic welfare reforms show examples of both de- and recentralisation (Minas et al. 2018). In Finland, the aim of the income benefit reform was centralisation. The income benefit was transferred from the local municipal social work to the National Social Insurance institution (Kela) at the beginning of 2017. The contents of the scheme remain unchanged; it is only the implementation of the basic benefit that has changed, with social workers still providing additional or preventive income support. The reform involves mandatory institutional cooperation between officials in Kela and municipal social work (see Minas et al. 2018). However, from the clients' perspective, it means that they should first apply for the basic income benefit in Kela, and if additional support is needed, the client has the possibility to apply supplementary or preventive income benefit from the municipality. The system has thus become more complicated. The strictly means-tested benefit has faced considerable criticism both before and after the reform (Krok 2008; Linnavirta, Kroll and Blomberg 2018).

Economic vulnerability of lone mothers

Lone parenthood is strongly gendered, because the majority of single-parent households are headed by women (Nieuwenhuis and Maldano 2018). Lone-parent families are not a marginal phenomenon in Finland: 20% of families are currently lone-parent families (Official Statistics of Finland 2020a). Compared with other OECD countries, the poverty rate of lone-parent families is low in Finland, but 20% of them are still considered poor. When compared with two-parent families in Finland, whose poverty rate is 7%, lone parents are more often poor than other families (Nieuwenhuis and Maldano 2018; Official Statistics of Finland 2020b).

Lone mothers go against many prevailing norms and values pertaining to a family. Morag Treanor (2018, 82) argues that being a lone mother is the most stigmatised position in the UK. On the other hand, Vanessa May (2001) shows that there are more neutral attitudes towards lone parenting in Finland, which might have to do with the weakness of the male breadwinner model. The vast majority of lone mothers of school-age children in Finland, around 80%, are in full-time employment compared with many other countries, such as the UK where only 40% are in full-time employment (Zagel and Hübgen 2018).

Finnish social policy provides a wide safety net for families (Hakovirta and Jokela 2018). In the family policy system, lone-mother headed families are seen as just one of many possible family types, all of which are valued equally, and lone mothers or their children do not receive any special attention or specific benefits (Zagel and Hübgen 2018). The government guarantees the minimum payment of child maintenance for the lone mothers until the child turns 18, if the father is unable or unwilling to pay maintenance. Of lone mothers, 80% receive child maintenance, but its contribution as an income source is less significant, forming only 10% of the total income of lone mothers (Hakovirta and Jokela 2018).

On the other hand, the Finnish social policy is still based on the dual-breadwinner model. In the Nordic societies, the standard of living demands two earners in the family (Hobson 1990). For most lone-mother families, employment and benefits alone cannot provide an adequate standard of living. The explanation of the lone mothers' high poverty risk can also be that women earn, on average, less than men (Official Statistics of Finland 2020b). Women are more likely to face lower wages and have fewer career opportunities, thus making it harder for lone mothers to gain financial autonomy (May 2001, 22). Finnish women have also fought hard to combine motherhood and working life (Sevon 2005), and especially lone mothers have difficulties to reconcile work and care. The lack of the second earner makes it harder for lone-mother households to have adequate earnings, but it also makes them more vulnerable to the financial consequences of unemployment, sickness and maternity and parent leaves. Moreover, the absence of a partner living in the same household or without co-parenting limits care possibilities and flexibility (Horemans and Marx 2018).

Bureaucracy and financial struggles

The interviewed lone mothers all had financial struggles in common. They described their everyday life as being worried about money all the time. The lone mothers had difficulties to make ends meet. Some of them were either employed full-time or part-time while others were not in paid work. They were either students, unemployed, on family leave or received rehabilitation support. They described their situation as 'struggling to keep their head above the surface' or as 'a nightmare'. Despite varying degrees of contact with the father of their children, all of the mothers retained primary responsibility for the children. The fathers were rarely actively involved in the lives of their children, and a large part of mothers received the minimum child maintenance benefit from the state. Despite their financial problems, the lone mothers were both carers and breadwinners, so they had to take care of their children and ensure that their children had food, clothing and a home.

The mothers suffering financial hardship felt that they did not receive any financial help from the income benefit system. Mothers described the process of claiming the income benefit as frustrating. They felt that the income benefit system was bureaucratic and did not care about their vulnerable life situation. Bureaucracy was an obstacle and the reason why some of the mothers said that they had been refused social assistance and had not applied for it even if their financial situation was bad.

> Applying for social assistance is laborious, always pushing the papers and collecting the documents and always thinking about the bank account. That all makes me feel like 'oh my God'. Providing all the documents stresses me out.
>
> (Meeri)

In the above excerpt, Meeri, the mother of a teenager, is describing the bureaucratic process of applying for the income benefit. She found it difficult to make ends meet because she was studying. She said that she was not applying for income benefit even though her family did not have anything to eat at home. She preferred to ask for food handouts through the church. Linnavirta, Kroll and Blomberg (2018) had similar findings from their interviews with people queuing at food banks.

A reason for the bureaucratic procedures is that the income benefit is strictly means and needs tested. The claimant must prove a family's poverty by producing various documents, including the family's income, bank account and expenditures, rent, an electric bill and possible assets such as a car or a family's summer cottage. The claimant should apply monthly, and it is uncertain how much money she will get. The claimant must also provide documented information about her private life, if additional information is requested, concerning, for example, persons who are living in the household, the agreement of child maintenance or an official medical record. According to Blomberg, Kroll and Kallio (2018), the procedures have become more bureaucratic when the implementation of the last-resort financial assistance was transferred from municipal social service to the Weberian-type of bureaucracy of an institution that traditionally handles a statutory universal social security.

Those of the lone mothers who were in the serious or unexpected situation and requiring immediate financial help felt judged and not listened to in their interactions with Kela. Some of the mothers even described the encounters as 'soul destroying'. Unexpected situations included, for example, when the mother or her children fell seriously ill. Poor families have a high incidence of poor health (Daly and Kelly 2015, 35–39), and lone mothers typically have more health problems than does the general population in

Finland (Sierminska 2018). In the following excerpt, the poor health of a lone mother or her children inevitably caused financial problems.

> I need to access my own online medical data to print my child's medical information. But this part of the income benefit was rejected. There are no humans in this rigmarole; there is only a machine that calculates. I'll make a supplementary application and in it I will write that I want to meet a social worker. So I will go fill out a third application for the same request.
>
> (Marja)

Marja's children had been in an accident, and one of the children was seriously injured. She could not pay the medical expenses. The mother had financial difficulties because she was waiting for a decision on rehabilitation support and she had to apply for the income benefit. For the mother, being in the income benefit process meant that she had to constantly complete different forms. This bureaucracy made her feel that the application process was dehumanising at a time when her family needed urgent help.

The income benefit reform has increased bureaucracy because mothers must first apply for the basic income benefit from Kela. After they receive a decision on basic income, they can then apply for supplementary and preventive assistance from the social office and meet a social worker. Yet before mothers can get a decision of basic income benefit, they must first apply for other universal or earnings-related benefits as well as have an official agreement for child maintenance. Some of the lone mothers did not apply for the income benefit because they did not want to be under the control of the income benefit system, and the bureaucratic application process made them feel as though they were begging scrounging. One reason for not applying for the income benefit is that women were ashamed of applying for financial assistance. The negative public views that question recipients' morals and motives can also be one reason for the underuse of the income benefit (Blomberg, Kroll and Kallio 2018). The mothers did not care whether they received their financial support from the municipal social services or from the social insurance institution. What mattered to them were the encounters with the officials. Despite being poor, they wanted to feel that they had independence and self-respect.

Everyday copying strategies

The lone mothers' lives were marked by complex difficulties, and they struggled to find feasible solutions. Help and support from other people were necessary to mothers, especially when caring for infants. The mothers needed help with transportation, childcare, small financial help and emotional support. Because of the breakdown of the traditional family structure, the local community, neighbourhood and friends became an important support network for mothers (Nelson 2000, 299, 314; Krok 2009).

If I have an urgent need for childcare, I ask if a neighbour can take the children and the neighbour helps if she is at home. My children are infants so it is hard to take care of them when I have had a stomach flu and nobody wanted to come to my home because they were frightened of getting the same illness, but the neighbour helped and brought lunch.

(Tiina)

Tiina, with two children under three years of age, describes the importance of a neighbour's support and help when she urgently needs it in childcare or when she herself is ill and needs help.

TIINA: I have occasional financial hardship, but I wouldn't move to a cheaper apartment just for that. I was studying for two months and I couldn't work because I was pregnant and I must take care of my child in the evenings and on weekends.
INTERVIEWER: Did you ask for financial help from your uncle?
TIINA: Yes.

Tiina was pregnant at the same time she was studying and had to take care of her child. She had applied for the income benefit when the family had been suffering financial hardship, but she did not receive any because her rent was too high for the criteria and she had a private pension. The friends in the neighbourhood were also important to her, so Tiina did not consider moving away from her apartment even if it left her without financial help from the benefit system. She went through hard financial times by getting help from relatives, who loaned her money for her everyday expenditures.

The next excerpt also shows that the income benefit system fails to account for lone mothers' everyday coping strategies, which are based on their routines and everyday environment. In this case, Kela's official required the mother to move to a cheaper apartment, which would have meant moving away from her current neighbourhood to a poor residential area.

Now in the last income support decision they said that my rent is too high and that I should move to a cheaper home. My child is starting school and we should change residences because we pay a hundred euros more rent than we should. Take my kid away from school. I have neighbours here that can take care of my kid sometimes.

(Tanja)

Tanja, with a school-age child, was a student and that is why the family had difficulties to make ends meet. One's immediate environment and place of residence are very important for a mother to provide a safe neighbourhood for the child. The school is near home, so the mother does not have to worry about the child walking alone to school, and she can trust that the neighbours will take care of the child if needed. These two cases show that a safe neighbourhood is one of the everyday coping strategies and that routines increase the sense of security.

The common stereotype associated with poor people is that they live hand-to-mouth and that their lives are simple. It has been shown (Shildrick et al. 2012; Daly and Kelly 2015) that the reality is the opposite. Most poor people have complex and diverse strategies to cope with everyday poverty (Lister 2004; Krok 2009). Poor people use different coping strategies to reduce their risk in poverty, increase adaptability and seek a degree of autonomy (Chambers 1989). The lone mothers' main copying strategy was based on locality and routines. The important part of the everyday strategy was repetition: social reproduction, cleaning, preparing meals and caring for children. The everyday rituals safeguard a sense of personal autonomy and dignity, while one's neighbourhood and home create a space of familiarity and security (e.g. Felski 2001; Krok 2009).

In many ways, the income benefit system organises the lone mothers' everyday life by deciding which expenditures are necessary, such as the level of acceptable rent, and by requiring a move to a cheaper apartment which would eliminate the supporting routines. Daly and Kelly (2015, 178) show that those who were required to find alternative housing suffer significant hardship, because they lost the support of family and friends in their immediate environment.

Strategies for preventing persistent poverty

The second important strategy of lone mothers was to cope with poverty so that it does not cause permanent damage, such as hurting one's credit rating or harming their families' nutrition. The mothers were confused by the income benefit principles, which fail to support their strategies to minimise the damages caused by poverty.

The interviewed lone mothers wanted to be good mothers and work for their children's wellbeing. It can be said that motherhood is part of their identity (see Krok 2009), and the welfare of children is the mission of women (Rich 1986, 49). The mothers were constantly worrying about getting too tired to take care of their children and worried about their welfare. They questioned if their children were suffering from poverty or because they lived without their father. The lone mothers were afraid that they were not able to be good mothers and that child welfare services would take their children away from them (see Chapter 5, Veenstra in this book). They tried to minimise the damages of poverty that can prevent them from being good mothers (see Vincent, Stephen, and Braun 2010; Daly and Kelly 2015).

> I shouted at the woman [the Kela official] that you can't play with someone's health and I have small children at home and I can't stop the medicine suddenly because there could be some side effects.
>
> (Sini)

Sini was angry about being left without financial aid. The poverty of her family meant that she had no money for medicine although it was necessary for her wellbeing and so that she could take care of her children. The income benefit system refused to pay because the Kela official decided that the medicine was not obligatory.

Mothers assumed that they had the right to receive financial help from the welfare state in situations of ill-health, and they felt that it was unfair that the income benefit system, as the last resort, failed to help them despite their vulnerable situation. The sickness of a lone mother, as the breadwinner of the family, also caused a loss of earnings.

> Debts are not taken into account, but if you hurt your credit rating, the debt becomes expenses which you get money for. The advice is to not take care of your business. I needed only one or two months of financial help. So they advised me to make irreversible mistakes to be in debt, so that my financial problems would be worse.
>
> (Sari)

Sari, who has a permanent full-time job, was on sick leave at the time of the interview. She said that she had to apply for income benefit so she can pay her monthly expenses and debts. Sari was chronically ill and not able to work and no longer receiving earning-related sickness benefits. Her family suffered occasional poverty because of her sickness. The income benefit officer refused to help the family with the debts until the lone mother had damaged her credit rating. If she had followed this advice, the family would have been stuck at the lowest poverty levels. It is very hard to move out of poverty if you have damaged your credit rating and you are in low-paid work (see Shildrick et al. 2012, 12–16). The mother's strategy was to prevent occasional poverty from becoming persistent poverty.

After its reform, the income support system failed to support the lone mothers' own coping strategies. Before the reform, the frontline social workers had discretion in their decision-making, so each case could be handled as an individual case. This freedom to decide what should be done in a particular situation has been eliminated from the current decision-making processes (see Blomberg, Kroll and Kallio 2018).

Conclusion

This chapter questions our assumptions about the economic vulnerability of lone mothers by investigating what lone mothers themselves want and need. Poverty should be understood as more than just having a low income (measured as 60% of the median household income) and material deprivation, such as not being able to afford clothes, furniture and so on (Treanor 2018, 85). Even though the lone mothers felt guilty that their children could not afford to participate in activities as their schoolmates did, poverty, for them, does not mean exclusion from society (see also Daly and Kelly 2015, 8). Instead, poverty for lone mothers is an experience of disrespect, humiliation, powerlessness and denial of rights (Lister 2004, 7). Those who are living in poverty report a stigma as part of their everyday experience (Chase and Walker 2013).

Lone mothers have complex and diverse strategies in coping with everyday poverty. Living with a low income has a negative effect on parenting, because stress is generally a part of the experiences of low-income parents, especially those of lone mothers (Daly and Kelly 2015, 91–104; Treanor 2018). Thus, the local neighbourhood offered important coping strategies for the lone mothers. According to Daly and Kelly (2015), poverty and low income weaken mobility, and poor people have no other choice but to live locally. The importance of neighbourhoods and local services for low-income families should not be underestimated. The experiences of lone mothers show that the Finnish income benefit system does not support everyday coping strategies based on one's neighbourhood, which they adopt to be good mothers and carers and to guarantee their children's wellbeing.

Living on benefits and low-paid work means poverty and insecurity. One of the main reasons for the financial hardship of lone mothers was the ill-health of either their children or the mothers themselves. Ill-health also weakens their capability to be a good mother. In Finland, the costs of ill-health have risen in recent years. For example, it is difficult for chronically ill unemployed people to retire, and at the same time, after the income benefit reform, the criteria for getting assistance for medical expenditures has become stricter. The second strategy for the lone mothers was to avoid persistent poverty. The benefit system failed to support lone mothers' strategies to mitigate the damages of poverty, such as avoiding debts, and in doing so, prevent impoverishment of the family and the risk of future dependency on the income benefit system.

From the standpoint of the lone mothers interviewed in this study, the system failed to support their own coping strategies in everyday life, by which they tried to guarantee their independence, income mobility, security and self-respect. Instead, the reform of the system has increased lone mothers' insecurity. The experiences of lone mothers deepen our understanding of how the income benefit system works for them and organises their everyday lives. The aim of the income benefit reform was to promote the equality of citizens so that the rules would be the same for all recipients throughout the country (Blomberg, Kroll and Kallio 2018). Even as the reform adopted the quantitative conceptualisation of poverty, it fails to recognise individual vulnerable situations, local conditions and variance and thus loses its main purpose of preventing social exclusion. These findings of lone mothers' experiences indicate that poverty should be understood through more than statistics.

References

Blomberg, Helena, Christian Kroll, and Johanna Kallio. 2018. "On the Changing Frontline of Welfare Delivery: Views on Social Assistance Recipients among Finnish Frontline Workers." *Journal of Poverty and Social Justice* 26 (2): 263–280. doi:10.1332/175982718X15232796966637

Chambers, Robert. 1989. "Editorial Introduction: Vulnerability, Coping and Policy." IDS *Bulletin* 20: 1–7.

Chase, Elaine, and Robert Walker. 2013. "The Co-Construction of Shame in the Context of Poverty; Beyond a Treat to the Social Bond." *Sociology* 47 (4): 739–754. doi:10.1177/0038038512453796

Daly, Mary, and Grace Kelly. 2015. *Families and Poverty: Everyday Life on a Low Income*. Bristol: Policy Press.

Felski, Rita. 2001. "The Invention of Everyday Life. New Formation." *A Journal of Culture/Theory Politics* 39: 15–31.

Hakovirta, Mia, and Merita Jokela. 2018. "Contribution of Child Maintenance to Lone Mothers' Income in Five Countries." *Journal of European Social Policy* 29 (2): 257–272.

Hobson, Barbara. 1990. "No Exit, No Voice: Women's Economic Dependency and the Welfare State." *Acta Sociologica* 33 (3): 235–250.

Horemans, Jeroen, and Marx Ive. 2018. "Doesn't Anyone Else Care? Variation in Poverty among Working Single Parents across Europe." In *The Triple Bind of Single-Parent Families: Resources, Employment and Policies to Improve Wellbeing*, edited by Rense Nieuwenhuis, and Laurie C. Maldonado, 195–221. Bristol: Policy Press.

Kettunen, Pauli. 2001. "The Nordic Welfare State in Finland." *Scandinavian Journal of History* 26 (3): 225–247.

Krok, Suvi. 2008. "Vähävarainen yksinhuoltajaäiti etuusjärjestelmässä." In *Sosiaalityö aikuisten parissa*, edited by Arja Jokinen, and Kirsi Juhila, 145–174. Tampere: Vastapaino.

Krok, Suvi. 2009. *Hyviä äitejä ja arjen pärjääjiä: Yksinhuoltajia marginaalissa*. Tampere: Acta Universistatis Tamperensis 1437. https://trepo.tuni.fi/bitstream/handle/10024/66494/978-951-44-7783-6.pdf?sequence=1

Kuivalainen, Susan, and Mikko Niemelä. 2010. "From Universalism to Selectivism: The Ideational Turn of the Anti-Poverty Policies in Finland." *Journal of European Social Policy* 20 (3): 263–276. doi:10.1177/0958928710364432

Linnavirta, Suvi, Christians Kroll, and Helena Blomberg. 2018. "The Perceived Legitimacy of a Basic Income among Finnish Food Aid Recipients." *The international Journal of Social Welfare* (0): 1–11. doi:10.1111/ijsw.12362

Lister, Ruth. 2004. *Poverty*. Cambridge: Policy Press.

May, Vanessa. 2001. *Lone Motherhood in Finnish Women's Life Stories. Creating Meaning in a Narrative Context*. Åbo: Åbo Akademi University Press.

Minas, Renata, Vibeke Jakobsen, Timo Kauppinen, Tomas Korpi, and Thomas Lorentzen. 2018. "The Governance of Poverty: Welfare Reform, Activation Policies, and Social Assistance Benefits and Caseloads in Nordic Countries." *Journal of European Social Policy* 28 (5): 487–500. doi:10.1177/0958928717753591

Nelson, Margareth K. 2000. "Single Mothers and Social Support: The Commitment to and Retreat from Reciprocity." *Qualitative Sociology* 23 (3): 291–317. doi:10.1023/A:1005567910606

Niemelä, Heikki, and Kari Salminen. 2006. *Social Security in Finland*. Helsinki; Kela: Research Department.

Nieuwenhuis, Rense, and Laurie C Maldano. 2018. "The Triple Bind of Single-Parent Families: Resources, Employment and Policies." In *The Triple Bind of Single-Parent Families: Resources, Employment and Policies to Improve Wellbeing*, edited by Rense Nieuwenhuis, and Laurie C. Maldonado, 1–30. Bristol: Policy Press.

Official Statistics of Finland (OSF). 2020a. Families [e-publication].ISSN=1798–3231. Helsinki: Statistics Finland. Accessed 2 February 2020a. http://www.stat.fi/til/perh/index_en.html

Official Statistics of Finland (OSF). 2020b. Income Distribution Statistics [e-publication].ISSN=1799-1331. Helsinki: Statistics Finland. Accessed 2 February 2020b. http://www.stat.fi/til/tjt/index_en.html

Perusturvan riittävyyden III arviointityöryhmä. 2019. *Perusturvan riittävyyden arviointiraportti 2015–2019*. Discussion Paper 6/2019. Helsinki: National Institute for Health and Welfare.

Rich, Adrienne. 1986. *Of Woman Born. Motherhood as Experience and Institution*. New York: W.W Norton & company.

Sevon, Eija. 2005. "Timing Motherhood: Experience and Narrating the Choice to Become a Mother." *Feminism & Psychology* 15 (4): 461–482.

Shildrick, Tracy, Robert MacDonald, Colin Webster, and Kayleight Garthwaite. 2012. *Poverty and Insecurity: Life in Low-Pay, No-Pay Britain*. Bristol: The Policy Press.

Sierminska, Eva (2018) ""The Wealth-Being" of Single Parents." In *The Triple Bind of Single-Parent Families: Resources, Employment and Policies to Improve Wellbeing*, edited by Rense Nieuwenhuis, and Laurie C. Maldonado, 51–79. Bristol: Policy Press.

Smith, Dorothy E. 1987. *The Everyday Life as Problematic. A Feminist Sociology*. Milton Keynes: Open University Press.

Smith, Dorothy E. 2005. *Institutional Ethnography. A Sociology for People*. Oxford: AltaMira Press.

Treanor, Morag C.2018. "Income Poverty, Material Deprivation and Lone Parenthood". In *The Triple Bind of Single-Parent Families: Resources, Employment and Policies to Improve Wellbeing*, edited by Rense Nieuwenhuis, and Laurie C. Maldonado, 81–100. Bristol: Policy Press.

Vincent, Carol, Stephen J. Ball, and Annette Braun. 2010. "Between the Estate and the State: Struggling to Be a 'Good' Mother." *British Journal of Sociology of Education* 31 (2): 123–38. doi:10.1080/01425690903538976

Warren, Carol. 2002. "Qualitative Interviewing". In *Handbook of Interviewing Research: Context & Method*, edited by Jaber Gubrium, and James Holstein, 83–102. London: Sage Publications.

Zagel, Hannah, and Sabine Hübgen. 2018. "A Life-Course Approach to Single Mothers' Economical Wellbeing in Different Welfare States." In *The Triple Bind of Single-Parent Families: Resources, Employment and Policies to Improve Wellbeing*, edited by Rense Nieuwenhuis, and Laurie C. Maldonado, 171–193. Bristol: Policy Press.

9 Social framework for understanding women's substance abuse, treatment and vulnerability

Teija Karttunen

Introduction

The increase in alcohol and drug abuse among women has attracted political attention and raised public health concerns. A growing body of research has also focused on specialised substance abuse treatment interventions for women (Grella and Greenwell 2004). Historically, attitudes towards female substance use have been negative, punitive and moralising (Measham 2002). Nowadays, these attitudes are conflicting: it is culturally and socially acceptable for women to use alcohol, and female substance use includes images of enjoyment, pleasure and freedom. On the other hand, the social stigma remains, and female substance abusers face negative labelling (Leppo 2012; Simonen, Törrönen and Tigerstedt 2014).

This chapter focuses on women's substance abuse problems and treatment issues in the context of Finnish society and its welfare service system. The medical framework is nowadays widely dominating women's substance abuse and its treatment (Martin and Aston 2014). As a social work researcher, I find it important to understand and examine women's substance abuse problems and treatment connected with vulnerability by tracing social, structural and cultural determinants combined with them. The social framework for understanding these questions comprise here (1) the psychosocial dimensions of women's substance abuse, (2) socially produced shame in women, (3) challenges of the Finnish welfare service system and its ideology and (4) issues of societal integration and social suffering. Examining these dimensions increases our understanding of women's vulnerability and how it is shaped and constructed by social and cultural context, not reduced as an individual feature.

The chapter is based on results in my dissertation and on further reflections (Karttunen 2019). The focus of my dissertation was to study a women-specific substance abuse treatment intervention. The study was conducted in a women's community in a larger residential facility, and data collection was based on ethnographic fieldwork. The aim was to propose alternative concepts and approaches for women's substance abuse and issues of recovery and to promote social interpretations of them.

Women's substance abuse and the question of vulnerability

Substance use disorders take a different course in women than they do in men. Research has demonstrated the gender differences of female substance abuse as well as its biological, health-related, social and psychological consequences (e.g. Tuchman 2010; Becker, McClellan and Glover 2016). Providing and promoting interventions designed especially for women have been seen as a way to meet women's distinctive needs and reduce the barriers they experience in receiving help and remaining in treatment (Greenfield and Grella 2009).

When considering addiction problems, women are seen as, on the whole, more vulnerable than are men. A research review by Martin and Aston (2014) proposes that research identifies substance-abusing women as a special population based on their relative vulnerability or on their reproductive capacity and childcare responsibilities. Vulnerability is here linked to women's susceptibility to harms regarding experiences of violence, abuse, trauma and victimisation, high rates of psychiatric comorbidity and physical risks for medical problems. Martin and Aston, however, take a critical attitude to this research finding. They state that social determinants affecting women's substance abuse and treatment are rarely discussed.

Martin and Aston's critical thinking is based on Foucault's concepts of knowledge, power and discourse. In line with this theorising, they propose that the literature they analysed has discursive effects that contribute to the ways of thinking and talking about substance-abusing women and their treatment needs. They conclude that the relative vulnerability of substance-abusing women and their treatment needs and the representations of them in research literature may reinforce the limited understanding instead of promoting gender-sensitive approaches (Martin and Aston 2014).

The critical perspective of Martin and Aston presents a challenge for the use of concepts and language, interpretations, problem definitions and goal-setting in research and in professional practices. The history of substance abuse treatment programmes for women – and especially for pregnant women and women with young children – is short and sparse (Grella and Greenwell 2004; Kaltenbach 2013). Emphasising women's unique treatment needs, their personal and sensitive experiences related to addiction problems, gender differences and defining substance-using women as vulnerable has been a way to promote and ensure the development, availability and delivery of substance abuse treatment services suitable for women (LaFave, Desportes and McBride 2008; Greenfield and Grella 2009). The clinical interest of professionals in substance abuse treatment settings is also to encourage, support and empower women who seek help and wish to recover from their addiction (Karttunen 2019), not to reinforce 'practices of othering'.

Intentions and purposes can be good and honest, but ageism, sexism and dogmatism exist if we fail to reflect carefully and critically on our use of concepts, working approaches and professional attitudes and beliefs. These shape treatment practices and even research priorities (Becker, McClellan and Glover 2016). The vulnerability can be reinforced and contributed to through language and professional strategies, beliefs and sociocultural attitudes (Crinall 1999; Aguilar and Jackson 2009). We should recognise women's agency, the capability to make choices, express their own thoughts and create alternative femininities (see also Virokannas, Liuski and Kuronen 2020). In terms of vulnerability, women's substance abuse should not thus be conceptualised within an individualised framework because drug abuse cuts across social divisions and is shaped by social, structural and cultural contexts, including social and health care services.

Psychosocial dimensions of women's substance abuse

A more sophisticated conceptualisation of female substance abuse problems is needed if we want to understand the question of vulnerability. Women's substance abuse problems are multidimensional and socially embedded. This gender-sensitive approach views female substance abuse, the recovery process and issues of relapse in the context of women's relationships, including broader relational and multigenerational systems (Claus et al. 2007; Sun 2007).

Women's substance abuse problems are intertwined with their whole life. Intersecting circles surrounding women's addiction problems include family and other social relations, housing, social functioning, physical health and psychological wellbeing, financial resources, crime, violence, abuse and traumatic experiences. These contribute to the risk of accumulating social deprivation (Stevens, Andrade and Ruiz 2009; Kruk and Sandberg 2013). Research demonstrates the social complexity of these problems in their gendered nature and structural factors producing social exclusion, social labelling, distrust and institutional barriers affecting access to welfare services and difficulties in re-integrating into society (Leppo 2012; Virokannas 2019). Focusing narrowly on substance abuse is thus insufficient. It overpowers social issues like poverty and other forms of material deprivation, homelessness, fragile systems of informal social support and deficits in the fulfilment of basic needs such as food, clothing and shelter (Marcellus 2004; Jones and Kaltenbach 2013).

Substance abuse has an impact on women's social networks and relationships. According to relational, self-in-relation theory, women's addictions are intertwined with poor interpersonal relationships and isolation. Substance use is a way to make or keep connections or to fit into a relationship even if this relationship is destructive, harmful or violating (Byington 1997; Covington 2002). Ambivalence regarding the role of social support and social relationships for substance-abusing women in their commitment to treatment, treatment outcomes and maintaining outcomes is also recognised (Falkin and Strauss 2003; Tracy et al. 2010).

Research also indicates the risk for intergenerational transmission of psychosocial problems related to female substance abuse (e.g. Dunlap et al. 2002; Belt 2013). In my own research, there were women with a family history of serious mental illness, substance abuse and child welfare problems throughout several generations. In these cases, only minor or slight social, material and emotional support was available for women from their family members or significant others. The accumulation of psychosocial stressors and constant chaos was a prevailing element in their social network, providing a rather risky and non-supportive environment for their recovery efforts and abstinence.

Hostile social environments, neighbourhood instability and social stressors linked to living conditions should also be considered when assessing and intervening in women's substance abuse and related psychosocial problems (e.g. Mulia et al. 2008). Breaking out from destructive lifestyles and social circumstances with many hardships and with a high tolerance towards violence, abuse and substance abuse as a part of women's normal life course can be an overwhelming task. The role of socialisation and habituation is evident here (Dunlap et al. 2002; James, Johnson and Raghavan 2004).

Research implies the existence of many social and health-related determinants behind and embedded in female substance abuse (e.g. Kahila et al. 2010; Kahila 2011; Sarkola et al. 2011). Kahila and others (2010) have, for example, investigated long-term morbidity, mortality and welfare outcomes among women with alcohol and/or substance misuse identified during pregnancy. The comparison group consisted of women with no addiction problems. The research results indicate that the lifestyle of these women is risky, dangerous and violent. Women with substance abuse problems are more likely to be victims of relational violence, and they are at heightened risk for untimely deaths (Kahila et al. 2010). Their unemployment rates and comorbidity rates are higher than they are among women with no addiction problems. Substance-abusing women were more often in need of disability pensions and the use of rehabilitation services. Their children were more likely to be taken into care at a very young age, even as babies (Sarkola et al. 2011). Overall, the prognosis of these women was estimated to be poor (Kahila 2011).

Sociodemographic factors and psychosocial stressors seem to have a profound impact on female substance abuse and its manifestations. The constellation of psychosocial problems related to female substance abuse can be understood in relation to social, health and economic disadvantages. These dimensions are likely to accumulate in certain socioeconomic positions (see Ohisalo, Laihiala and Saari 2015). This heightened risk of social deprivation requires access to crucial resources such as material support and income assistance, safe and secure housing, educational and employment opportunities and social support.

Shame in women

Among women, shame is a key contributor to the denial of addiction problem, often preventing women from seeking help. In the service system, 'the female junkie' is regarded as more deviant than a woman without an addiction problem (Virokannas 2017a). Professional attitudes can be labelling and negative, resulting in fear among women of losing their autonomy, moral worth, children and other important social relations. There is social and cultural ambivalence towards female substance use prevailing in Finnish society: there is acceptance as well as control and regulation. Moral and punitive discourses are easily detected in public discussion, media portrayals and in professional language (Leppo 2012). This ambivalence both creates and reinforces shame on women.

Shame is a strong 'social signal' of our moral sense, values and culturally accepted norms of conduct. The function of shame is to preserve social bonds (Scheff 2000). Shame is a culturally and socially structured way to make distinctions between 'the good and the bad', and it mediates our social status in a wider community and society. It is far more common that shame is inflicted on women with substance abuse issues than on men with similar problems. For men, it remains possible to preserve some honour or pride. Addicted women clash with society's view of femininity and the roles of wife and mother (Covington 2002; Howard 2015). Brown has stated that women experience shame as "a web of layered, conflicting, and competing expectations about how women are supposed to be" (Brown 2006, 46). Substance-abusing women might feel themselves to be unfit, not worth being nurtured, cared for and recovered because they believe that they are violating social norms (Virokannas 2013; Karttunen 2019).

Even within drug abuse subcultures, there are distinctions made between women that produce inequality and differing positions. Power imbalances and social divisions in mainstream society are reproduced in the drug abuse subculture, and its structures reinforce shame and humiliation for women. Shame is thus induced both inside and outside of the substance abuse subculture. In both of these two distinct social environments, women with addiction problems are at the margins (Measham 2002). In treatment settings, conflicts, distrust and disrespect can appear between women from different drug subcultures. Labelling another woman as a whore, displaying verbal aggression or targeting body shaming through humiliating language are ways of using social power between women.

Despite the social, cultural and structural roots of shame, it is experienced at a very personal level and expressed in a woman's relation to herself, her body and her femininity. Shame and guilt are often used interchangeably, but these are distinct emotions with different implications for motivation and adjustment. Feelings of guilt are also less disabling (Dearing, Stuewig and Tagney 2005) than is shame, which can lead to social isolation. Shame can be internalised in a way that even within a very nurturing and caring treatment environment, women might feel bad, unfit and undeserving to receive any care and support offered by the professionals or peers. In the case of relapse, the negative cycle of guilt and shame is reinforced again. The consequences of socially and culturally produced shame include rejection, fear, denial, hostility and dropping out of treatment (Karttunen 2019).

Women may feel threatened or irritated if professional interventions are too direct or forceful. The risk of treatment drop-out can be increased by confrontational interaction styles, potentially shame-inducing treatment strategies, negative and moralising attitudes. These can be produced by peers as well as by professionals. Shame-inducing strategies in treatment are based on traditional male-dominant treatment practices and are thus unsuitable for women. They may also increase women's risk for depression and feelings of helplessness or of being 'out of control'. Treatment approaches that rely on strong confrontation, provoke ambivalence and use verbal humiliation aimed at 'breaking the denial of the addict' does not alleviate women's internalised experiences of stigma, shame, guilt and fear – in fact, the contrary is true (Hernandez and Mendoza 2011; Karttunen 2019).

In mixed-gender treatment groups, shame can lead to women remaining silent, withdrawing into themselves and other difficulties in participating actively. Even in female-only treatment settings, shame can be experienced as nearly petrifying, and women may openly express resistance or unintentional defences to protect themselves. Open and encouraging discussion about feelings of shame and guilt in a safe and secure treatment environment can be helpful, and peer support can alleviate these emotions. Shame can be reduced by showing acceptance, understanding, respect and using non-labelling language (Karttunen 2019).

Challenges of the welfare service system

Research findings presented earlier in this chapter refer to the wider problem of social deprivation among substance-abusing women. A heightened risk of social deprivation requires access to crucial resources such as material support and income assistance, safe and secure housing, educational and employment opportunities, and social support. The ability of the Finnish welfare service system to provide enough social and material support for these women to break out from destructive lifestyles and social conditions seems to be poor (Kahila et al. 2010). For substance-abusing women, social and health care services are not integrated but too loosely and ineffectively coordinated and fragmented. Problems are treated piecemeal, which results in losing sight of the person as a whole (Isola, Siukola and Kukkonen 2019).

The structures and organisations of the welfare service system seem to be inflexible and too strict. The system's sensitivity and ability to take into account women's unique service needs and personal life situations are weak (Virokannas 2017a, 2017b). There is considerable variation in how much weight is put on a woman's engagement in decision-making or when planning her substance abuse treatment options. The research shows how negative attitudes and prejudices held by professionals, strict demands or admission criteria for services are constructed in daily practices (Leppo 2012; Virokannas 2017a). The power relationship between women and professionals is usually asymmetrical, and encounters may be riddled with tension. Women may feel that they are not suited for the services that are available or they have to try to negotiate, adjust or attune their behaviour or interaction style in order to achieve their personal goals (Leppo 2012; Virokannas 2011, 2017a, 2017b).

My research also shows that the clinical assessments of treatment staff in residential care and their recommendations for continuity of care are not automatically assumed to be competent or relevant in the decision-making process in municipal social welfare. For women, this uncertainty and their continuous efforts to reassure the authorities of their need for a longer stay in residential treatment were extremely stressful. Women felt that their personal motivation for treatment and recovery was questioned. This negatively affected their treatment retention. Their motivation to bond and to participate as active members of the therapeutic community decreased. This impairs the role and power of the therapeutic community as an intentional treatment method and as a resource for the individual change process. Overall, difficulties in treatment retention may have a negative effect on treatment outcomes (Karttunen 2019).

Exclusion or inequality is produced and maintained between women in the social welfare system. Services that women are offered vary in their treatment contents, availability, intensity and other resources (Karttunen 2019). Services are organised in local health and social care clinics and not necessarily with any clinical expertise. Local service systems are different in their policies and ways of allocating money and other resources to treatment (Kuussaari and Partanen 2010; Hirschovits-Gerz et al. 2019). Women's need for comprehensive services and holistic treatment approaches are not thus fulfilled. Treatment ideologies and welfare services relying strongly on professional expertise and authority may exclude women, fail to meet their expectations and thus exacerbate their problems and social conditions. According to my findings, many women were progressing well in their recovery process during the treatment phase in residential care. Continuity of care was urgently needed, but there was a lack of services suitable for them. Weak connections between treatment facilities and women's social environment and social networks may further complicate this (Karttunen 2019).

One of the challenges in the treatment system is how to apply a gender-sensitive approach appropriately and to avoid the universal 'gender-blind' approach. On the other hand, there's a danger of narrow-mindedly applying gender-perspective approaches in substance abuse treatment settings. This could result in stereotyped perceptions of femininity (and masculinity), thus ignoring women's unique and personal characteristics. At worst, stereotyped assumptions or prejudices may produce discriminatory effects in services by defining women as passive, vulnerable and exposed. Strict or definite views on femininity or motherhood expressed and maintained by practitioners can cause feelings of being alienated, strange or unfit (Samuelsson 2015; Karttunen 2019).

Societal reintegration and social suffering

Addiction as a social event refers to "the way people connect with other people and with other things in their lives" (Adams 2008, 6). Addiction disrupts social ties and connections between the self and other aspects of life and produces fragmentation. It alienates one from institutional roles and positions and weakens the commitment to act as an active citizen as well as the trust between the individual and her social environment. As a consequence of addiction, women suffer emotionally and socially from this disconnection. Violence and trauma further impair this disconnection. Within a social framework, the success of treatment requires mobilising a person's social environment. Treatment focusing exclusively on the individual is thus not sufficient. Wider societal and community relations have to be restored (Adams 2008).

Understanding recovery as a reintegration process emphasises the social and cultural understanding of addiction, recovery and personal change. Reintegration is a process of socialisation aiming at restoring and sustaining social connections disrupted by addiction (Adams 2008). It refers to the rebuilding of vital family, community and societal ties. Eventually, the ideological aim of substance abuse treatment is to help and support women to return to society as productive and healthy citizens (Travis, Solomon and Waul 2001; Adams 2008). Recovery and individual change is, in essence, a relation-based process, and these relations include a woman's relation to herself and her gender, to other people and to society and its institutions.

Societal reintegration is a challenging task for women. First of all, women may lack experience of belonging, acting and being a member of society. Without these previous experiences, it is difficult to integrate into society. Severe substance abuse during adolescence or in young adulthood and prolonged trauma alienates and excludes (Virokannas 2013). Second, the lack of socially supportive relations, an unstable social situation and a variety of co-occurring psychosocial problems may hinder women from successfully reintegrating with society. Third, societal expectations of participating in vocational training or getting established in the labour market are highly valued in Finnish society.

The Finnish cultural and societal ethos is demanding, with a tendency to moralise and call for individual responsibility in participating and acting. In the eyes of Finns, these are essential characteristics of a decent citizen. For substance-abusing women burdened with many hardships, traumatic experiences and limited resources to cope with these expectations may be too overwhelming and distressing. They do not see themselves as good enough citizens with full rights. Requirements for a good and satisfying life, motives and ambitions outside vocational training or the labour market are not easily defined and argued for (Mattila-Aalto 2009; Granfelt 2013; Karttunen 2019).

Women's experiences of rejection, social isolation, exclusion from social institutions and alienation even from everyday routines can be understood in terms of social suffering. The lives of women can be reduced to a struggle, which results in social isolation and decreased levels of social functioning. Women may have difficulties behaving in places, settings and institutions common in our society. This alienates them from everyday routines and social connections, and they may feel like strangers (Karttunen 2019).

Social suffering is structured through the social order and produces experiences of losing one's social recognition and further increases experiences of humiliation, resentment and disappointment. Providing and securing material support and services for people in fragile social positions is thus not sufficient. It is a basic human need to long for recognition and approval, but in case of social suffering, these are not fulfilled (Frost and Hoggett 2008). Social suffering can be very destructive because it isolates one from society. The critical question is whether society and the welfare service system recognise and acknowledge the social suffering that frames the lives of many substance-abusing women and how society's moral impetus to intervene is understood.

Traumatic life events, intertwined feelings of shame and guilt, oppression, abuse, exclusion and inequality, and fragmented social relations are experienced on a very personal level. Women may feel themselves to be victims – powerless, alienated, insecure and broken. What is crucial is the practitioners' ability to see the possibilities, personal capability and resources of these women – to see the women as acting subjects. To this end, some principles of practice are proposed here. First, there should be a strong emphasis on a woman's personal responsibility to participate and act in order to combat her addiction. Second, it is a woman's duty to personally set goals for her treatment. Third, there is a lesson to be learned about how to give and receive feedback, how to form and express your opinions and to believe they are valuable and worth arguing.

The professional's duty is to encourage and motivate women to be active, make personal choices and move forward. The aim is to strengthen women's generalised self-efficacy. This may have a positive impact on recovery. Overall, the aim is to reduce women's dependency on professionals by using empowering strategies. It is the woman who knows what is best for her and what her ambitions, motives and personal goals are. Empowerment is a personal and social process at the individual level. This personal process can be supported and endorsed by peers, professionals and social network members.

How society reflects women's attempts to experience bonding, social approval, respect and recognition has an impact on the success of the reintegration process. Remaining in socially marginalised positions regardless of women's efforts to reintegrate and to participate hinders the attempt to maintain treatment results. Relational issues are important for women, and therefore the question of how to reintegrate into society is crucial for women's process of change. Reintegration implies a mutual obligation to participate in the change process (Adams 2008). The communities based on peer support may improve rebuilding relationships and trust (see Chapter 12, Virokannas in this book). They offer experiences and feelings of belonging to the community, having social connections and bonding with others. From a social work perspective, these are the crucial elements in the recovery process for women.

Conclusions

Current clinical and epidemiological research on female substance abuse focusing on parenting responsibilities, sex differences, health issues and victimisation obscures the complexity of women's substance abuse (Martin and Aston 2014). Women's substance abuse is shaped by many social and cultural dimensions. Examining these increases the understanding of vulnerability in the context of female substance abuse. This shifts the view from an individual framework to define addiction as a social event and, in the case of women, socially embedded. This implicates treatment orientations that include family- and community-level interventions and engagement.

There is a need for integrated social and health care services that are effectively coordinated. Challenges related to the welfare service system can be partly explained by the ideology of the Finnish welfare state, which may overshadow women's individual treatment needs and gender-specific issues. This is because of the invisibility of gender that prevails in our society as a whole. We tend to see our professional practices, social and health care professionals and social policy strategies as gender neutral. Consequently, women's substance abuse and its gender-related dimensions are not easily recognised or taken into account. This may contribute to the vulnerability of substance-abusing women.

The essential challenge for the welfare service system is thus the question of diversity of women and multiple interpretations of femininity. Women with substance abuse issues are a diverse group, and they demonstrate unique psychosocial characteristics: women enter treatment from various socioeconomic, educational, marital status, sexual orientation, health status and age backgrounds. They are also likely to represent various identities because they define themselves not only based on their gender but on other identity dimensions, such as their age or class or sexual orientation. Focusing exclusively on gender may ignore other identities (Bright, Osborne and Greif 2011). Mutual understanding and sharing between women cannot be taken for granted. We should recognise the need for carefully planned and tailored treatment programme content that respects differences and heterogeneity (Samuelsson 2015).

Finnish culture is overall highly tolerant towards alcohol use at different social events and in a leisure time context. On the other hand, responsibility and the social cost of problematic substance abuse remain highly individualised. The shame induced in substance-abusing women is combined with this cultural ambivalence. Developing shame-alleviating strategies must be one of the key elements in substance abuse treatment for women. The feelings of being trapped, isolated and powerless can be reduced by implementing treatment approaches that increase awareness and understanding about shame and the sociocultural and gender-based expectations that trigger it (Hernandez and Mendoza 2011). Understanding shame as well as its cultural and structural roots along with its effects on women's social functioning is thus an important aspect of understanding vulnerability in the context of female substance abuse.

Women suffering from substance abuse have difficulties when trying to restore the social relations disrupted by addiction. Social relations and wider community ties are vital and integral parts of the recovery process, but these are often fragmented and mutual trust has to be restored. A marginalised position in society is a consequence of structurally produced social suffering framing the lives of these women. Experiences of social exclusion and isolation deteriorate women's trust in professionals and service delivery systems; they do not see themselves as worthy of care and recovery. Rejection and mistrust are created and maintained by structural forces, which may further hinder women from seeking help. The eventual goal of societal reintegration might be almost impossible to achieve if there is no chance to receive social support, recognition and appreciation from society and its institutions.

References

Adams, Peter. 2008. *Fragmented Intimacy. Addiction in a Social World*. New York: Springer.

Aguilar, Jamile P., and Anna K. Jackson. 2009. "From Streets to Institutions: Female Adolescent Drug Sellers' Perceptions of Their Power." *Affilia* 24 (4): 369–381. doi:10.1177/0886109909344058

Becker, Jill B., Michelle McClellan, and Beth Glover. 2016. "Sociocultural Context for Sex Differences in Addiction." *Addiction Biology* 21 (5): 1052–1059. doi:10.1111/adb.12383

Belt, Ritva. 2013. *Mother-Infant Psychotherapy Groups among Drug-Abusing Mothers. Preventing Intergenerational Negative Transmission*. Acta Electronica Universitatis Tamperensis 1269. Tampere: University of Tampere.

Bright, Charlotte Lynn, Victoria Osborne, and Geoffrey Greif. 2011. "One Dozen Considerations When Working with Women in Substance Abuse groups." *Journal of Psychoactive Drugs* 43 (1): 65–68. doi:10.1080/02791072.2011.566503

Brown, Brené. 2006. "Shame Resilience Theory: A Grounded Theory Study on Women and Shame." *Families in Society* 87 (1): 43–52. doi:10.1606/1044-3894.3483

Byington, Diane. 1997. "Applying Relational Theory to Addiction Treatment." In *Gender & Addictions. Men & Women in Treatment*, edited by Sulamith Lala Ashenberg Straussner, and Elizabeth Zelvin, 33–14. Northvale, NJ: Jason Aronson.

Claus, Ronald E., Robert G. Orwin, Wendy Kissin, Antoinette Krupski, Kevin Cambell, and Ken Stark. 2007. "Does Gender-Specific Substance Abuse Treatment for Women Promote Continuity of Care?" *Journal of Substance Abuse Treatment* 32 (1): 27–39. doi:10.1016/j.jsat.2006.06.013

Covington, Stephanie. 2002. "Helping Women Recover: Creating Gender-Responsive Treatment." In *The Handbook of Addiction Treatment for Women: Theory and Practice,* edited by Sulamith Lala Ashenberg Straussner, and Stephanie Brown, 52–73. San Francisco, CA: Jossey-Bass.

Crinall, Karen. 1999. "Challenging Victimization in Practice with Young Women." In *Transforming Social Work Practice. Postmodern Critical Perspectives,* edited by Bob Pease, and Jan Fook, 70–83. London; New York: Routledge.

Dearing, Ronda L., Jeffrey Stuewig, and June Price Tagney. 2005. "On the Importance of Distinguishing Shame from Guilt: Relations to Problematic Alcohol and Drug Use." *Addictive Behaviors* 30 (7): 1392–1404. doi:10.1016/j.addbeh.2005.02.002

Dunlap, Eloise, Andrew Golub, Bruce D. Johnson, and Damaris Wesley. 2002. "Intergenerational Transmission of Conduct Norms for Drugs, Sexual Exploitation and Violence: A Case Study." *British Journal of Criminology* 42 (1): 1–20. doi:10.1093/bjc/42.1.1

Falkin, Gregory P., and Sheila M. Strauss. 2003. "Social Supporters and Drug Use Enablers. A Dilemma for Women in Recovery." *Addictive Behaviors* 28 (1): 141–155. doi:10.1016/S0306–4603(01)00219-2

Frost, Liz, and Paul Hoggett. 2008. "Human Agency and Social Suffering." *Critical Social Policy* 28 (4): 438–460. doi:10.1177/0261018308095279

Granfelt, Riitta. 2013. "Naisten kokemuksia kodittomuudesta ja vankeudesta." In *Varjoja naiseudessa,* edited by Elina Virokannas, and Sanna Väyrynen, 199–219. Helsinki: UNIpress.

Greenfield, Shelly, and Christine Grella. 2009. "What Is" Women-Focused" Treatment for Substance Use Disorders?" *Psychiatric Services* 60 (7): 880–882. doi:10.1176/ps.2009.60.7.880

Grella, Christine, and Lisa Greenwell. 2004. "Substance Abuse Treatment for Women: Changes in the Settings Where Women Received Treatment and Types of Services Provided, 1987–1998." *Journal of Behavioral Health Services & Research* 31 (4): 367–383. doi:10.1007/BF02287690

Hernandez, Virginia Rondero, and Carmen Mendoza. 2011. "Shame Resilience: A Strategy for Empowering Women in Treatment for Substance Abuse." *Journal of Social Work in the Addictions* 11 (4): 375–393. doi:10.1080/1533256X.2011.622193

Hirschovits-Gerz, Tanja, Kristiina Kuussaari, Kerstin Stenius, and Tuukka Tammi. 2019. "Estimating the Needs of Substance Problem Use Services: An Exercise in Seven Finnish Municipalities Using Nationally Collected, Municipal-Level Survey and Register Data." *Journal of Studies on Alcohol and Drugs* (S18): 76–86. doi:10.15288/jsads.2019.s18.76

Howard, Heather. 2015. "Reducing Stigma: Lessons from Opioid-Dependent Women." *Journal of Social Work Practice in the Addictions* 15 (4): 418–438. doi: 10.1080/1533256X.2015.1091003

Isola, Anna-Maria, Reetta Siukola, and Minna Kukkonen. 2019. "Gendered Experiences of Poverty and Recognition in the Finnish Welfare State." *Nordic Journal of Feminist and Gender Research* 27 (3): 152–165. doi:10.1080/08038740.2019.1604570

James, Susan E, Janice Johnson, and Chitra Raghavan. 2004. "I Couldn't Go Anywhere" Contextualizing Violence and Drug Abuse: A Social Network Study." *Violence against Women* 10 (9): 991–1014. doi:10.1177/1077801204267377

Jones, Hendrée E., and Karol Kaltenbach. 2013. *Treating Women with Substance Use Disorders during Pregnancy. A Comprehensive Approach to Caring for Mother and Child.* New York: Oxford University Press.

Kahila, Hanna. 2011. *Substance Misuse Problems during Pregnancy with Special Emphasis on Buprenorphine.* Helsinki: Helsingin yliopisto.

Kahila, Hanna, Mika Gissler, Taisto Sarkola, Ilona Autti-Rämö, and Erja Halmesmäki. 2010. "Maternal Welfare, Morbidity and Mortality 6–15 Years after a Pregnancy Complicated by Alcohol and Substance Abuse: A Register-Based Case-Control Follow-Up Study of 524 Women." *Drug and Alcohol Dependence* 111 (3): 215–221. doi:10.1016/j.drugalcdep.2010.04.014

Kaltenbach, Karol. 2013. "Bio-Psychosocial Characteristics of Parenting Women with Substance Use Disorders." In *Parenting and Substance Abuse*, edited by Nancy E. Suchman, Marjukka Pajulo, and Linda C. Mayes., 185–194. New York: Oxford.

Karttunen, Teija (2019) *Naiserityistä päihdehoitoa. Etnografinen tutkimus päihdehoitolaitoksen naistenyhteisöstä.* Jyu Dissertations 118. Jyväskylä: Jyväskylän Yliopisto. http://urn.fi/URN:ISBN:978-951-39-7839-6

Kruk, Edward, and Kathryn Sandberg. 2013. "A Home for Body and Soul: Substance Using Women in Recovery." *Harm Reduction Journal* 10: 39. doi:10.1186/1477–7517-10–39

Kuussaari, Kristiina, and Airi Partanen. 2010. "Administrative Challenges in the Finnish Alcohol and Drug Treatment System." *Nordic Studies on Alcohol and Drugs* 27 (6): 667–684. doi:10.1177/145507251002700611

LaFave, Linda, Laura Desportes, and Christine McBride. 2008. "Treatment Outcomes and Perceived Benefits: A Qualitative and Quantitative Assessment of a Women's Substance Abuse Treatment Program." *Women and Therapy* 32 (1): 51–68. doi:10.1080/02703140802384743

Leppo, Anna. 2012. *Precarious Pregnancies. Alcohol, Drugs and The Regulation of Risks.* Publications of the Department of Social Research 2012:3. Helsinki: University of Helsinki.

Marcellus, Lenora. 2004. "Feminist Ethics Must Inform Practice Interventions with Perinatal Substance Users." *Health Care for Women International* 25 (8): 730–742. doi:10.1080/07399330490475584

Martin, Fiona, and Shaughney Aston. 2014. "A "Special Population" with "Unique Treatment Needs": Dominant Representation of "Women Substance Abuse" and Their Effects." *Contemporary Drug Problems* 41 (3): 335–360. doi:10.1177/009145091404100304

Mattila-Aalto, Minna. 2009. *Kuntoutusosallisuuden diagnoosi. Tutkimus entisten rappiokäyttäjien kuntoutumisen muodoista, mekanismeista ja mahdollisuuksista.* Kuntoutussäätiön tutkimuksia 81/2009. Helsinki: Kuntoutussäätiö.

Measham, Fiona. 2002. ""Doing Gender" – "Doing Drugs": Conceptualizing the Gendering of Drug Cultures." *Contemporary Drug Problems* 29 (2): 335–373. doi:10.1177/009145090202900206

Mulia, Nina, Laura Smith, Jason Bond, Laurie Jacobs, and Rachel Korsa. 2008. "Stress, Social Support and Problem Drinking among Women in Poverty." *Addiction* 103 (8): 1283–1293. doi:10.1111/j.1360–0443.2008.02234.x

Ohisalo, Maria, Tuomo Laihiala, and Juho Saari. 2015. "Huono-osaisuuden kasautuminen ja ulottuvuudet leipäjonossa." *Yhteiskuntapolitiikka* 80 (5): 435–446.

Samuelsson, Eva. 2015. "Substance Use and Treatment Needs: Constructions of Gender in Swedish Addiction Care." *Contemporary Drug Problems* 42 (3): 188–208. doi:10.1177/0091450915592912

Sarkola, Taisto, Mika Gissler, Hanna Kahila, Ilona Autti-Rämö, and Erja Halmesmäki. 2011. "Early Healthcare Utilization and Welfare Interventions among Children of Mothers with Alcohol and Substance Abuse: A Retrospective Cohort Study." *Acta Paediatrica* 100 (10): 1379–1385. doi:10.1111/j.1651-2227.2011.02317.x

Scheff, Thomas. 2000. "Shame and the Social Bund: A Sociological Theory." *Sociological Theory* 18 (1): 84–99. doi:10.1111/0735-2751.00089

Simonen, Jenni, Jukka Törrönen, and Christoffer Tigerstedt. 2014. "Femininities of Drinking among Finnish and Swedish Women of Different Ages." *Addiction Research and Theory* 22 (2): 98–108. doi:10.3109/16066359.2013.779676

Stevens, Sally, Rosi A. C. Andrade, and Bridget S. Ruiz. 2009. "Women and Substance Abuse: Gender, Age, and Cultural Considerations." *Journal of Ethnicity in Substance Abuse* 8 (3): 341–358. doi:10.1080/15332640903110542

Sun, An-Pyng. 2007. "Relapse among Substance-Abusing Women: Components and Processes." *Substance use & Misuse* 42 (1): 1–21. doi:10.1080/10826080601094082

Tracy, Elizabeth M., Michelle R. Munson, Lance T. Peterson, and Jerry E. Floersch. 2010. "Social Support: A Mixed Blessing for Women in Substance Abuse Treatment." *Journal of Social Work Practice in Addictions* 10 (3): 257–282. doi:10.1080/1533256X.2010.500970

Travis, Jeremy, Amy L. Solomon, and Michelle Waul. 2001. *From Prison to Home. The Dimensions and Consequences of Prisoner reentry.* Washington, DC: Justice Policy Center. Urban Institute.

Tuchman, Ellen. 2010. "Women and Addiction: The Importance of Gender Issues in Substance Abuse Research." *Journal of Addictive Diseases* 29 (2): 127–138. doi:10.1080/10550881003684582

Virokannas, Elina. 2011. "Identity Categorization of Motherhood in the Context of Drug Abuse and Child Welfare Services." *Qualitative Social Work* 10 (3): 329–345. doi:10.1177/1473325011408480

Virokannas, Elina. 2013. "Vailla suojelua — huumehoidossa olleiden äitien kertomuksia lapsuudenkokemuksistaan." In *Varjoja naiseudessa*, edited by Elina Virokannas, and Sanna Väyrynen, 52–82. Helsinki: UNIpress.

Virokannas, Elina. 2017a. "Eriarvoisuuden kokemuksia ja hallinnan suhteita hyvinvointipalvelujärjestelmässä. Huumeita käyttävien naisten 'standpoint'". *Yhteiskuntapolitiikka* 82 (3): 274–283.

Virokannas, Elina. 2017b. "Rajoitettuja avunsaannin kokemuksia ja hallinnan suhteita huumeita käyttävien naisten keskusteluissa hyvinvointipalvelujärjestelmässä." *Janus* 25 (2): 111–126.

Virokannas, Elina. 2019. "Treatment Barriers to Social and Health Care Services from the Standpoint of Female Substance Users in Finland." *Journal of Social Service Research*, doi:10.1080/01488376.2019.1598532

Virokannas, Elina, Suvi Liuski, and Marjo Kuronen. 2020. "The Contested Concept of Vulnerability – A Literature Review." *European Journal of Social Work* 23 (2): 327–339. doi:10.1080/13691457.2018.1508001

Part III
Contradictions of informal support

10 Low-income breadwinning Israeli mothers negotiating economic survival

The exchange of sex for material resources

Einat Lavee

Introduction

The ability of women in general, and mothers in particular, to rely on state support for economic survival has been drastically reduced during last few decades. This shift was generated by changes in the protection the welfare state offers its citizens as well as the positions at the bottom of the labour market available to welfare recipients (Collins and Mayer 2010). Hence, women living in poverty turn to other paths or combine survival strategies, relying on social networks of support and agency-based support (Offer 2010). However, studies have shown that the neoliberal ideology, which both celebrates independence and stigmatises dependence, makes it virtually impossible to use these paths to attain sufficient material resources (Kissane 2012; Lavee and Offer 2012).

Additional studies have focused on material support received from men. From Edin and Lein's (1997) classic research onward, such support has been described as a central survival strategy for low-income mothers. Edin and Lein (as do others, e.g. Nelson 2004) define men's support as part of a broader strategy of interpersonal social support. Yet, it appears that understanding the receipt of material resources from men as just another type of social support is problematic for two main reasons. First, the receipt of support from men usually involves sexual exchange, wherein the woman has to give her body in exchange for material resources and thus is significantly different from all other kinds of support, such as that of the family or friends. Second, placing the understanding of the receipt of men's material support under the vast umbrella of social support ignores the linkage between macro-level structural constraints and women's daily struggles on the micro-level. Understanding this linkage is crucial in light of research claiming that welfare reforms (macro-level structural constraints) encourage women's reliance on partnerships with men (micro-level daily struggles) (Scott, London, and Myers 2002; Weigt 2010).

Economic and institutional harm can accumulate in a vulnerable individual life, compounding the experience of vulnerability and causing greater harm (Fineman 2010). In this chapter, I focus on the ways the state's with-drawal from its responsibility to poor mothers increases their gender and class vulnerability, exposing them to various oppressions. In doing so, I examine the case of Israeli mothers who provide for their families in poverty.

Israeli society is an ideal site for revealing processes of exclusion and inclusion that underlie renewed forms of interaction between class and gender. Although initially established as a social democratic welfare state, Israel underwent massive policy changes upon adopting neoliberalism (Ajzenstadt 2009), similar to other Western countries. These changes occurred since the mid-1980 but increased dramatically since the welfare reform of 2003. Whereas previous welfare policy was relatively generous to low-income women, especially single mothers, the new welfare order has radically decreased these women's abilities to rely on state support to provide for their families (Lavee 2016).

I draw on Dorothy Smith's (2005) method of institutional ethnography, which begins with micro-level experiences and continues to the macro-level in order to explain how social relations, structures and institutional control organise the everyday world of individuals. In-depth interviews of Israeli mothers living in poverty demonstrate how the withdrawal of the public safety net makes material resources received from men, who are not fathers of their children and with whom they are not cohabiting, central to their economic survival.

Sex exchange: social support or prostitution?

A review of the literature on women's reliance on men for material survival reveals this to be a controversial survival strategy that has not been properly addressed. Research has framed the exchange of sex for material resources either as an aspect of a survival strategy involving partnership support or as a continuum ranging from partnership to prostitution. For example, some theoreticians frame all sexual exchange for material resources as prostitution (O'Neill 1997; Phoenix 1999). Others, such as Edin and Lein's (1997) and Seccombe's (1999) comprehensive ethnographies, distinguish between support received from men within romantic relationships and prostitution in its common sense. They describe the reliance of mothers who live in poverty on 'serial boyfriends', based on the accounts of women who described frequent changing of partners, with such partnerships usually based on the man's ability to contribute financially to the household. The rule for staying in the relationship, and usually for the man's residing in the woman's house, was 'no pay, no stay'. The close correlation between receiving material resources from the man and the woman's willingness to remain in the relationship raised the possibility of a continuum between partnership and prostitution, as described by Edin and Lein: "The mercenary nature of these relationships occasionally made it difficult for mothers to distinguish between serial boyfriends and outright prostitution" (1997, 157).

A similar approach was taken by Seccombe (1999), who distinguished between the categories of prostitution and boyfriend in terms of the length of the relationship, that is, a one-night stand or longer-term. Nelson (2004) proposed framing this as a mutual relationship that involves the exchange of sex, emotions and money. However, her interviewees often stopped short of defining the relationship in romantic terms, and similar to Edin and Lein's and Seccombe's interviewees, they spoke of the practical or material aspects of these relationships.

We thus seem to lack an appropriate conceptualisation for this bread-winning path involving the exchange of sex for material resources. I suggest framing this exchange as an oppressive survival strategy that stems from inequality in power relations, entailing the activation of institutional/hegemonic power, together with the decrease of power among the women involved (Dominelli 2002). This strategy occurs against a backdrop of reduced structures of opportunity and under socioeconomic policy that withdraws state support. The analytical frameworks for understanding the exchange of sex for material resources, as proposed up until now, address the problematic nature of this path – mainly as harmful, unequal relationships. However, they do not address women's entering into these arrangements as an aspect of macro-level, structural gender and class inequality and as a response to institutional changes that drastically reduce alternative paths of obtaining material resources. Focusing on this aspect will enable us to shift the discussion from the continuum between romantic relationships and prostitution toward understanding the social relations in which these women act (Smith 2005): entering into these arrangements in the absence of other alternatives and under institutional hegemonic power.

Welfare reform and the return to traditional gender scripts

Over the last few decades, there has been a drastic change in the protection the state offers its citizens in many Western countries (Hacker 2004; Fineman 2005), including Israel (Ajzenstadt 2009). Among other changes, the provision of opportunity to many individuals has been severely compromised. Fineman (2010) explains that, increasingly, governments become unresponsive to those who are disadvantaged, blaming individuals for their situation and ignoring the inequities woven into the systems in which people are mired. Although the reduction in state support comes to the fore in different forms in different contexts, it usually includes lowered welfare allocations, stricter eligibility rules and cutbacks in social services (Abramovitz 2012).

Scholars have linked the reduction of welfare benefits with the dictate to participate in a low-wage labour market and with women's dependence on men (Scott, London, and Myers 2002). They argue that, as a result of the narrowing breadwinning paths available to low-income women, these women may increase their 'dangerous' dependence on men who were or are abusive. Similarly, Weigt explains: "Welfare reform aims to transfer women's reliance from a state-supported mode of income distribution (welfare) to privately supported income sources (men)" (2010, 566).

Weigt emphasises the problematic aspect of welfare reforms that actively encourages marriage as a buffer from poverty and a way to defeat welfare dependence. Moreover, the relationships into which low-income women enter are generally characterised by a traditional gender division of labour – the breadwinning man and the caregiver woman. This standpoint reflects Hobson's (1990) classic argument, which posits that variations in women's economic dependency often reflect the ways in which distributive systems in welfare states are gendered in their benefit provisions, policy incentives and support for women. From this framework, the state increases women's familialisation and decreases the possibility of their defamilialisation – that is, the maintenance of autonomous households that are not dependent upon male breadwinners (Orloff 1996; Christopher 2002), mainly by state family policy which provides the services and benefits that allow women to live an independent life (Kröger 2011). Moreover, Cooper (2017) stresses that this is a deliberate policy made by neoliberal economists, who wish to re-establish the private family as the primary source of economic security and a comprehensive alternative to the welfare state. Such a policy establishes the formation of specific class and gender relations.

Following these arguments, I examine the meaning of the exchange of sex for material resources in the lives of low-income Israeli women. I seek to link previous insights to concurrent understanding of women's vulnerability, not as an individual characteristic but rather as a life circumstance and a response to social processes that produce, and reproduce, their vulnerability (Virokannas, Liuski and Kuronen 2020). Taking the standpoint of feminist literature that describes the influence of macro-level social institutions on micro-level individual actions (Smith 2005), I frame this exchange as oppressive survival strategy, stemming from unequal power relations and therefore as particularly offensive to women.

Low-income mothers in Israel

Israel was originally established as a social democratic welfare state, and, for years, maintained a strong collectivist ethos (Doron 2003). Since the late-1980s, however, it has gradually adopted market-oriented economic policies. This trend, which has considerably intensified since the Israeli welfare reform of 2003, was dramatically influenced by neoliberal welfare ideology, similar to other Western countries, and has led to serious retrenchment in social expenditures and a restructuring of welfare (Maman and Rosenhek 2011). Together with reducing state responsibility for its weakened populations (Lavee and Cohen 2019), unemployment benefits have become more limited in scope and difficult to obtain; welfare allowances have been severely cut; new eligibility requirements have been imposed and welfare-to-work programmes have been implemented.

Whereas previous welfare policy aimed at allowing low-income women to support autonomous households independent of marriage and the market, the new welfare order has radically decreased the ability of mothers living in poverty – in their changed roles as both caregivers and providers – to attain independence. While single mothers have been increasingly pressured to join the work force, additional childcare or other family-friendly policies have not been enacted. Mothers who have lost eligibility for (reduced) government support and who have not entered the work force are accused by politicians, policy-makers and the press of being undeserving and deviant (Herbst and Benjamin 2016). Similarly, the labour market conditions of low-income women under the new order are paving the way for increased dependence: most of the jobs available to them often entail low-wage, precarious employment (Benjamin 2016).

Alongside these changes, inequality and poverty rates have increased. Israel currently has the highest rates of poverty among OECD countries. In 2016, the rate of poverty was 19% of all families and 25% of single-parent families (Israeli National Insurance Institute 2017).

It is within this context that the current research took place. I conducted semi-structured in-depth interviews with 75 low-income mothers who fit three criteria for participation: (a) living in poverty, defined by the subjective experience of economic distress and repeated welfare dependence rather than income; (b) being the sole earner of the household and (c) having at least one child living at home. The vast majority of the women were single mothers; only seven were married.

A negotiation over control and vulnerable positioning

Virokannas and her colleagues (2020) suggest that people, including those considered and constructed as 'extremely vulnerable', are capable of acting and activating agency. Taking this stance as my point of departure, in this section, I propose framing the survival strategy of exchanging sex for material resources as having a dual meaning: as increasing women's ability to negotiate over power relations, enabling them to resist their vulnerable inferior positions; and as an oppressive strategy that reproduces and reinforces gender scripts of the breadwinning man and the dependent woman.

Negotiation over control: serial partners

The possibility to negotiate power relations and the dual meaning of this survival strategy emerge from the story of Coral, a mother of one:

> I always survived. If I was short on money, I always had someone to ask … I always had a boyfriend, you see? What I'm trying to tell you is that I had relations with guys … they wanted me, and I was there because of the economic part. They…it was very convenient for me, and I benefited a lot.
> (Coral)

Coral describes the material resources she received from boyfriends as essential to her survival. She does not speak of one permanent boyfriend, but rather multiple partners. Further, when asked how the material support from men is received, she explained:

> It comes naturally. Even he proposes it … it's like, how I can describe it? It's like out of emotion. Because when he proposes it, you tell him about your mess, and he says "If you need to, you can ask me, there's no problem, I can give you [money]." I don't really know how to explain this to you. That's how it is. It's like, I had a lot of times when someone I went out with bought things for my house, even when he wasn't living with me, because he loved me, wanted to please me, wanted to show me that he's a man.
>
> (Coral)

There are two ways to understand the described dynamic. First, it can be seen as the reproduction of traditional gender scripts, where the woman is vulnerable and dependent, and the man is the provider and dominant. The other possibility is examining these relations as manifesting the woman's power and challenging traditional gender and class relations. Coral does not present herself as vulnerable nor as passively adapting to circumstances wherein she must be dependent on a male breadwinner. When she speaks of her relationships with men, she portrays herself as having control over her life and her income resources, citing the benefits embedded in these relationships.

However, Coral does not mention the social relations and institutional change within which she is embedded, which could have shed light on her ability to negotiate alternative breadwinning paths. From her interview, it becomes apparent that she is almost totally isolated from interpersonal networks of support. She has no connection with the father of her child, at the hands of whom she suffered severe abuse during their marriage, and thus she insists on distancing her child from him. Moreover, due to policy changes, she was compelled to leave her previous better-paying job and now works as a cleaner. Under these circumstances, it appears that being dependent on cash or other material support from men, even while insisting on possession of power during the exchange, is not only a return to traditional gender scripts, but explicitly reinforces them.

Limited negotiation possibilities: "slippery slope of dependence"

Engaging in a survival strategy that involves the exchange of sex against the backdrop of reduced institutional support emerges in sharp relief in Maly's story. The single mother of one child, Maly was injured in a terror attack but does not receive institutional support, as the welfare authorities refuse to

acknowledge that her disabilities are related to the attack. Following meetings with her case manager, which she describes as 'humiliating', where the
caseworker told her, "I'm sick of you already, go out and do something with
your life!" Maly realised that this source of support is blocked. She explains
that she realised "I'm all alone. What can I do?"

Maly is sight impaired and suffers from PTSD, following a terrorist attack in which she was present, making it very difficult for her to find a job.
Having no sources of income, she entered into an arrangement of exchanging sex for money. At the time of the interview, she had ongoing relationships with four different men:

> I began corresponding with men online, and one day I get an offer of
> a date in exchange for money. I reacted, What? What?! I've heard of
> it, but…What? I'm in shock! How did he put it? I want a relationship,
> but with no strings. And he was willing to pay. It's not called a date
> for money; it's called 'support.' Then I thought to myself, Why not? I
> admitted that it would help me pay the bills; our lives – mine and my
> son's – would improve until I could get back on track, and so it began….
> At first it was like a bad dream – this isn't me – that you expect to wake
> up from. Then I started getting similar propositions online, and had
> four 'benefactors' at once.
>
> (Maly)

How to interpret the above story in the context of reduced public safety
nets? Alongside the exchange of sex for money being defined as 'commercial
sexual activity' (Bernstein 2007), that is, prostitution, it is rarely discussed
in terms of poverty, gender and the welfare state. Instead, the research addresses related, yet differing aspects, such as in the context of poverty and
illegal activity (Venkatesh 2006); economic-global changes and concurrent
changes in sex and sex work (Bernstein 2007) or the relationships between
violence, drug use and prostitution (Raphael 2015). Indeed, few studies
have conceptualised the exchange of sex for material resources as a survival
strategy (Phoenix 1999). However, the main difference between these studies
and the present discussion is that the focus I place on this strategy is not
on its 'commercial'[1] aspect, but rather in terms of the feminist debate over
gender relations, women's vulnerability and the welfare state. The findings
demonstrate how, in the absence of social protection, mothers who provide
in poverty enter harmful arrangements, reproducing and amplifying the inequality between women and men.

Women who live in poverty and who are the sole providers of their family often describe their lives as a daily struggle for survival. For them, the
money transferred in this exchange, as well as the arrangement in general,
might appear on the micro-level 'everyday world of mothers' (Smith, 2005)
as 'less bad' than other options for providing for the family. Take the case of

Karen, a single mother of three who extricated herself from a violent marriage and who was making very little money as a cleaner:

KAREN: There are lots of tourists here. So this older guy approaches me and starts talking to me in French, which I know. Right away I know what he wants. After a few minutes, he asks me if I want to come with him to his hotel. I told him to fuck off, and he kept trying to persuade me. Then suddenly – to this day I don't know where I got the courage – I told him I would if he'd pay me... He immediately asked me how much, and I recall being surprised that he agreed so readily to pay me. I told him 300 shekels...It had been maybe twenty years since I'd seen the inside of a hotel. We drank some wine, it wasn't too bad. I was in such shock that I virtually didn't think. I just did it and walked out with 300 shekels – for less than an hour! I couldn't believe I'd done it, or that I'd earned the money, and just...like...I looked at myself, like, from outside myself. Then he asked when we could meet again. So for that entire summer, we met weekly. That was last year. Since then he's gone back to France, and he's supposed to come back this summer.

INTERVIEWER: And will you see him again?

KAREN: I think so. I won't lie, I wouldn't see him if money weren't involved, but this way, at least short term, I can give the kids a little something extra.

Karen's response elucidates the ways in which this strategy reinforces traditional gender scripts and reveals its oppressive character. An analysis that focuses on women's ability to provide for themselves and their families independently, without the compulsion to be dependent on breadwinning men, shifts the discussion from the 'slippery slope of prostitution' (Nelson 2004, 450) to what I call the 'slippery slope of dependency'. Karen's use of this strategy enabled her to provide for her family almost independently from her salary. However, without continuous institutional support, and under inferior labour market conditions – which do not enable sufficient breadwinning even for those who fully participate – the road back to gender patterns and female dependence on male resources is short indeed.

No possibility of negotiations: "forced dependences"

The narrowing paths to economic survival under neoliberal welfare reform mean increased dependence on sources of support other than the state and the labour market. Specifically, as Scott and her colleagues (2002) explained, this dynamic exposes the most isolated women to 'dangerous dependencies', as described in the story of Sonia, a single mother of one:

SONIA: Nothing you see here [her apartment's furnishings, etc.] is mine; it's all my landlord's. I found him by happenstance, and it's a good thing, because we're more friends than we are tenant and landlord. So once in a while he takes [my] kid to a hotel – he has an aparthotel unit – or takes us both there. He also helps us with groceries. We're more like friends: I ask his advice, confide in him. Because of our good relationship, I still have a place to live. If he were any other landlord, I'd've been sleeping in the street a long time ago. On holidays, like Passover, he tells me, Don't pay this month's rent. But I pay a high price to stay here [silence].

INTERVIEWER: What do you mean?

SONIA: I do pay to live here. Along with him being a good friend, he exploits my situation. He knows how desperate I am. That's it. Figure it out for yourself. Come up with the most desperate scenario.

INTERVIEWER: He exploits you sexually?

SONIA: Yes. I can't say no, because then he starts in with threats. It's compartmentalized. I see him about once a week.

INTERVIEWER: How did this arrangement come about?

SONIA: It didn't come about. It just is. He has this aparthotel unit, and it began when I asked him to find me work. I'd go there once a week and 'clean', and he'd pay me. After a couple times, we were already a 'going thing'. We've never actually talked about it; I just know that when he calls and says, Come over, I go. I tell myself that I know why he does it: I need a roof over my head. Lodging a complaint? What good would it do me? Who am I against all his lawyers? So I keep quiet and go there whenever he asks. I have no choice. If I could…I do it so he'll let me stay in the apartment. If I can just cater to his wishes…because if I lose the apartment, I'll lose my kid. Otherwise I have nowhere to go, so it's for my kid's sake. So, yeah, it's a type of prostitution, right?

INTERVIEWER: Survival, prostitution. There are lots of ways to define it.

SONIA: So it is a kind of prostitution. I'm not at peace with it, but I have no choice. I've already been raped; [so] with this rape, I cooperate, instead of getting beaten up.

Within minutes, the description of a close friend who helps a tenant with her economic distress, forgives the rent and takes her and her son on vacation becomes a description of sexual exchange and exploitation. When Sonia tried to refuse the arrangement, its true nature was exposed as rape under intimidation. Sonia is isolated from any social networks, including her family, who ignore her due to her inability to hold down a job or provide for her child. During the interview, she expressed what was seen through my (nonprofessional) lens as harsh emotional distress. She also described frustration with her caseworker, who she perceives as impervious and not offering adequate care. Under this extreme lack of possibilities, and under the threat of losing child custody if she has no permanent residence, Sonia is compelled to 'cooperate' with her landlord.

While Sonia's case is extreme, mainly due to the compulsion under which the exchange takes place, many interviewees described how their multiple vulnerabilities – as poor women, mostly single mothers – expose them to situations where men in power positions have identified their lack of options and taken advantage of their own economic superiority to increase female dependence. Single mothers are especially vulnerable to suggestions of exchanging sex for material resources, as manifested in Ronit's story:

> I had a client who used to tell me, "You're so stupid. I can take care of you." He wanted me to be his mistress, you know, this is one more aspect of being a single parent and struggling to provide for your family. They think they can buy you.

Another woman said:

> I was in many situations where men asked me to "make them feel good" once a week in exchange for paying my bills, my rent and more. You get many, many propositions like that.

The women's stories suggest that reducing the possibilities for women to support their families in an independent manner increases their dependence on men's resources, in a way that men see very clearly, as manifested in the quote above: "you're so stupid" – that is, it would be a stupidity not to accept the men's suggestions of help. In this way, policy that increases women's dependence reinforces the significance of gender differences in social interactions and increases gender and class inequality.

Discussion

Women's dependence on men's resources has been discussed broadly in the literature in various contexts. Research that addresses interpersonal networks of support demonstrates how low-income women, especially sole-provider single mothers, are forced to depend upon sexual exchange for their economic survival. However, this literature usually avoids a systematic examination of the terms under which the engagement of women in sexual exchange with serial partners becomes 'outright prostitution' (Seccombe 1999).

At a differing theoretical location, feminist scholars have claimed that, in a patriarchal society, any material benefit given in exchange for sex can be understood as prostitution and that this is also the case within marital relationships (Pheterson 1996). Likewise, Ryan (1997) argued that prostitution is simply an exaggeration of economic conditions wherein most women are compelled to exchange sex for many kinds of support.

This chapter presented the voices of low-income mothers who were embedded in complexities of social relations that limited their options and shaped both their breadwinning paths and their survival strategies. Drawing on their stories, I sought to posit a different framework for conceptualising the exchange of sex for material resources. The analysis which examines everyday practices of mothers against the structures of opportunities open to them, allow me to move beyond existing definitions of such exchange and to define it as an oppressive survival strategy. By stepping from the gender and welfare state context, which examines the terms under which defamilialisation becomes possible, it is useful to shift our focus from the 'slippery slope of prostitution' (Nelson 2004) to the 'slippery slope of dependence'. My proposed framework goes beyond examination of the dichotomy between 'prostitute' and 'normative' woman, focusing instead on the social relations within which low-income women are embedded and act. The analysis presented here expands feminist literature on the relationship between gender and the welfare state, specifically women's ability to attain defamilialisation. In this context, Fineman explains that an individual experience of vulnerability varies according to the quality and quantity of resources one possesses or can command. While society cannot eradicate individual's vulnerability, it can mediate, compensate and lessen vulnerability through programs, institutions and structures (Fineman 2010, 269).

The findings presented in this chapter demonstrate how recent social policy reforms have reduced the women's ability to gain defamilialisation, bringing them to what Jordan describes as being "a husband away from poverty" (Jordan 2006, 1114), against the backdrop of reduced social protection which leads them to high dependence on men's economic resources. In other words, welfare states, at least those based on the social democratic model, had been seen as woman-friendly (Hobson 1990), but contemporary policies increased their vulnerabilities and need to rely on the dependences on men.

The main purpose of institutional ethnography, which constituted the methodological lens for this study, is to explore the ways in which the experiences and knowledge of individuals are socially organised (Smith 1999). Thus, the purpose of this chapter was not to explain women's behaviours, but rather to understand the ways in which their experiences are embedded in social relationships and how they participate in those relationships. Listening to the women's voices enables me to portray the ways in which current welfare policy does not provide sufficient public protection and support for low-income mothers and thus exposes them to a variety of vulnerabilities. It is the narrowing structure of opportunities available to low-income women and especially mothers – as part of the accelerating adoption of neoliberal socioeconomic policy – which compels them to apply oppressive survival strategies in order to obtain material resources. Smith (1999) defined this dynamic as 'ruling relations', relationships that contain a complex field of collaboration and control, related to the structural and discourse processes that take place in the social environment of individuals and subordinate them to the social organisation of the field in which it functions. All the while experiencing this obedience as an expression of their free will. Thus, while one might argue that the negotiation over this exchange might have implications for women's power positions as well as their ability to own resources they could not obtain in other ways, my findings negate this possibility. Instead, they suggest that current welfare policy *reinforces* gender, amplifying gender differences in social interactions and increasing both gender and class inequality.

This social process supports the understanding that we have to consider women's vulnerability not as an individual characteristic, but rather as a response to, or consequence of, multiple life circumstances, together with institutional conditions that produce and reproduce vulnerability. By defining the circumstances under which the route of 'normative' women intersects the resource of their sexuality, I have sought to portray a social process that reveals the ongoing negotiation between independence and dependence among breadwinning low-income mothers as well as the ways these women identify their sexuality as the only resource they can activate in this negotiation. The formulation of this process revealed not only increased dependence of women on men but also their dependence on the (missing) state safety net – the very system that ought to have enabled defamilialisation.

Note

1 By 'commercial', I refer to work that focuses on the exchange of sex for money, such as street prostitution or brothels.

References

Abramovitz, Mimi. 2012. "Theorising the Neoliberal Welfare State for Social Policy." In *The SAGE Handbook of Social Work*, edited by Mel Gray, James Midgley, and Stephen A. Webb, 33–50. London: Sage. doi:10.4135/9781446247648.n3

Ajzenstadt, Mimi. 2009. "Moral Panic and Neo-Liberalism: The Case of Single Mothers on Welfare in Israel." *The British Journal of Criminology* 49 (1): 68–87. doi:10.1093/bjc/azn067

Benjamin, Orly. 2016. *Gendering Israel's Outsourcing: The Erasure of Employees' Caring Skills*. Cham: Palgrave Macmillan.

Bernstein, Elizabeth. 2007. *Temporarily Yours: Intimacy, Authenticity and Commerce of Sex*. Chicago, IL: University of Chicago Press.

Christopher, Karen. 2002. "Welfare State Regimes and Mothers' Poverty." *Social Politics* 9 (1): 60–86. doi:10.1093/sp/9.1.60

Collins, Jane L., and Victoria Mayer. 2010. *Both Hands Tied: Welfare Reform and the Race to the Bottom of the Low-Wage Labor Market*. Chicago, IL: University of Chicago Press.

Cooper, Melinda. 2017. *Family Values: Between Neoliberalism and the New Social Conservatism*. New York: MIT Press.

Dominelli, Lena. 2002. *Anti-Oppressive Social Work Theory and Practice*. New York: Palgrave Macmillan.

Doron, Abraham. 2003. "The Israeli Welfare Regime: Changing Trends and Their Societal Effects." *Israeli Sociology* 5 (2): 417–434 (Hebrew).

Edin, Kathryn, and Laura Lein. 1997. *Making Ends Meet: How Single Mothers Survive Welfare and Low-Wage Work*. New York: Russell Sage.

Fineman, Martha Albertson. 2005. *The Autonomy Myth: A Theory of Dependency.* New York: The New Press.

Fineman, Martha Albertson. 2010. "The Vulnerable Subject and the Responsive State." *Emory Law Journal* 60: 251–275.

Hacker, Jacob S. 2004. "Privatizing Risk without Privatizing the Welfare State: The Hidden Politics of Social Policy Retrenchment in the United States." *American Political Science Review* 98 (2): 243–260. doi:10.1017/S0003055404001121

Herbst, Anat, and Orly Benjamin. 2016. "Between Activation and Supporting Women: Alternative Operation of Welfare-to-Work Programmes." *Social Policy & Administration* 50: 501–519. doi:10.1111/spol.12112

Hobson, Barbara. 1990. "No Exit, No Voice: Women's Economic Dependency and the Welfare State." *Acta Sociologica* 33 (3): 235–250. doi:10.1177/000169939003300305

Israeli National Insurance Institute. 2017. *Annual Report of the Dimensions of Poverty and Social Gaps.* https://www.btl.gov.il/Publications/oni_report/Documents/oni2017.pdf

Jordan, Jason. 2006. "Mothers, Wives, and Workers: Explaining Gendered Dimensions of the Welfare State." *Comparative Political Studies* 39 (9): 1109–1132. doi:10.1177/0010414005284215

Kissane, Rebecca Joyce. 2012. "Poor Women's Moral Economies of Nonprofit Social Service Use: Conspicuous Constraint and Empowerment in the Hollow State." *Sociological Perspectives* 55 (1): 189–211. doi:10.1525/sop.2012.55.1.189

Kröger, Teppo. 2011. "Defamilisation, Dedomestication and Care Policy: Comparing Childcare Service Provisions of Welfare States." *International Journal of Sociology and Social Policy* 31 (7/8): 424–440. doi:10.1108/01443331111149860

Lavee, Einat. 2016. "Low-income Women's Encounters with Social Services: Negotiation over Power, Knowledge and Respectability." *British Journal of Social Work* 47 (5): 1554–1571. doi:10.1093/bjsw/bcw131

Lavee, Einat, and Nissim Cohen. 2019. "How Street-level Bureaucrats Become Policy Entrepreneurs: The Case of Urban Renewal." *Governance* 32 (3): 475–492. doi:10.1111/gove.12387

Lavee, Einat, and Shira Offer. 2012. "'If You Sit and Cry No One Will Help You': Understanding Perceptions of Worthiness and Social Support Relations among Low-Income Women under a Neoliberal Discourse." *The Sociological Quarterly* 53 (3): 374–393. doi:10.1111/j.1533–8525.2012.01240.x

Maman, Daniel, and Zeev Rosenhek. 2011. *The Israeli Central Bank: Political Economy, Global Logics and Local Actors.* London: Routledge. doi:10.4324/9780203830444

Nelson, Margaret K. 2004. "Reciprocity and Romance." *Qualitative Sociology* 27 (4): 439–459. doi:10.1023/B:QUAS.0000049242.21417.d8

Offer, Shira. 2010. "Agency-Based Support: A 'Last-Resort' Strategy for Low-Income Families?" *Social Science Quarterly* 91 (1): 284–300. doi:10.1111/j.1540–6237.2010.00693.x

O'Neill, Maggie. 1997. "Prostitute Women Now." In *Rethinking Prostitution: Purchasing Sex in the 1990s*, edited by Graham Scambler, and Annette Scambler, 3–28. London: Routledge.

Orloff, Ann Shola. 1996. "Gender in the Welfare State." *Annual Review of Sociology* 22: 51–78.

Pheterson, Gail. 1996. *The Prostitution Prism.* Amsterdam: Amsterdam University Press.

Phoenix, Joanna. 1999. *Making Sense of Prostitution*. New York: Palgrave.

Raphael, Jody. 2015. *Listening to Olivia: Violence, Poverty, and Prostitution*. Boston, MA: Northeastern University Press.

Ryan, Lorna. 1997. *Reading "The Prostitute."* Farnham: Ashgate.

Scott, Ellen K., Andrew S. London, and Nancy A. Myers. 2002. "Dangerous Dependencies: The Intersection of Welfare and Domestic Violence." *Gender and Society* 16 (6): 878–897. doi:10.1177/089124302237893

Seccombe, Karen. 1999. *"So You Think I Drive a Cadillac?" Welfare Recipients' Perspectives on the System and Its Reform*. Boston, MA: Allyn and Bacon.

Smith, Dorothy E. 1999. *Writing the Social: Critique, Theory, and Investigations*. Toronto: University of Toronto Press.

Smith, Dorothy E. 2005. *Institutional Ethnography: A Sociology for People*. Lanham, MD: AltaMira Press.

Venkatesh, Sudhir A. 2006. *Off the Books: The Underground Economy of the Urban Poor*. Cambridge, MA: Harvard University Press.

Virokannas, Elina, Suvi Liuski, and Marjo Kuronen. 2020. "The Contested Concept of Vulnerability – A Literature Review." *European Journal of Social Work* 23 (2): 327–339. doi:10.1080/13691457.2018.1508001

Weigt, Jill. 2010. "'I Feel Like it's a Heavier Burden…': The Gendered Contours of Heterosexual Partnering after Welfare Reform." *Gender and Society* 24 (5): 565–590. doi:10.1177/0891243210382865

11   Vulnerability and agency

Women after prison in the Basque Autonomous Community, Spain

Estibaliz de Miguel-Calvo

Introduction

This chapter focuses on the vulnerabilities generated by institutions, specifically the carceral institution and its effects on criminalised women. Thus, I draw on a non-individualistic understanding of vulnerability, with the aim of putting at the forefront the structural and social processes that cause certain groups or individuals to find themselves in vulnerable situations (e.g. Freedman 2019; Virokannas, Liuski and Kuronen 2020). I suggest that understanding gendered, classist and racialised forms of punishment oriented to women by penal institutions could inform better understanding of experiences of reintegration. This could also suggest the improvement of providing services to women prior to and after incarceration.

I understand these women acting as agents, which counteract the assumption that vulnerability and agency are incompatible. Agency presupposes the existence of a subject, while vulnerability is often understood as the condition that prevents acting as a subject (Martínez 2019). In searching for ways to resist to the material and symbolic effects of imprisonment, through the support of welfare services and/or family and partners, they act as subjects who are striving to counteract their vulnerabilities. The discussion is structured around formal and informal support, that is, the provision of services to women prisoners offered by civil associations in the prison context as well as the support they seek from relatives and partners. Women use formal and informal support as a means to practice their agency. Subsequently, criminalised women do not position themselves as passive individuals, but rather act as agents navigating through the daily difficulties they face after prison.

This chapter is based on qualitative empirical research carried out in one women's module of a prison in the Basque Autonomous Community (BAC) (De Miguel-Calvo 2015b). As part of a wider project focused on women's romantic relationships both in prison and in their life paths, I discuss here their future perspectives, difficulties and needs that they forecast after their release from prison. The research, carried out with 49 in-depth interviews and participant observation inside prison, is a rare exception in the field of qualitative research in prisons in the Basque Country, due to the persistent

reluctance of the Spanish penitentiary institution about letting social researchers get to know what happens behind prison walls.

The chapter opens with a brief overview of critical and feminist criminology, emphasising that vulnerability in the penitentiary context results
from the criminalisation of socially stigmatised groups. It is also noted that
the forms of punitive control exercised to women have gender traits, insofar
as the workings and agents of the penal system contribute to the construction of the 'bad woman' and to a gendered punishment. Having described
the context of incarcerated women in the BAC with respect to the Spanish
penitentiary system and the Basque provision of welfare services, empirical
evidence on the views of incarcerated women is presented in relation to their
future prospects once they are released.

Institutional construction of vulnerabilities to criminalised women

In the articulation between the penal and welfare systems, vulnerabilities
of criminalised women after prison are related to the process of criminalisation, marginalisation (Smith and Pittis 2005) and social exclusion (De
Miguel-Calvo 2014). Specifically, I propose that vulnerabilities of women
prisoners at the time of their re-entry to society are related to three aspects:
first, criminalisation processes that cause imprisonment of poor, racialised
women and those labelled as deviants such as drug users. Second, the stigmatisation derived from the actions of different penitentiary agents based
on hegemonic discourses on femininity, social class and race. Third, the impact of prison that does not disappear once released (Dodge and Pogrebin
2001). In this section, I will develop the first two aspects, while the consequences of imprisonment will be discussed in the section devoted to the
empirical analysis of voices of criminalised women.

Regarding the processes of criminalisation, prison generates vulnerability mainly among those women that already have some trait of social vulnerability. Scholarship highlights the overrepresentation of certain groups
in prison such as poor women, foreigners and migrants (Ribas, Almeda, and
Bodelón 2005), ethnic minorities and racialised groups (Richie 1996; Equipo
Barañi 2001), together with drug users (De Miguel-Calvo 2015a, 2016; Malloch 2000). Thus, the general pattern of women in prison is characterised by
a low level of education, a weak position in the labour market, low income
and precarious housing. In relation to their role in the domestic sphere, they
generally are the main providers of the family. Although imprisoned women
are mostly single mothers, often with absent partners, pair relationships are
important in qualitative terms (De Miguel-Calvo 2015b, 2017).

Considering the complex combination of axes of vulnerability, intersectionality provides a useful theoretical tool in the criminological field
(Bernard 2012; De Miguel-Calvo 2016), as it fosters an understanding of
complex articulation of structural determinants whilst paying attention to

the individual's creative actions (Platero 2012). This notion, therefore, addresses the tension between vulnerability and agency I am bringing forward in this chapter.

Feminist criminology describes the mechanisms of criminal punishment of women and the social construction of the criminal woman (Nicolás et al. 2009), through hegemonic notions of femininity combined with social class. Poor women who commit crimes embody 'the abject' as they transgress not only laws but also gender norms. The judicial and the criminal systems contribute to the creation of a 'normal' woman (Larrauri 1994), as opposed to the abnormal and deviant criminal, on the basis of discourses of femininity clustered around notions of domesticity, sexuality and pathology (Carlen and Worrall 1987). In this sense, criminal women are conceived as monstrous since their behaviour do not correspond to the normative definition of women – passive, caretaking and conforming to the norms. Not only patriarchy but also capitalism and racism conform to the basic structures of oppression mutually articulated in our contemporary societies. Female criminalisation, then, is classist and strongly racialised (Rice 1990; Richie 1996; Davis 2003).

Incarcerated women in the Basque Autonomous Community

In December 2018, women made up 7.6% (3,846) of the total prison population (50,521) in Spain (SGIIP 2019). In the Basque Autonomous Community (BAC), there were 1,300 prisoners, 128 of whom were women, located in modules for women inside two of the three prisons in the territory. This is in line with the general pattern to locate women in specific wings inside 'mixed prisons', which are usually not only outnumbered by men but also managed according to an androcentric perspective (Almeda 2005). There is no specific prison for women in the Basque territory nor any unit for mothers. Unlike Catalonia, the BAC is not in charge of the administration of prisons, but it is in the hands of the General State Administration. Since 2011, however, the BAC has had power over prison health, so that the health service offered within prisons is embedded in the Basque public health services (Zulaika et al. 2012).

The Spanish penitentiary system is characterised by long sentences compared to many other European countries, also by the scarce use of parole, rigidity as well as the difficult access to alternative measures to prison and the lack of effective regulation of restorative justice (ROSEP 2015). Prison social services are part of the prison administration. As Almeda (2002) points out, the gap between prison social services and the general welfare services implies several problems and limitations, such as lack of efficiency in the practice of social service professionals, significant difficulties in coordinating with the basic network of social services, lack of knowledge of existing resources and obstacles in developing alternatives to prison. According to Almeda, prison social assistance has a subsidiary role and a marginal position in the prison structure. The separation between penitentiary social services and the general social services generates obstacles for implementing alternative measures to prison as well as for the preparation of life in freedom (Almeda 2002).

The role of non-governmental organisations (NGOs) is relevant when it comes to articulating relations between the penitentiary system and civil society as well as providing services for prisoners and former prisoners, especially in an underdeveloped social welfare model as that of Basque territory. According to Almeda (2002), there are three kinds of associations working in prisons: religious associations, professional associations, which provide services for prisoners and for released former prisoners, and social entities oriented towards defending the rights of prisoners. These latter associations often encounter many obstacles to intervene in prison, as the prison denies entry to those associations that show criticism towards the prison institution (Almeda 2002).

The BAC counts on a dense network of associations that have been working in a coordinated manner for several decades. Grouped together in the ESEN Network (Espetxe Sarea Euskadi-Navarra), they make up the most important group of associations working in prisons in Spain. Most of these associations are of a professional nature, that is, providers of services to (ex-)prisoners. Moreover, many of the social entities form part of the portfolio of welfare services agreed with the Basque Government and the Provincial Councils. In this way, not only do they offer services to imprisoned people but also they are key actors in the resocialisation processes offering alternatives to prison. In short, the activities and actions by the NGOs are crucial for guaranteeing the social rights of prisoners, especially with regard to the social services for released prisoners. However, prisoners do not rely solely on the formal support of institutions and associations. They generally seek informal support of family and partners to move forward in their post-prison phase.

Incarcerated women's voices about getting out of prison

This section brings together the voices of women prisoners in relation to the prospect of re-entry. When it comes to coping with release from prison, through the various modalities provided by law, criminalised women face a complex combination of vulnerabilities arising both from their pre-entry situation and from the consequences of their stay in prison. This diversity of vulnerabilities might be summarised in twofold challenges: returning to society after prison and dealing with the problems they faced already before entering prison.

The gap between imprisonment and re-entry into society

Many women interviewed referred to the vision of going out into the street as an abyss, with numerous difficulties to face and bearing the consequences of imprisonment:

It will take me a little while to adapt because four years here you move away from the world, you are between four walls, you always see the same faces, you always see the same ones... And then you go out and you see so many people. I think I might be a little scary.

(Celia[1])

It is not surprising that women prisoners feel overwhelmed by the prospect of being released. Empirical investigations highlight the limited intervention of prison social work. Prison social services do not ensure sufficient preparation for social reintegration and do not monitor released prisoners (Pérez Villalba 2017).

The stigma attached to prisoners and the consequences of the imprisonment weigh heavily on facing the future outside prison:

I can find many difficulties, many and more because of my way of being. You can see that I have been in prison because you can see us. When we get out of prison, after serving a long sentence, you notice that I have been imprisoned. People get a certain fear, and more being a woman ... maybe rejection.

(Esperanza)

Emotions of fear of facing life in freedom and fear of experiencing stigma (Goffman 2008) in interactions with others. This experience of the self arises from previous experiences of marginalisation and criminalisation as well as from the time spent in prison. As Goffman (1993) states, the degradation of the self is produced in the context of 'total institutions', in the relations with the norms of the institution and with the surveillance personnel, which gradually strip the inmates of control over their acts.

The forms of stigmatisation often intersect not only because they are former prisoners but also, for example, for being drug users (De Miguel-Calvo 2016). When talking about their needs when they return to society, incarcerated women often mention work and housing as the main means to rebuild their lives. With short, precarious or almost non-existent work trajectories before being incarcerated (De Miguel-Calvo 2014), they generally aspire to achieve feminised and highly precarious jobs.

Empirical research highlights the gendered character of the activities and programmes for incarcerated women in Spain. They are offered courses in hairdressing or recreational activities of embroidery, but there are no proposals that are adjusted to the demands of the labour market (Cruells and Igareda 2005). In addition, criminal records are obstacles to finding a job.

For those who are mothers, eight out of ten women prisoners (Gea-Fernández 2017), attending to their children is one of the priorities for their release from prison. It is urgent for them to leave as soon as possible to take care of children. Being a mother, then, generates particular conditions that position women in prison and at the time of their release (Dodge and Pogrebin 2001). Getting children back home is usually a major motivation for women to change their life and reintegrate into society (Ferraro and Moe 2003; Leverentz 2014; Easterling, Feldmeyer, and Presser 2019; Chapter 7 Salovaara in this book). Notwithstanding, imprisonment can generate changes in the way they see themselves as women and as mothers. Mara described these shifts in terms of taking up full responsibility of children to return home:

> Focusing on the home is going to be hard. Yes, because I'm made to be alone, to be without the children. And then the responsibility, that you have the children again. And everything is going to be very difficult for me.
>
> (Mara)

Certainly, this does not mean that she does not wish to return to her role as a full-time mother, but it is clear that distancing herself from the role during incarceration produces ambiguity in the way she understands motherhood and is likely to bring about an awareness of wear and tear it entails.

For those women who are not mothers but whose life project is to have children, the time of imprisonment delays their plans. Therefore, one of the urgencies when they get out is to achieve the material conditions necessary to have children:

> The first thing when I go out, I go out the first thing I do is to look for work, look for my house again, start all over again. And then my mother is the first, and then I think about the children. I go out and I am 30, 31, 32 [years old]. I'm going to think about the children, about having children.
>
> (Aisha)

Motherhood is part of the life project of most incarcerated women, who may see their plans delayed because of imprisonment. Motherhood is a source of positive identity and meaning in life that can counteract damaged identity and provide a purpose in life.

To summarise, finding a job, having a job and to form a family are the common aspirations among criminalised women. These are conformist aspirations, desires to be part of the normality from which they have been denied because of labelling and stigmatisation. As Gålnander (2019) puts it, their motivations for change, that is, the mobilisation of their capacity to be agents, are aimed at achieving an active and productive social life within the parameters of gender, class and race. Big dreams are not reserved for them since future aspirations are regulated by the resources available.

Without formal support: Aminah's story

At this point, I present Aminah's account summarising the difficulties and aspirations that women prisoners have regarding their release from prison. Her words express how the different aspects of vulnerability are interrelated: material, relational, symbolic and emotional. At the same time, Aminah has somewhat higher aspirations than most women prisoners do, as she aspires to a skilled job, which positions her with particular challenges.

Aminah is a 35-year-old French citizen who was detained carrying drugs in the Spanish territory in transit from Morocco. Single and with no children, she has a working-class background and a migrant family origin. Living independently since she was young, she has gone through vulnerable situations to the extent of sleeping rough for some time. Sleeping on the street is now also a possibility at the prospect of getting out of prison:

> I don't know where I'm going to sleep when I go out. As I have already gone from sleeping 3 months in the street once because I do not want to go through the same experience because once you fall into the street it is very difficult to get out of the street.
>
> (Aminah)

Her aspirations are higher than the average of women prisoners because she wants to access professional training that allows her to have a job that not only gives her money but also personal satisfaction.

> My biggest concern is that the day I'm going to leave here [the prison] all the problems that await me, how am I going to do it? Where am I going to live? How am I going to look for a job and what kind of job is it going to be? Is it going to be cleaning? Am I not going to have the possibility of doing professional training to be able to have a job with value and dignity, a job that I like, can make me happy? Because most of the time you spend at work, so if at work you're not happy and on top of that you don't have the love of a partner, then fucked. And when I leave here, can I afford to do professional training? Well, no. Why? Because who is going to feed me? Who is going to pay my rent? Who is going to pay for my water and electricity while I am studying? No one. So I can't afford … the luxury of studying or having professional training to get a decent job, can I? That's the reality.
>
> (Aminah)

Having an apartment is a basic need and crucial for re-entry to society. In case of homelessness, Aminah would be in an extremely vulnerable situation if she was not able to get a roof and a job (Lewinson, Thomas, and White 2014). These aspirations are very difficult to fulfil without external support, bearing in mind the vulnerabilities created by imprisonment together with the criminalisation of vulnerable women:

> Let's see who gives me a hand without judging me, who gives me the chance to get up, who gives me the chance to do professional training to be independent, I don't like being dependent on anyone, I hate being dependent on a person.
>
> (Aminah)

Aminah is in a situation of vulnerability because she is a foreign woman, without social bonds in the BAC. As far as the formal support of associations is concerned, most alternatives to prison sentence are contemplated for drug users, not as often for profile like hers. The ADAP – 'Asociación de Apoyo a Personas Presas' (Association of Support to Prisoners), which has shelters for women (former) prisoners, is one of the main references for criminalised women in the BAC. However, Aminah does not feel very optimistic about her chances of getting into the supported housing:

> In case this association cannot help me because I'm not a drug user, I'm not a single mother, I'm not this, I'm not that. Then there is nothing for me.
>
> (Aminah)

ADAP usually takes in foreign women, so it would not be impossible for Aminah to access the resource. However, she is right that rehabilitation programs in Spanish prisons have specialised greatly in the care of drug users (De Miguel-Calvo, 2015a). The attention to foreign people is more limited because there are not so many resources destined to them and because the legal obstacles make it very difficult to undertake a rehabilitation process with women who, in many occasions, do not have legal residence or do they plan to live in Spain.

Beyond formal support: the role of family and intimate relationships

The support of a social network, family or partners is paramount in the process of social reintegration, especially for those women in the most vulnerable situations. Having someone can make a big difference in rebuilding their lives:

> For now, we [are planning to] go to my mother-in-law's house, if God wants and she doesn't die because, if she dies, we lose everything. If my mother-in- law is still alive, then there is no problem because we go to my mother-in- law's house, but if not... I don't know if some brother or sister-in-law of mine would open the doors of her house for us.
>
> (Cristal)

In this vein, decisions in the realm of emotions and relationships may function as an act of agency for criminalised women (De Miguel-Calvo 2017), understanding agency as the capacity to act as an agent in various ways, resisting creatively the 'pains of imprisonment' and the gendered punitive regimes (Bosworth 1999). According to Fili, "we need to go beyond the victim-or-resisters paradigm and take seriously the meanings and workings of women's imprisonment" (2013, 18). Thus, friends, acquaintances, family and intimate relationships form a means to survive the deprivations of imprisonment (Comfort 2008), a coping mechanism (Severance 2005) or a way of getting security (Ojeda 2013).

Research on women in prison emphasises the tendency of criminalised women to have a relationship. Regarding intimate relationships, findings of the study in the BAC showed that eight out of ten women interviewed had a partner. This tendency to be in a couple relationship has been interpreted and discussed as 'emotional dependency' of women on men (Cruells and Igareda 2005; Aróstegi et al. 2008). 'Dependency' on man is also dependency on money, apartment, safety, clothes and so on (Leverentz 2006), a bond that may expose women to more vulnerable life situations.

Incarcerated women usually suffer from multiple traumas beginning in their early childhood. Women's strategies for coping with the trauma are typically substance abuse and rushing into relationships with abusive men (Almeda 2005). These strategies are eliciting further violence and traumas. It seems that women are making 'bad choices', but these may be the best of extant choices (Fuentes 2014). Thus, heterosexual romantic love generates conditions for the perpetuation of the vulnerabilities of criminalised women.

Nevertheless, and following the line of analysis in the tension between vulnerability and agency, romantic relationships in prison may also be interpreted as a resource for resisting the consequences of confinement, as they break the logic of separation and disagreement and constitute a socially valued resource. By constituting a source of validation of the self, couple's love is the reparative element of the deteriorated identity, since it allows the inclusion in a socially shared and collectively valued paradigm. In this way, imprisoned women attenuate the stigmatisation and social exclusion to which they are subjected, inserting themselves into frameworks of love that emphasise personal worth and the sense of being part of a shared utopia. Moreover, the current concept of love as a space for personal freedom, a way of 'redemption' and 'escape', is especially valuable in the context of confinement (de Miguel-Calvo 2017, 2020). Couple love plays an important role in this context characterised by a lack of freedom, material and emotional scarcity and a painful reality according to which people are 'condemned' criminally, socially and subjectively.

In Luna's story, it is possible to grasp that emotional and material support are intimately intertwined in the love practices, aspects that are very important for daily survival behind bars, but also for the future prospects to re-entry to society. Luna is 25 years old, single and childless. She had been imprisoned several times in her life, after living in several shelters for children and suffering violence and abandonment by her family. This loneliness and lack of support that she has experienced throughout her life are repeated inside the prison. The loneliness that is relieved by strong ties of friendship established with a partner, and a relationship that she has had with a man she met in prison, whom she has been partnered for more than two years.

> I've been with him for two years and three months. I've been in prison for 2 years and 6 months. And I am with him. At first, he worked, he was in workshops, he sent me some money, he helped me, and he told his sister to put clothes on me. He's been here for many years, he's been here for 11 years, now he's on leave and he's giving me the little he has.
>
> (Luna)

Relationship offers not only a resource for the present but also the possibility of a project for the future:

> I hope it lasts and that it fulfils what we have in mind. We have been together for two and a half years now. I hope that everything will be as he says. If so, great to me but, if not, I will be alone, alone and with no one.
>
> (Luna)

Not for all women in prison, intimate relationships are of equal importance. Some have life projects that are more focused on getting a job and training, along with fostering children. Women with higher social exclusion profiles who lack family support seem to be the ones who are more attached to pair relationships, as it seems to be the only resource they have to get ahead.

Patricia's story has many parallels with Luna's in terms of her life trajectories, and how she approaches her relationship as a couple in prison. Patricia is 24 years old, single, and despite being in prison for the first time, she has already experienced confinement in juvenile facilities. She has a history of incarceration on several members of her family, including her father and mother. In fact, she was born in prison. Her life is characterised by extreme social exclusion: she has lived on the streets, is homeless, has used drugs and has suffered violence. Once in prison, she talks about her current partner as her lifeline. She does not receive visitors from the outside nor does she have any money, so the man with whom she has established a relationship in prison is all she has and provides her with both material and emotional support, something she badly needs:

> He sends me tobacco... And now I have ADAP's too. They told me they were going to send me clothes because my family doesn't send me clothes. I came here naked. All the clothes I'm wearing, this (pointing)

and this (pointing) I put on for the first time. It's the only clothes I have...I have very strong pain, my family doesn't come to see me because they don't have a car...I need affection, he's the only man who gives me the affection I want.

(Patricia)

Romantic relationships are therefore a lifeline for criminalised women, especially those who have no other economic and social resources. Love makes it possible to generate disruptions in the logic of the prison institution, restoring a deteriorated identity, achieving its own resources and generating socially valuable bonds. Not all love stories in the biographies of criminalised women are at all positive. The tension between agency and vulnerability generates ambiguous views about relationships.

Conclusion

Building on a contextual and structural understanding of vulnerability, I have analysed in this chapter the complex intersection of vulnerabilities in the lives of criminalised women, both prior to incarceration and as a result of the gendered penitentiary punishment.

Frictions in the articulation of the penal and welfare system arise when we focus on the specific context of the BAC. The role of the NGOs in providing services for prisoners and former prisoners is important in relation to the Basque general social services. Social movements, thus, fill the gap between prisons and society as well as between the social services and the penitentiary system. This is crucial to facilitate the transition of women from prison to the outside. Still, criminalised women deal with the vulnerabilities after prison not only through formal resources but also looking for informal support of family and couple relationships. Criminalised women act as subjects in their aspiration of a 'normal life' where informal and formal support are crucial for overcoming the vulnerabilities arising from imprisonment and previous background.

Aspirations to find a job, obtain housing and being a mother tend to be based on hegemonic notions of gender, class and race. For those who, like Aminah, aspire to higher levels of education and skilled employment, difficulties seem to be much greater, especially given their precarious past, including homelessness. This is compounded by a prison sentence that delays and hinders access to decent living conditions. Chances of obtaining formal or informal support are much lower for foreign women in prison. Their status as foreigners is added to the axes of gender and class inequality. Even so, Aminah has her own life project, where she is not looking for a relationship.

There is another profile of women in prison. Extremely poor women, who have accumulated several stigmatising factors (such as drug use, imprisonment of family members, and a life in contact with crime) and who find themselves in prison without any further support. As in the case of Luna and Patricia, having a partner is crucial for their material and emotional survival in prison as well as for their re-entry to society.

In any case, love is saturated by meaning behind bars. Symbolic connotations of 'freedom', 'escape', 'autonomy' or 'salvation' acquire dense connotations in the environment of confinement. The damaged stigma can be repaired through participation in the collective utopia of love. Social inclusion and repair of the self occur having a partner. It has been called 'dependence' but goes beyond a personal and psychological trait. Navigating the tensions between vulnerability and agency and assuming that social relationships can be harmful and violent, relationships with family and romantic love with a partner are here interpreted as particular dimensions of agency, as much as they distort prison logics and offer symbolic resources that are especially valuable in carceral contexts.

Note

1 All the names that are mentioned are fictional.

References

Almeda, Elisabet. 2002. *Corregir y Castigar: El Ayer y Hoy de Las Cárceles de Mujeres*. Barcelona: Bellaterra.

Almeda, Elisabet. 2005. "Women's Imprisonment in Spain." *Punishment & Society* 7 (2): 183–199. doi:10.1177/1462474505050442.

Aróstegi, Elisabete, A. Fernández, N. García del Moral, and Aurora Urbano. 2008. *Prisión y Género*. Bilbao: Zubiko.

Bernard, April. 2012. "The Intersectional Alternative: Explaining Female Criminality." *Feminist Criminology* 8 (1): 3–19. doi:10.1177/1557085112445304

Bosworth, Mary. 1999. *Engendering Resistance: Agency and Power in Women's Prisons*. Aldershot: Ashgate.

Carlen, Pat, and Anne Worrall. 1987. *Gender, Crime and Justice*. Milton Keynes: Open University Press.

Comfort, Megan. 2008. *Doing Time Together. Love and Family in the Shadow of the Prison*. Chicago, IL: University of Chicago Press.

Cruells, Marta, and Noelia Igareda. 2005. *Mujeres, Integración y Prisión*. Barcelona: Aurea.

Davis, Angela. 2003. *Are Prisons Obsolete?* New York: Seven Stories Press.

De Miguel-Calvo, Estibaliz. 2014. "Encarcelamiento de Mujeres. El Castigo Penitenciario de La Exclusión Social y La Desigualdad de Género." *Zerbitzuan* 56 (Septiembre): 75–86. doi:10.5569/1134–7147.56.05.

De Miguel-Calvo, Estibaliz. 2015a. "Mujeres Usuarias de Drogas En Prisión." *Praxis Sociológica* 19: 141–159.

De Miguel-Calvo, Estibaliz. 2015b. *Relaciones Amorosas de Las Mujeres Encarceladas*. Bilbao: UPV/EHU Servicio Editorial.

De Miguel-Calvo, Estibaliz. 2016. "Mujeres, Consumo de Drogas y Encarcelamiento. Una Aproximación Interseccional." *Política y Sociedad* 53 (2): 529–549.

De Miguel-Calvo, Estibaliz. 2017. "Explorando La Agencia de Las Mujeres Encarceladas a Través de Sus Experiencias Amorosas." *Papers. Revista de Sociologia* 102 (2): 311–335. doi:10.5565/rev/papers.2340.

De Miguel-Calvo, Estibaliz. 2020. "Free to Love: Experiences with Love for Women in Prison." In *International Handbook of Love. Transcultural and Transdisciplinary Perspectives*, edited by Claude-Helene Mayer, and Elisabeth Vanderheiden. London: Springer.

Dodge, Mary, and Mark R. Pogrebin. 2001. "Collateral Costs of Imprisonment for Women: Complications of Reintegration." *Prison Journal* 81 (1): 42–54. doi:10.1177/0032885501081001004

Easterling, Beth A., Ben Feldmeyer, and Lois Presser. 2019. "Narrating Mother Identities from Prison." *Feminist Criminology* 14 (5): 519–539. doi:10.1177/15570 85118773457

Equipo Barañi. 2001. *Mujeres Gitanas y Sistema Penal*. Madrid: Metyel.

Ferraro, Kathleen J., and Angela M. Moe. 2003. "Mothering, Crime, and Incarceration." *Journal of Contemporary Ethnography* 32 (1): 9–40. doi:10.1177/0891 241602238937

Fili, Adriani. 2013. "Women in Prison: Victims or Resisters? Representations of Agency in Women's Prisons in Greece." *Signs: Journal of Women in Culture and Society* 29 (1): 1–26. doi:10.1017/CBO9781107415324.004

Freedman, Jane. 2019. "The Uses and Abuses of 'Vulnerability' in EU Asylum and Refugee Protection: Protecting Women or Reducing Autonomy?" *Papeles Del CEIC* no. 1: 1–15. doi:10.1387/pceic.19525

Fuentes, Catherine Mitchell. 2014. "Nobody's Child: The Role of Trauma and Interpersonal Violence in Women's Pathways to Incarceration and Resultant Service Needs." *Medical Anthropology Quarterly* 28 (1): 85–104. doi:10.1111/maq.12058

Gålnander, Robin. 2019. "Desistance from Crime — To What? Exploring Future Aspirations and Their Implications for Processes of Desistance." *Feminist Criminology* 1–23. doi:10.1177/1557085119879236

Gea-Fernández, Mª José. 2017. "Maternidad en prisión. Situación de los hijos e hijas que acompañan a sus madres compartiendo condena." *Papers. Revista de Sociologia* 102 (2): 287–310. doi:10.5565/REV/PAPERS.2339

Goffman, Erving. 1993. *Asylums. Essays on the Social Situation of Mental Patients and Other Inmates*. London and New York: Penguin Random House.

Goffman, Erving. 2008. *Estigma. La Identidad Deteriorada*. 6ª. Buenos Aires-Madrid: Amorrortu.

Larrauri, Elena. 1994. *Mujeres, derecho penal y criminología*. Madrid: Siglo XXI.

Leverentz, Andrea M. 2006. "The Love of a Good Man? Romantic Relationships as a Source of Support or Hindrance for Female Ex-Offenders." *Journal of Research in Crime and Delinquency* 43 (4): 459–488. doi:10.1177/0022427806293323

Leverentz, Andrea M. 2014. *The Ex-Prisoner's Dilemma: How Women Negotiate Competing Narratives of Reentry and Desistance*. New Brunswick, NJ: Rutgers University Press.

Lewinson, Terri, M. Lori Thomas, and Shaneureka White. 2014. "Traumatic Transitions: Homeless Women's Narratives of Abuse, Loss, and Fear." *Affilia: Journal of Women and Social Work* 29 (2): 192–205. doi:10.1177/0886109913516449

Malloch, Margaret S. 2000. *Women, Drugs and Custody*. Winchester: Waterside Press.

Martínez, María. 2019. "Una (Breve y No Muy Sistemática) Aproximación a La Noción de Agencia Desde La Vulnerabilidad." *Papeles del CEIC. International Journal on Collective Identity Research* 1 (205): 1–9. doi:10.1387/pceic.20616 ISSN

Nicolás, Gemma, Encarna Bodelón, Roberto Bergalli, and Iñaki Rivera. 2009. *Género y Dominación. Críticas Feministas Del Derecho y Del Poder*. Barcelona: Anthropos.

Ojeda, Natalia-Soledad. 2013. "Cárcel de Mujeres. Una Mirada Etnográfica Sobre Las Relaciones Afectivas En Un Establecimiento Carcelario de Mediana Seguridad En Argentina." *Sociedad y Economía* 25: 237–254.

Pérez Villalba, Lorena Geraldine. 2017. *Desigualdad de género y reinserción socio-laboral de mujeres expresas en Navarra*. Pamplona: UPNA.

Platero, R. Lucas. 2012. *Intersecciones: Cuerpos y Sexualidades En La Encrucijada: Temas Contemporáneos*. Edited by Raquel Platero Méndez. Serie General Universitaria. Barcelona: Bellaterra.

Ribas, Natalia, Elisabet Almeda, and Encarna Bodelón. 2005. *Rastreando Lo Invisible. Mujeres Extranjeras En Las Cárceles*. Barcelona: Anthropos.

Rice, Marcia. 1990. "Challenging Orthodoxies in Feminist Theory: A Black Feminist Critique." In *Feminist Perspectives in Criminology*, edited by Lorraine Gelsthorpe, and Alison Morris, 57–69. Milton Keynes-Philadelphia: Open University Press.

Richie, Beth. 1996. *Compelled to Crime: The Gender Entrapment of Battered Black Women*. New York and London: Routledge.

ROSEP. 2015. Informe ROSEP Red de Organizaciones Sociales Del Entorno Penitenciario.

Severance, Teresa A. 2005. "You Know Who You Can Go to': Cooperation and Exchange between Incarcerated Women." *The Prison Journal* 85: 343–365.

SGIIP. 2019. Informe General 2018. Madrid.

Smith, Anthony, and Marian Pittis. 2005. "Researching de Margins: An Introduction." In *Researching the Margins. Strategies for Ethical and Rigorous Research with Marginalised Communities*, edited by Anthony Smith, and Marian Pittis, 3–41. New York: Palgrave.

Virokannas, Elina, Suvi Liuski, and Marjo Kuronen. 2020. "The Contested Concept of Vulnerability – A Literature Review." *European Journal of Social Work* 23 (2): 327–339. doi:10.1080/13691457.2018.1508001

Zulaika, D., P. Etxeandia, A. Bengoa, J. Caminos, and J. M. Arroyo-Cobo. 2012. "A New Prison Health Care Model: The Experience of the Basque Country." *Revista Española de Sanidad Penitenciaria* 14 (3): 91–98. doi:10.4321/S1575-0620 2012000300004

12 Peer support among female substance users in Finland

Elina Virokannas

Introduction

Welfare service users easily 'fall in-between' complex systems, do not have their individual needs met or fail to have their specific life situations recognised (e.g. Määttä 2013; Lavee 2016). Further, people in vulnerable life situations (Virokannas, Liuski, and Kuronen 2020) such as women who use illegal drugs encounter multiple barriers and prejudices in the public service system (Hines 2013; Virokannas 2019). They might have severe health, financial, and housing problems but are labelled as unsuitable customers or they are unaware of the services they are entitled to (Paylor, Measham and Asher 2012, 47–48). In such situations, the unofficial help of other people sharing a similar life situation might play an important role (Barker and Maguire 2017).

In this chapter, I am interested in how peer support is enabled and arranged on a practical level between female drug users. The data were obtained from seven group discussions and three individual meetings with 13 women aged 25–55, gathered between August 2015 and August 2016 in Helsinki, the capital city of Finland. I contacted the women through a health and social care project that aimed at reaching the most marginalised female substance users and to help them receive the social and health services they needed. The project was organised by the NGO A-Clinic Foundation, and funding was received from Finland's Slot Machine Association (RAY). Ethical approval was granted by the ethics committee of the A-Clinic Foundation.

The group discussions were open to everyone who used the project's services. Participants did not receive any financial compensation for their participation, but coffee, snacks and fruit were offered during the meetings. The women had been informed beforehand that the aim of the study was to consider their experiences with the social and health service system.[1] The meetings were contrived to be as informal as possible, and no interview protocol or structured questions were used. Thus, women's experiences of peer support were not asked by the researcher but it was an issue that frequently stood out. One to five women participated in each discussion. The participating women could choose to remain anonymous, and their names or other identification information were changed as the audiotapes were transcribed.

Emphasising women's voice and reciprocal support has been the focus of several feminist studies (e.g. Reinharz and Chase 2001), but these are rarely studied in the field of substance use or peer support as such. I view the life situation of the women as vulnerable because they face complex problems and stigmatising attitudes by society (see Fawcett 2009; Brown 2011). Moreover, mutual support among women who use drugs could be questioned in the official welfare service system. There might be doubts that unofficial advices concerning, for example, injecting or avoiding certain services have bad influences on women's attitude to the official system (see Chapter 6 Mejak and Leskošek in this book). However, my aim in this chapter is not to evaluate the moral aspects of peer support. According to previous studies (e.g. Fletcher et al. 2016), there seems to be more doubts than support for the claim that people in vulnerable life situations try to manipulate the system. On the contrary, focusing on hidden ways that women support each other reveals an opportunity to evaluate the official welfare service system and emphasise the strength and empathy among female drug users that often remains unseen.

Service user involvement organised by the welfare system versus unofficial peer support

The concepts of peer support, service user involvement and expert-by-experience have similarities and connections. However, those are given different meanings in different contexts as well as in different countries and between different service sectors. Furthermore, meanings and hierarchical power relations that are attached to the different terms vary (see McDonald 2006; McLaughlin 2009). Peer support is traditionally defined as to being based on shared life experiences (Nylund 2000), and it does not necessarily have anything to do with social and health care services. On the contrary, the so-called service user involvement has widely and internationally been recognised as an important part of developing practice in the welfare service system (Beresford, Adshead and Croft 2007; Warren 2007; Fox 2011; Nelson 2012). In addition, as stated by Meriluoto (2018, 20), the concept of expertise-by-experience has become a marker for an inclusive and empowering welfare organisation, and as such, it is an obligatory concept to provide proof of the organisations' innovative and participatory attitude for the funders. In this chapter, my focus is mostly on unofficial peer support, but I also discuss its connections with the official welfare services and the idea of service user involvement.

On the one hand, the idea of service user involvement is to strengthen the role of service users and benefit from the knowledge gained through personal experience. On the other hand, this idea is also connected to the consumerist discourse in which the role of service users and their relation to service providers in public services are understood more like the role of a customer conforming to the market model (Simmons, Powell and Greener 2009). In Finland, service user involvement is often associated with the concept of experts-by-experience, since they get some amount of education, and some compensation for their work and their own recovery process has proceeded (Falk et al. 2013). Instead, 'peers' are people who are still using services, and they do not have to be, for example, clean from drugs or other problems. By that definition, as experts-by-experience cooperate mainly with professionals aiming to develop the services, peers support each other. In some other contexts, peers and experts-by-experience are used synonymously (e.g. Barker and Maguire 2017).

Recently, the concept of 'peer recovery support' in which the relationship between the peer recovery provider and service user is understood to be asymmetrical and the emphasis is on the recovery process (Reif et al. 2014) or 'intentional peer support' (Barker and Maguire 2017) have been used to address peer support that is fostered and developed by professional organisations. In the case of intentional peer support, the element of sharing personal experiences is present but the status of peer support is defined in relation to official helping organisations as peers are viewed as distinct from professionals (see Barker and Maguire 2017, 599). Furthermore, in the context of the US, 'peer-based recovery support services' refers to nonprofessional assistance to achieve long-term recovery from substance use disorders by 'recovery coaches' who have experiential knowledge (Bassuk et al. 2016). Unlike peers in the Finnish context, recovery coaches are in most cases expected to be sober for a certain duration to be able to qualify as peer workers.

A study by Barker and Maguire (2017) in the UK shows that peer support has been utilised in diverse ways. According to their large research review concerning homelessness, the main outcomes of peer support intervention were increased social relationships and social esteem, reduced harm related to substance addiction, improved physical health and developed life skills. Peers influenced the overall quality of life through shared experiences of homelessness, mental illnesses and addiction. Similar results have been attained in the field of substance abuse even if there is a shortage in the quality and amount of research concerning the issue (Reif et al. 2014; Bassuk et al. 2016). In Finland, some recent projects targeted at people with substance abuse problems (Virokannas 2014) have developed activities where peer supporters motivate and encourage other substance users to take part in health and social care services, share information of safe injecting and deliver clean injection equipment to each other.

I understand peer support as a specific kind of service user involvement because it is related to the gaps the official welfare service system creates, but I do not define it only in relation to the formal welfare system. Hence, in this chapter, improvements in the quality of life have been defined from the women's standpoint (see Smith 1987, 2004, 75) and not from the perspective of the service system. On the basis of the group discussions with women, I will focus on both illustrations of women's informal peer-to-peer support and descriptions of more formal peer activities as several women participated in the project's peer support activities, which were partly supervised by project workers.

Informal help in the group discussions

The elements of informal help and peer support came out either as spontaneous comments like advising other women or sharing recommendations with them during the group discussions or as descriptions of events where women or their acquaintances have supported each other. Moreover, those women who had taken part in peer activities for a long time and had gained significant experience of intentional peer support (see Barker and Maguire 2017) shared their experiences in some discussions.

I present my analysis in three main themes and give examples of each. First, I focus on ad hoc giving of and asking for advice or information and sharing experiences and empathy during the group discussions. I then present women's descriptions of times how they have helped each other in their everyday life and how reciprocity was defined as an essential element of such help. Finally, I address reflection on acting as a peer supporter intentionally and in a more formal way.

Advice, information and empathy

All discussions between women contained ad hoc advising and showing empathy and taking part in other women's experiences. Women shared experiences especially concerning the welfare service system in which they had experienced similar obstacles and difficulties (see Virokannas 2019). Advice was mostly offered spontaneously but was sometimes also asked for. Most often, advice and recommendations concerned the welfare service system, different treatments, such as how certain therapy methods work or how to find services. Financial problems and housing issues were widely shared. Advice related to income support and social benefits were also given. Housing services were discussed widely as women have had many problems with housing, including periods of homelessness.

In the first extract, six women, a researcher and a social work student are discussing housing issues and division of housing services. Outi has told other women about her past experiences of homelessness. She had left her violent relationship and moved to a safe house. In this process, she lost her apartment and lived for a while with her sister. Finally, she had got a place in a supportive housing called 'Clover' where she lives at present. The other women are interested how she managed to get the place from Clover as they find it difficult.

KAISA[2]: How did you get the place from the Clover / [were you at some rehab?

OUTI: [Well, it went kind of, I mean / I should be in a way / kind of come straight from rehab / [straight

KAISA: [Yeah

OUTI: I have been in [opioid] substitution therapy for several years / so / I had [give a laugh] / you know / relapse, and after / you know [...

KAISA: [So you had to be in fact / kind of / [some time

HENNA: [So that place was a rehab institution [and this was ...

OUTI: [Yeah but I had already been, kind of, you know, get already out of rehab and / I mean / then in the day centre / meeting centre, there was a former / resident who kind of arranged the place for me

KAISA: Yeah

HENNA: But it can't be so, it is not easy to have a place from the Clover. Last spring, I applied for a place / [to Clover / and did not get any and...

OUTI: [Well it depends kind of or / I mean [Venla [refers to her friend who is not present] and I got access in two weeks

[Overlapping speech about queues to Clover by several women.]

KAISA: [People don't change so much there all the time / and...

ANNA: [It depends where you...

PAULA: [There are queues now

HENNA: Now and then there are queues and other times aren't, for example in the Pinewood [another supportive housing] there are free places now but last summer there were none

OUTI: Yeah, ymm and in the Clover there have been vacancy all the time [...

HENNA: [The new unit was open

OUTI: Yeah, you know Venla / she will also get the place now, she only had to apply and go to the interviews and she is in. It took two weeks after I overall heard about the Clover and I was in and /...

RESEARCHER: Where did you hear?

OUTI: Mmm from that former resident who now works at the day centre

The extract begins with Kaisa's question to Outi about how she has got access to Clover. It is commonly known among women that the normal route to Clover goes straight from a rehab period and Outi has not said anything about being in rehab. As the conversation proceeds, it emerges that Outi has actually had a short rehab period but she did not go to Clover straight after it. Instead, she had learned the possibility to apply for Clover from her friend. According to Outi's description, her friend arranged her fast access to Clover.

Henna questioned Outi's story since Henna herself has not got access to Clover in spite of her efforts. As Outi defended her story by saying that her other friend Venla also got the fast access, the conversation increases and continues by overlapping talk, where women share their experiences and information about getting access to housing services and present queue situations to different units. Obviously, authorities, for example social work-ers, did not have any role in women's discussions either as a source of knowl-edge or as service provider or enabler. On the contrary, support and help have been entirely received through women's informal social networks.

The women also shared information of certain social workers who should be avoided. They discussed and shared experiences of how to manage situ-ations in which drug-using mothers get tired with their children and how to deal with custody issues. In one conversation, it came out that some women in the group had received a so-called red label in their health care files. Ad-vice was given on how to get rid of those labels. Recommendations were given on how to obtain help from the patient ombudsman or professional mentor working in the project, in the case of malpractice or submitting a formal complaint.

In the next conversation, Jaana has just told the others that she has lost her faith in health care services after several disappointments. She has had problems with her back for many years, but it had not been examined prop-erly. Jaana thought that the reason was her stigma as a drug user. The other women begin to think of different ways Jaana could get help and offer ad-vice to her.

IRENE: We have a service counsellor here, you know. They can help you in meetings with authorities and things, can't they? // I mean really, if you would take someone like that with you / it would be much more difficult for them to treat you badly, if there is someone // you know [...
REETTA: [Someone who [...
IRENE: [beside you looking [gives a laugh] I mean, what is [going on
JAANA: [You mean here is some service counsellor or?
IRENE: Yeah, here are
HENNA: Anne is [service counsellor [–] she is service counsellor
JAANA: [Umm, okay // okay
IRENE: You can get help from them
JAANA: Umm, okay // yeah

Irene interpreted Jaana's reason for avoiding services as the result of bad treatment, so she recommended Jaana to have someone with her the next time she goes to the doctor. She advised Jaana that they can ask for a service counsellor's help in difficult situations. Jaana did not know about this pos-sibility and accepts the information. Reetta and Henna confirmed Irene's advice. Unlike in the first extract where women shared information but dis-agreed and questioned each other's experience, in this case, all participants shared a similar opinion about solving the problem.

In addition to sharing information about different services and getting access to them, advice was related to substance use. There were occasional discussions about how to give clean drug tests in situations where some-one has not been drug-free. However, the option of cheating was defined as something that happened in the past but not anymore. In addition, how to lower the tolerance in order to reduce drug use and medication during the opiate substitution treatment were discussed. One woman talked about peer groups on the internet where drug users share information about the effects of different substances and dosing limits. She was the only one who stated that her drug-using career has started with the help of her friend, who introduced her to new drugs. Ideas of getting rid of alcohol addiction were also discussed. It was common to all conversations that professionals – other than third-sector's project workers – and the welfare service system had no significant role.

Reciprocal help

In addition to the ad hoc advice and information shared in the discussions, women described several events in the past where informal concrete help were offered and received. Along with mental support, women had received help from other drug users when they had moved apartment or needed place to stay overnight. If someone had spent hours in food bank queues received food might have been shared with others. Reciprocity was a common element in women's descriptions. In the next extract, Reetta describes her peer work as a clean needle and syringe deliverer. Even if delivering clean equipment has its origin in a project's peer activities that are supervised by professional workers, Reetta arranges to implement it in her own way.

REETTA: I have / couple of places where I actually / deliver // right at the home // I mean I get so much other things back
RESEARCHER: Okay / yeah
REETTA: I can protect myself. I get place to stay overnight. I mean I exchange that way. You know / mm even if this // other person does visit XX [a needle exchange service] frequently I mean as often as she can // but / she has not visited YY [another needle exchange service] so she does not get more than hundred // and there are users of zero-three and zero-five / So she gets one hundred of each from me.
RESEARCHER: Okay yeah
REETTA: And / the thing that / I am at their home and I have a key for them and / It is kind of my second home
RESEARCH: Right
REETTA: She is my childhood friend and // from the fourth class / I mean / of they are rare to whom I deliver at home

Reetta's extract about delivering clean needles and syringes to someone's home – usually the equipment must be collected from Reetta's place – creates a win–win situation. She delivered a sufficient amount of clean, different-sized equipment to her friend, and as a 'return service', she got a safe overnight place when needed. Reetta emphasised that this kind of arrangement is exceptional and based on the trust that is built from her and her friend's shared childhood and long-lasting relationship. Housing issues are also addressed in the next extract, where Leila describes how she offers temporary accommodation to her friends.

LEILA: We have sort of / a small homeless co-operative here / well it has always been in fact but I mean / we do not take just anyone to our flat / we have mattress and things but a few have come you know who have been / have been helped to put an announcement about seeking an apartment to 'Tori' (a website) and kind of been pushed to take a shower and been given clean [clothes

RESEARCHER: [Okay

LEILA: You go now looking clean to the apartment introduction and / and like that but no they have not been lucky in any open house but anyway have tried to help them

STUDENT: [Yeah

LEILA: And then quite often / guys have stolen food in the evening and then they offer it to us you know // do not have to even ask or anything

Just as in the previous case with Reetta, in Leila's extract, the peer support contains elements of reciprocity. Leila and her unnamed roommates offered a mattress on the floor to their acquaintances and gave advice on how to make an apartment announcement. As a 'return service', the overnighter shared stolen food with the hostesses. Even if the return favour does not seem to be a condition for help, some kind of previous relationship is a basis for opening one's home to others. However, Leila described offering help more as an ongoing way of life than rare exceptions.

There were several other descriptions of unofficial help in past events. These considered, for example, situations where accidents had happened to family members or in the neighbourhood and people have ended up in difficult situations because they could not take care of their everyday needs but did not get help from the service system either. In these situations, women helped each other by, for example, bringing food from grocery stores or giving advice on how to apply for benefits. Help was also given as a sort of 'nursing care' because there was a lack of professional home care. In these situations, the unofficial help was not so much based on reciprocity but on the observation that someone in the neighbourhoods cannot manage without help.

Reflections concerning work as peer supporter

Acting as a peer supporter was something that was explicitly reflected on in some discussions. In these cases, the women referred to the project's peer activity group, which was aimed at recovering addicts who wanted to share their experiences and support other drug users. Women shared the view that in order to work as a peer supporter, one's own problems should somehow be in control. Many women had offered help to others several times even if they have not identified themselves as peer supporters. Furthermore, women considered that the help does not have to be something huge, but small things and acts might be significant, such as sharing one's own experiences to others in a similar life situation. Or as Kaisa puts it: "It could be that we just have a chat".

The other aspect of peer support addressed women's own resources and having enough strength to support others. In their study, Leppo and Perälä (2009) have concluded that as compensation for the lack of professional support, working as a peer supporter does not necessarily lead to the empowerment of service users. In the women's discussions, the issue of having enough strength to support others was discussed a few times. The next extract begins with Kaisa's advice to Niina on how to take care of oneself when working as a peer supporter.

KAISA: You can always delegate hard situations to [someone else or something
NIINA: [Ymm // yeah I have, I am going to take, I mean, I might / I might be the one whohhh [laughs] gets burnout and / worries too much about those people's future and /
RESEARCHER: [Yeah / yeah right
NIINA: [Try to take the kind of attitude that keep it kind of // work / You know, take that role and when you are / kind of / off you know / then / try to // be merciful to oneself and think hey now I won't think these / peer issues but // I mean
KAISA: You can say to yourself or others / to your friends that / for instance / after eight or nine you don't answer the phone / I mean it is your own time / you are not / anymore /working
NIINA: Yeah / okay

Niina was just going to begin to work as a peer supporter, and she wondered how she would manage in her new post. By saying that she might get tired and worry too much over other people's problems, she actually showed that she was aware of those risks. From her position as a more experienced peer supporter, Kaisa gave her several pieces of advice, starting from delegating jobs to confirming Niina's own ideas of taking care of one's free time.

Other aspects of peer support activities also emerged in the conversations. Kaisa talked about her feelings that in some treatment units, unpaid peer supporters are used to replace professionals.

KAISA: I think that those peer supporters // fuck // they are as many / in some rehab / department as / clients themselves / and staff / I mean / real staff that get salary // have education / do they have you know / more time to do something

RESEARCHER: Right /

KAISA: I do not / disregard you know I think it is great / in the department / because it could be often much easier with a peer supporter / but I mean // you cannot suppose that / they take so much responsibility that professionals [can load to them I mean everything

RESEARCHER: [Right / yeah / it is not meant to be like that

KAISA: I mean yeah this is it you can go or / take them with you but I mean there / have to be / some / professional worker // even around

Even if Kaisa thought that it could be easier to discuss with a peer supporter with similar experiences instead of a professional, she emphasised that the responsibility should be on professionals. She also describes the division of work between paid staff and peer supporters as something that is controlled by professionals, who 'load' the responsibility onto peers and might not even be present. The researcher confirms that the division of work is not supposed to be like that. As a summary, women who intentionally identified themselves as peer workers critically reflected on their position and were aware of the power relations related to their relationships with professionals.

Conclusion: multifaceted peer support

Women who use drugs support each other in various ways outside of the official welfare service system. It is important to critically analyse the idealistic picture of the service user involvement and emphasise service users' own perspectives (e.g. Leppo and Perälä 2009; McLaughlin 2009; Beresford 2010; Virokannas 2016). I have referred to any kind of giving advice and information and sharing of experiences that are intended to participate in other women's life situation as peer support. Thus, my definition of peer support is more diverse than, for example, peer recovery support or the traditional Alcoholics Anonymous ideology. My definition is not bound to a certain programme or place, and the goal is not to accept a certain way of living or achieve certain recovery goals (see Barker and Maguire 2017).

It was obvious that women had several needs for different services, including medical, financial and social ones, but they did not necessarily seek help or receive enough support from the official service system (see also Virokannas 2019). In their peer-to-peer discussions concerning difficult life situations, professionals or authorities of the official welfare service system played almost no significant role except that the system and professionals were criticised. The main purposes of sharing experiences were indented to help other women to improve the quality of their life by reducing harms or just to survive. Even if the women also shared experiences of different effects of substances or ways to avoid sanctions in the treatment system, the purpose was not to manipulate the system but somehow to manage with it (see also Fletcher et al. 2016).

Bassuk et al. (2016) highlight that more research is needed on the impacts of providing peer support on the peer workers themselves. Based on my study, there were several benefits of both spontaneous and intentional informal help, such as reciprocity, having information and empathy, but the benefits cannot be measured, for example, by efforts to get sober or by integrating better into the society in the dominant way. Leppo and Perälä (2009) have emphasised that realisation of the benefits concerning unofficial help alongside the official system depends on the institutional context, gender and changing modes of professionalism. Utilising experience-based knowledge is essential, but it should not mean replacing paid professionals with unpaid peers, whose own strengths are limited. Thus, I find it even more important to critically study the risks that overloading responsibilities on peers might cause and the power relations and the gaps in the official system.

At the same time, the importance of informal woman-to-woman support should be recognised as meaningful. It is important to provide such spaces where service users can meet and share experiences and provide mutual help. Further, what makes the peer supporters' accounts interesting from the perspective of social work practice is the silent knowledge that is based on several years' experience of living in a stigmatised subculture. Through their stories, it is possible to see the social and health care system from an outsider's point of view. Unofficial support gives women safety that the official system often cannot provide. However, such support cannot be the excuse to neglect the human rights and service needs of women in vulnerable life situations.

Notes

1 The information letter given to women was as follows:

> My aim is to consider the social and health care system with the help of your experiences. It does not matter if you have not used these services for a while, you can still take part in XX-project. If you have needed services from doctors or social workers (for example) at some point in your life, but for some reason you had not sought support, you are just the right person to help me with my study. I would like to hear why you do not seek or receive support from the system. If you use some services (for example Vinkki [the Drop-In Needle Exchange program], health care centre, or social work office), I would like to hear why you use those services and what experiences of them you had. How have you been treated, what has gone well and what perhaps not so well?

2 All names are pseudonyms. Slashes refer to breaks in the speech, a short break is shown as one slash, /, and two slashes, //, mean a longer break of over one second. Empty parentheses, ( ), refer to unclear speech. Square brackets, [ ], between speakers show overlapping speech between speakers, while within the text, they show implied concepts that might be necessary in order to follow the direction of the speech. The discussions were conducted in Finnish. The extracts have been translated into English in a manner allowing for the original form to be preserved as much as possible.

References

Barker, Stephanie, L., and Maguire Nick. 2017. "Experts by Experience: Peer Support and Its Use with the Homeless." *Community Mental Health* 53: 598–612. doi:10.1007/s10597-017-0102-2

Bassuk, Ellen, L., Justine Hanson, R. Neil Greene, Molly Richard, and Alexandre Laudet. 2016. "Peer-Delivered Recovery Support Services for Addictions in the United States: A Systematic Review." *Journal of Substance Abuse Treatment* 63: 1–9. doi:10.1016/j.jsat.2016.01.003

Beresford, Peter. 2010. "Public Partnerships, Governance and User Involvement: A Service User Perspective." *International Journal of Consumer Studies* 34 (5): 495–502. doi:10.1111/j.1470–6431.2010.00905.x

Beresford, Peter, Lesley Adshead, and Suzy Croft. 2007. *Palliative Care, Social Work and Service Users: Making Life Possible.* London: Jessica Kingsley.

Brown, Kate. 2011. "'Vulnerability': Handle with Care." *Ethics and Social Welfare* 5 (3): 313–321. doi:10.1080/17496535.2011.597165

Falk, Hanna, Marjo Kurki, Päivi Rissanen, Sini Kankaanpää, and Niina Sinkkonen. 2013. *Kuntoutujasta toimijaksi – kokemus asiantuntijuudeksi.* Työpaperi 39/2013. Helsinki: Terveyden ja hyvinvoinnin laitos.

Fawcett, Barbara. 2009. "Vulnerability. Questioning the Certainties in Social Work and Health." *International Social Work* 52 (4): 473–484. doi:10.1177/0020 872809104251

Fletcher, Del, John F. Flint, Elaine Batty, and Jennifer McNeill. 2016. "Gamers or Victims of the System? Welfare Reform, Cynical Manipulation and Vulnerability." *Journal of Poverty and Social Justice* 24 (2): 171–185. doi:10.1332/175982716X 14650295704731

Fox, Joanna. 2011. "'The View from Inside': Understanding Service User Involvement in Health and Social Care Education." *Disability & Society* 26 (2): 169–177. doi:10.1080/09687599.2011.544057

Hines, Lisa. 2013. "The Treatment Views and Recommendations of Substance Abusing Women: A Meta-Synthesis." *Qualitative Social Work* 12 (4): 473–489. doi:10.1177/1473325011432776

Lavee, Einat. 2016. "Low-Income Women's Encounters with Social Services: Negotiation over Power, Knowledge and Respectability." *British Journal of Social Work* 47 (5): 1554–1571. doi:10.1093/bjsw/bcw131

Leppo, Anna, and Riikka Perälä. 2009. "User Involvement in Finland: The Hybrid of Control and Emancipation." *Journal of Health Organization and Management* 23 (3): 359–371. doi:10.1108/14777260910966771

McDonald, Catherine. 2006. *Challenging Social Work: The Context of Practice.* Basingstoke: Palgrave Macmillan.

McLaughlin, Hugh. 2009. "'What's in a Name: 'Client', 'Patient', 'Customer', 'Consumer', 'Expert by Experience', 'Service User'—What's Next?'" *British Journal of Social Work* 39 (6): 1101–1117. doi:10.1093/bjsw/bcm155

Määttä, Anne. 2013. "Perusturva ja poiskäännyttäminen." *Janus* 21 (2): 170–177.

Meriluoto, Taina. 2018. *Making Experts-by-Experience – Governmental Ethnography of Participatory Initiatives in Finnish Social Welfare Organisations.* Jyväskylä: University of Jyväskylä.

Nelson, Anna. 2012. *Social Work with Substance users.* London: Sage.

Nylund, Marianne. 2000. *Varieties of Mutual Support and Voluntary Action. A Study of Finnish Self-Help Groups and Volunteers.* Helsinki: Helsingin yliopisto.

Paylor, Ian, Fiona Measham, and Hugh Asher. 2012. *Social Work and Drug Use.* Berkshire: McGraw-Hill, Open University Press.

Reif, Sharon, Lisa Braude, Russel D. Lyman, Richard H. Dougherty, Allen S. Daniels, Sushmita Shoma Ghose, Onaje Salim, and Miriam E. Delphin-Rittmon. 2014. "Peer Recovery Support for Individuals with Substance Use Disorders: Assessing the Evidence." *Psychiatric Services* 65 (7). doi:10.1176/appi.pa.201400047

Reinharz, Shulamit, and Susan E. Chase 2001. "Interviewing Women." *In Handbook of Interview Research. Context & Method,* edited by J. F. Gubrium, and J. A. Holstein, 221–238. London: Sage Publications, Inc.

Simmons, Richard, Martin Powell, and Ian Greener, eds. 2009. *The Consumer in Public Services. Choice, Values and Difference.* Bristol: The Polity Press.

Smith, Dorothy E. 1987. *The Everyday World as Problematic. A Feminist Sociology.* Oxford: Open University Press/Milton Keynes.

Smith, Dorothy E. 2004. *Writing the Social. Critique, Theory, and Investigations.* Toronto: University Toronto Press.

Virokannas, Elina. 2014. "Vertaisten ja ammattilaisten jäsenyyskategoriat huumeidenkäyttäjille suunnatussa katuklinikkatyössä." *Yhteiskuntapolitiikka* 79 (6): 657–668.

Virokannas, Elina. 2016. "Exploring Relationships and Emotions through Reflexive Secondary Data Analysis: Peer Supporters', Professionals' and Clients' Experiences of a Finnish s Street-Level Substance Misuse Clinic." In *Relationship-Based Research in Social Work. Understanding Practice Research,* edited by Gillian Ruch, and Ilse Julkunen, 173–193. London: Jessica Kingsley Publishers.

Virokannas, Elina. 2019. "Treatment Barriers to Social and Health Care Services from the Standpoint of Female Substance Users in Finland." *Journal of Social Service Research.* doi:10.1080/01488376.2019.1598532

Virokannas, Elina, Liuski Suvi, and Kuronen Marjo. 2020. "The Contested Concept of Vulnerability – A Literature Review." *European Journal of Social Work* 23 (2):327–339. doi:10.1080/13691457.2018.1508001

Warren, Janet. 2007. *Service User and Carer Participation in Social* Work. Glasgow: Learning Matters.

13 Concluding remarks

A need for women-specific welfare services

Marjo Kuronen and Ulla Salovaara

The empirical findings presented in this book convincingly show that despite differences between the service systems and welfare state models in Finland, Canada, Israel, Slovenia, Spain and the UK, the difficulties that women face with the welfare service system and in their encounters with it have striking similarities. Women find it difficult to know how to apply for and receive the services, social support and protection they need to cope in the vulnerable situations they struggle with in their daily lives. They describe service systems as complex, fragmented and complicated, with no clear logic and rules about how to work with them. For these women, the systems look like 'a jungle with arbitrary rules', as Virokannas et al. put it in Chapter 3 of this book. Women also said it was merely 'good luck' when they encountered an understanding practitioner and received help. More often, they experienced encounters with the welfare system and its practitioners as stigmatising, frustrating and even humiliating. Women who were mothers were afraid of using the services and talking to professionals out of fear of losing their children or not getting them back. Women face expectations, moral judgement and categorisations that do not correspond to their own understanding of the situation and the service needs they require to improve their lives and integrate back into society as 'normal' women and citizens. Because of these negative experiences, women avoid and even resist the service system rather than actively search for help, support and social protection, which again might worsen their situation.

Many of the chapters discuss the service needs of women with substance abuse and related problems and the ways in which the service system responds and meets, or fails to meet, their needs. Other major themes are weak social security for poor women and its consequences. Economic vulnerability and poverty are related to the experiences of a vast majority of these women. Furthermore, many authors discuss the control of women's motherhood and sexuality and how women respond to it. None of the chapters focuses specifically on how the service system meets women who are victims of violence, even if this is one of the major women-specific problems throughout the world. Yet experiences of violence are often intertwined with other vulnerabilities women face. Service systems in different countries have problems in how to recognise, meet and help women victims of intimate violence (e.g. Virkki et al. 2015), even if the problem is widely recognised in the local, national and international policy statements.

It is not only that the service system puts negative labels on these women, but the stigma is also internalised, even if women might also resist being defined as vulnerable. Experienced stigma, awareness and sensitivity regarding one's background and vulnerable situation often frame women's encounters with the practitioners, and they interpret them through the experience of a 'stigmatised identity' (Juhila 2004). Patricia Easteal (2001) talks about learned rules of 'Don't talk, don't trust, don't feel', which might be reflected in women's relationship and encounters with the authorities and the service system.

Many of the chapters in this book also analyse the coping strategies that women have developed because they were not able to obtain or did not want to apply for formal services or benefits, or because they resist the way they were treated and defined in the service system. In these strategies, they often relied on social, emotional and financial support from their families, male partners, friends and peers or neighbourhood and community. However, some of these strategies might be harmful, oppressive or at least contradictory in their consequences. By deciding not to apply for services and benefits, women simultaneously might make their situation even more vulnerable. Especially in searching for or accepting support and protection from men, women might put themselves at risk of economic dependency, oppression, and physical and sexual abuse. Many of these women have suffered several traumatic experiences during their life course, and their harmful coping strategies might be related to these traumas (e.g. Fuentes 2014). However, even if it seems that women are making bad choices that are harmful to them, from their personal perspective, these are the best choices they have available for coping, surviving and supporting themselves and often their children as well.

Social support from other women, both family members and peers, is important, even crucial for women's coping in their daily lives. The service system should also create more opportunities for such support by developing women-only services, peer group activities, promoting community action and simply by providing safe spaces where women would be able to meet each other. Informal social support is important, but it cannot and should not replace formal services and social security from the state.

How then should service systems be developed to meet women's needs better? Overall, welfare service systems are fragmented and poorly integrated. Women often have multiple and long-term needs and answering them would require a holistic approach and better coordinated services from different sectors and organisations of the service system. There is also a lack of services and gaps in social protection to meet the very basic needs of women to survive, such as basic financial support and accommodation where they can feel at home and protected. In many countries, NGOs rather than the public welfare service system organise services for the most marginalised groups of people, including specific services for women. The problem is that often these services are organised only locally or on a temporary basis. Even though NGOs are a valuable part of the service system and often actively campaign for the social and human rights of these people, the state should not withdraw from its responsibility to provide adequate services (Fineman 2010). At the general policy level, there seems to be awareness of these problems, but it has not necessarily led to improvements in the service system.

In addition to improving and developing the welfare service system in general, there is also a need for women-specific services. By this, we mean sufficient availability of community-based services and institutional care provided with a gender-sensitive approach. These include counselling and therapy for individuals as well as groups, social work services, housing units, shelters for homeless women and victims of violence, and drug treatment and rehabilitation units, all of which would provide safe environments for women to receive care, counselling and treatment.

Early feminist social work literature of the 1970s and 1980s (e.g. Hanmer and Statham 1988; Dominelli and McLeod 1989) called for critical practice that would recognise women's oppression and social inequality in society, develop emancipatory action and empowering women-to-women practice free from professional power relations. In many ways, these aims and principles are still relevant even if they have since been problematised as well (see e.g. Orme 2012). It is now understood that women do not share the same experiences only because they are women, not even with women in a similar vulnerable situation, and even less with female professionals. Yet it might be better for women to deal with a female professional, especially if they have traumatic experiences of violent and abusive relationships with men. It has also been questioned whether power relations between women as service users and practitioners can ever be removed, but these hierarchies could at least be lowered and power relations made visible and open for discussion. Even though controlling aspects of the service system and professional practices cannot be avoided, those should not be hidden and denied either. However, a gender-sensitive approach and understanding is still needed and is widely missing not only in social work but also in all welfare services, in some countries more than in others (Kuronen 2020), and services specifically for women are rather marginal in the service system, especially in public welfare services.

What is important in developing women-specific services is to see, understand and work with the complexity of women's vulnerable situations and their relatedness to social structures and inequalities. For example, women's substance abuse often intersects with issues related to social relations, housing, psychosocial wellbeing, financial issues, crime, violence, abuse and traumatic experiences (see Chapter 9, Karttunen in this book).

Developing women-specific services requires challenging the ways the services are currently organised and provided as well as how women are viewed as service users. What we see as crucial in working with and encountering these women is understanding, respect and a safe environment. Understanding means recognition of the complexity of women's situations, internalised stigma and the consequences of their past, often traumatic experiences. Understanding also means hearing how women themselves see and interpret their situation, experiences and needs. Respect and a reciprocal relationship (Törrönen 2018) should be basic elements of interaction. Yet we should accept that these encounters unavoidably possess their own distinctions and facing of 'otherness'. The feeling of safety is based on understanding and respect, but it also means a safe physical environment to deal with difficult issues. Women-specificity is not only related to face-to-face interactions. In addition, practitioners should act as advocates for women in vulnerable situations, fight for their rights to services and make their voice heard in society.

Women's negative experiences with the service system are often personified in individual professionals, mostly women themselves. It is important to improve and develop the practices in which professionals encounter women as service users. However, we should not blame individual practitioners who are part of the organisational order of the service system (Høgsbro 2017; Kuronen 2020). Instead, the focus should be on developing the welfare service system as a whole to better meet the needs of women in vulnerable life situations and in the most marginalised positions in societies.

We are writing the final words of this book in April 2020 as the COVID-19 pandemic is spreading all over the world and putting the welfare service systems of all countries under great pressure. This exceptional situation might exclude marginalised groups of women even more, as many services have been forced to close or severely limited or are digitalised. There is an enormous risk that the pandemic will deepen their vulnerable situations and the struggles of their daily lives. This time is a test of sustainability for our service systems and especially for the services supporting and protecting people in the most vulnerable situations.

References

Dominelli, Lena, and Eileen McLeod. 1989. *Feminist Social Work*. London: Macmillan.

Easteal, Patricia. 2001. "Women in Australian Prisons. The Cycle of Abuse and Dysfunctional Environments." *The Prison Journal* 81 (1): 87–112. doi:10.1177/0032885501081001007

Fineman, Martha. 2010. "The Vulnerable Subject and the Responsive State." *Emory Law Journal* 60 (2): 251–275.

Fuentes, Catherine Mitchell. 2014. "Nobody's Child: The Role of Trauma and Interpersonal Violence in Women's Pathways to Incarceration and Resultant Service Needs." *Medical Anthropology Quarterly* 28 (1): 85–104. doi:10.1111/maq.12058

Hanmer, Jalna, and Daphne Statham. 1988. *Women and Social Work: Towards a Woman-centred Practice*. London: Macmillan.

Høgsbro, Kjeld. 2017. "Institutional Ethnography for People in a Vulnerable and Oppressed Situation." In *Social Work and Research in Advanced Welfare States*, edited by Kjeld Høgsbro and Ian Shaw, 117–130. London and New York: Routledge.

Juhila, Kirsi. 2004. "Talking Back to Stigmatized Identities. Negotiation of Culturally Dominant Categorizations in Interviews with Shelter Residents." *Qualitative Social Work* 3 (3): 259–275. doi:10.1177/1473325004045665

Kuronen, Marjo. 2020. "Institutional Ethnography as a Feminist Approach for Social Work Research." In *Institutional Ethnography in the Nordic Region*, edited by Rebecca W.B. Lund and Ann Christin E. Nilsen, 117–127. London and New York: Routledge.

Orme, Joan. 2012. "Feminist Social Work." In *Social Work Theories and Methods*, edited by Mel Grey and Stephen Webb, 87–98. 2nd ed. London: Sage.

Törrönen, Maritta. 2018. "Creating Wellbeing through Reciprocal Relationships." In *Reciprocal Relationships and Well-being: Implications for Social Work and Social Policy*, edited by Maritta Törrönen, Carol Munn-Giddings, and Laura Tarkiainen, 26–45. London: Routledge.

Virkki, Tuija, Marita Husso, Marianne Notko, Juha Holma, Aarno Laitila, and Mikko Mäntysaari. 2015. "Possibilities for Intervention in Domestic Violence: Frame Analysis of Health Care Professionals' Attitudes." *Journal of Social Service Research* 41 (1): 6–24. doi:10.1080/01488376.2014.917449

Index

Note: Page numbers followed by "n" denote endnotes.